CORN Publication Series 1[illegible]

In memory of María Teresa and Guy

This publication was supported by the GDR 2912 (Histoire des Campagnes Européennes) of the CNRS (FR).

ISBN 978-2-503-51986-9
D/2014/0095/179

Printed in the EU on acid free paper

Measuring Agricultural Growth

Land and Labour Productivity in Western Europe from the Middle Ages to the Twentieth Century (England, France and Spain)

Edited by Jean-Michel Chevet and Gérard Béaur

BREPOLS

CONTENTS

LIST OF CONTRIBUTORS

ANNIE ANTOINE	University of Rennes II, France
GÉRARD BÉAUR	Centre de Recherches Historiques, CNRS/ EHESS, Paris, France
JOSÉ MIGUEL LANA BERASAIN	Public University of Navarre, Iruña/Pamplona, Spain
PAUL BRASSLEY	University of Exeter, United Kingdom
BRUCE M. S. CAMPBELL	The Queen's University of Belfast, United Kingdom
JEAN-MICHEL CHEVET	INRA, ADES-UMR 5185, Bordeaux, France
JEAN DUMA	University of Paris X-Nanterre, France
TIM J. A. LE GOFF	York University Toronto, Canada / IRCOM, Paris, France
MARÍA TERESA PÉREZ PICAZO †	University of Murcia, Spain
DONALD M. G. SUTHERLAND	University of Maryland, USA

LIST OF FIGURES

LIST OF TABLES

without any critical distance. Surely all these teleological justifications in favour of the thesis of superior English agriculture simply come from the opinion that was widely expressed in the English administration, and no doubt everywhere in the world, at the beginning of the nineteenth century, that, as the author of an article in the *Quarterly Review* wrote in 1827: 'Better is it for us to be condemned to labour for our country's good than to luxuriate amid olives, vines, and vices'.[3] Is this intrinsic superiority of the northern races not a romantic legend? Is the history of the superiority of English agriculture not a myth, or just an assumption, of natural superiority, even in works which do not seem to have as strong an ideological bent as that of Gregory Clark?

In this suspiciously unanimous chorus, a few discordant voices have questioned this simplistic, not to say ideological, schema. The superiority of English yields has been strongly challenged (Béaur, 1999, Chevet, 1998, 1999a, Morineau, 1971, 1991). It has been shown that France was not behind in the introduction of artificial meadows (Chevet, 1999a). It makes no sense to compare the cereal production of the London region, or of Norfolk on its own, to that of the whole of France or Spain. It must be obvious that national data, which include areas not suitable for cereal production (such as the French mountains and the Castilian high plateaus) as well as fertile plains intensively cultivated since the Middle Ages, are totally artificial.[4] Geography exists, and comparisons only make sense at a regional level, as some authors have pointed out, for example Erik Thoen on the county of Flanders (Thoen, 2004). It is as presumptuous to try to adopt the Norfolk model in the Massif Central as it would be to plant vines and olives in Cornwall.

In any case, if England had a margin of security for its wheat supply in the modern period, it was partly because it had relatively few people to feed until at least the middle of the eighteenth century. From then on, one can make the case hypothetically that, at the national level, there was no other reason for the difference between the performances of French and English agriculture, either because demographic pressure was notoriously weak in England in the eighteenth century or because wheat cultivation was reserved for the best land in the nineteenth. If there was so much room for stock-raising in England, it was because there were reserves of land not needed for cereals, as they would have been in a densely occupied land. Around 1700, at a time when British agriculture had fewer than 7 million inhabitants to feed on 230,000 km^2, French agriculture had to meet the needs of at least three times as many people on a bit more than twice as much land. It is obvious that this difference in population pressure meant that attitudes to developing the land would not be the same. There is a striking counter-check for this theory. As soon as demographic growth started and population density came close to that which had long been known on the other side of the Channel, Britain, from being an exporter of cereals, became, after 1760, more and more an importer. This was a practical choice

---

3 Quoted by George Orwell (1967).

4 '[…] how is it possible to compare the performances of a country like France, universally praised or criticised for its diversity, with that of a country two and a half times smaller, when the examples used all have very particular settings and apply to particular moments in time? If the Paris region, or Normandy, or on a larger scale, the Paris basin are selected as examples. it is doubtful the same results would be obtained and that inequalities on the same scale, if any, would be found'. These remarks, in a review putting Jan Luiten van Zanden's conclusions (1994) into perspective, still remain valid 17 years later (Béaur, 1996: 422).

because of the strength of maritime trade and the relatively proximity to the sea of even the most remote villages.

Even though this takes us away from our main subject it is high time for the myth of Dutch exceptionalism to be finally demolished. Dutch and Flemish agriculture, supported by urban growth, which itself was linked to flourishing 'industry' and trade, were justifiably admired by contemporaries and put forward as models of development for the whole of Europe (Thoen, 2001; Dejongh and Thoen; Van Zanden, 2009). These advances are undeniable but they need to be put in context and it is quite reasonable to think that 'agriculture in some parts of the Paris Basin was no less competitive than the North Sea Area'. The yields obtained on the rich plateaus around Paris demonstrate the strength of cereal-growing in the region way back into the Middle Ages, and equal those in Britain, even those of the most fertile regions (Béaur, 1999: 146–154).

It is now beginning to be understood that 'gardening' around a prominent urban conglomeration was just one of the areas of activity that developed whenever urban demand, aristocratic, bourgeois or popular, provided an impetus. We are now able to go beyond the hackneyed, but accurate, picture in which cereal crops dominated the Paris region of and discover how imaginative Parisian peasants also planted masses of vines to supply the consumers of the metropolis (Lachiver, 1982), how they had cultivated artichokes, asparagus, fruits and vegetables in the city since at least the sixteenth century (Gurvil, 2010), how abundantly peaches grew in the suburb of Montreuil (Bennezon, 2009) and cherries and other fruit trees in the nearby Montmorency valley (Mérot, 2007, 2010), and how nursery gardens flourished just outside the city at Vitry (Traversat, 2001). In brief, a highly intensive agriculture with a strong value-added component, prospered wherever there was a market for producers. It is clear that Paris, the largest city in the West from the sixteenth to the beginning of the eighteenth century, was, as much as the Low Countries, and perhaps more by its size, a 'great market' (Abad, 2002), a model on a larger scale, but similar to those in other places, in Italy, in Spain and elsewhere.

Critics have also looked at the so-called institutional blockage in France (Béaur & Chevet, 2013). It has recently been shown that at the end of the nineteenth century the agricultural population for a given area was no greater in France than in England, though of course this needs to be examined at a regional level (Chevet, 2010). Finally, even the supposedly fundamental role of enclosures has been called into question (Meuvret, 1977, 1988; Neeson, 1993; Béaur, 2006; Chevet, 1998, 1999). Richard Hoyle casts doubt on their effectiveness as a means of redistributing land (Hoyle, 1990, 2003); Mark Overton displays scepticism about the great landowners' enthusiasm for the Agricultural Revolution (Overton, 1996); Gérard Béaur demonstrates with the aid of maps that the elimination of common land in eighteenth-century France would have had little effect in the areas where it would have been beneficial to extend cultivated land because common lands had already almost vanished there; they remained only in areas where they had a real economic function, that is, mainly in mountainous regions. Very recently the idea that property rights encouraged progress has been criticised as a representation of collective national imagination hiding behind one of many theories of economic science (Béaur & Chevet, 2013). This criticism, supported by 25 converging contributions (Béaur, Schofield, Chevet & Pérez-Picazo, 2013), has undermined the radical neo-institutionalist theory, which claimed to explain delays in development by institutional blockage and the take-off in growth by the arrival of perfect, absolute property rights, free from restrictions due to confused rights over the land (see Congost, 2003; Congost & Santos, 2010). But the 'English way' of capitalism set against the 'French way', the 'peasant way', is still a hardy old chestnut. It is tempting to look at the question from the beginning, to find reasonable and reasoned methods of evaluation and ways of accounting for the troublesome variables: production and productivity. This collective work is designed as a modest and precise aid to this endeavour, proposing new hypotheses, turning to new sources, and using methods adequate to the desired aims, while subjecting theories and models to critical evaluation.

III. Changing the level of analysis

III.1. Using new sources, combining the 'micro' and the 'macro'

It is clear that works inspired by Rostovian and Malthusian theories have in most cases only measured the development of cereal production for human consumption. This has led to neglecting other indicators of change, beginning with those showing progress in animal production, or even more, in 'alternative cultures'. Similarly, other signs of change in the agricultural sector, often slower and less spectacular, were left out of the picture. To fill this gap, which tends to distort our picture of innovations in the countryside, it is necessary to look at 'micro' data and no longer make do with unreliable estimates obtained from the traditionally-favoured aggregate data at the 'macro' level. Information obtained from monographs has the double merit of making production systems easier to understand and making it possible to reinvent a new theory of global labour productivity which accounts for a world where seasonal underemployment was endemic, which means that hasty estimates based on statistical manipulation of figures for the active population are likely to be false.

Measuring agricultural productivity is a difficult, if not impossible, task and is always complex and ambiguous. There are few statistical data until the twentieth century which give a precise idea of it, and even with these we need to ask questions about how trustworthy and representative they are, even at a recent period. Paul Brassley has shown that they cannot be simply taken at face value, and that they incorporate certain biases which must be corrected if they are to be interpreted correctly (this volume). There are various methods of calculation and they are always riddled with uncertainties and tainted with bias. The indicators are never unequivocal and can sometimes show contradictory findings; the case of England in the Middle Ages is a good illustration of such gaps, irritating, but inevitable and normal in economic history.

This is why historians have looked for indirect instruments that would enable them to show the performance of agricultural regions, and why they have a tendency to use different scales. This is what has been done here, mainly using the 'micro' point of view, sometimes alone, sometimes in association with more 'macro' data or even a definitely 'macro' point of view, but always with the idea that the agricultural holdings themselves should be at the heart of our investigations. That is really what matters. Accounts have been the main concern of the authors, though complemented, where possible, by other relevant data such as post–mortem inventories, agricultural treatises and leases: all of these have been used to make the farms tell us their story.

Although the account books left by religious communities and great landowning families and their farmers have been known for a long time they have not been employed in a systematic way, or have been insufficiently used, except by English historians (Afton, 2000; Afton, Beckett & Turner, 2001). Consulting this considerable body of material should make it possible to understand better not only changes in production but also in labour productivity. This mass of documents, of varying quality and precision, may contain information on innovations in cultivation, the process of specialisation and intensification, as well as parameters for measuring the quantity of labour invested in the productive cycle. Using this kind of source means that new methods of investigation have to be adopted and new indicators created.

III.2. Using new indicators

There are many different indicators that can be used in judging the state of an agricultural system. The productivity of the soil can be calculated, but first there has to be agreement on how to do it: productivity by seeding or by surface area, productivity in relation to the arable surface potentially cultivable or productivity compared to the surface actually sown with the cereal in question? Should one keep to gross product or take account of intermediate production, keep back the seed and deduct it from the gross product, or not? This assumes that all these details are available, which is rarely the case, as José Miguel Lana Berasain regrets (this volume).

If we look at labour productivity, are we to examine productivity per unit of labour or per unit of work actually performed? Here again there are many gaps: how should unpaid work, mainly that of the farmer's family, be measured; how should the work done by women and children be taken into account? There are certainly some sets of accounts that give explicit information on this last point but this is not general. This is why Jean-Michel Chevet preferred to concentrate on draught team productivity as an important first step to measuring overall productivity (Chevet, this volume).

But that is not all: do we consider productivity product by product or do we measure overall productivity by combining and weighting the proportion of each cereal? This has led to the WAGY (weighted annual grain yield) and WACY (weighted annual cereal yield), devised by Bruce Campbell and perfected by him with Mark Overton, taken from data in English probate inventories – a gauge that the two authors used with great ingenuity to measure agricultural production and productivity (Overton & Campbell, 1991, 1992, 1996; Overton, 1979, 1980, 2005). This elegant solution solves many problems of adjustment, although it still leaves many points not completely settled; what solutions do not? The inconvenience of using monetary values is also obvious. However, there is no point in deceiving ourselves; no source is perfect and it is only by comparing data, however affected it is by these biases, that we can hope to extract credible and scientifically acceptable information.

The Campbell/Overton composite indicator has limits, as its authors admit. The WAGY and WACY are by their nature limited to a few of the principal products and set the rest aside; they do not include 'alternative cultures', which might well have been significant on a farm, or the products of animal rearing. Bruce Campbell's solution, in the article in this volume, complements his earlier writings; it consists of turning the estimate of land value (unit of value) into the arbiter and thereby creating a highly useful method that makes it possible to cover all products, not just cereals.

Using monetary units of value magnifies the effects of supply and demand, which can also distort the values used. Though the values observed make up a geography of land productivity and land quality, and a map of the opportunities offered by different levels of access to markets, they are also based on the relative rarity of goods and on supply matched against demand. When arable lands were relatively scarce in proportion to pasture they tended to become more expensive, says Bruce Campbell (this volume). Conversely, when meadows were in demand the price difference was in the other direction. One could object that if meadows fell behind arable it was perhaps because only the best land was cultivated and that, if the opposite happened, it was perhaps because the greatest possible amount of land had been put under plough. In other words, in the first case the productivity of arable was high and in the second it was low. No doubt demographic pressure had something to do with it. But this only reinforces Campbell's hypothesis, because it is precisely this differential productivity that he is trying to prove, with maps in support. In all cases, how can we account for all inputs (land, capital, labour) and their respective productivity? This is what the Total Factor Productivity (TFP), used by Donald Sutherland, attempts to do (Sutherland, this volume). Historians are usually doubtful and somewhat suspicious of this indicator, either because of practical difficulties or because of theoretical objections. Economists, on the other hand, are very fond of this method of calculation, which seems to them to be the best, if not the only relevant one, and some historians have experimented with it, applying it to ancient history and also in this volume. It seems to solve a difficult problem by including in one index the result of the balance of all the inputs and outputs. Philip Hoffman has shown the kind of results that can be obtained by this method (Hoffman, 1996).

However, it is true that this method has deficiencies in the way it is worked out. Expressing all the variables in monetary terms is not totally outlandish, but it is a step based on a very bold assumption. There are also problems with its makeup. How are we to assign weights to land, capital and labour respectively? Further, in an economy where capital investment was very modest and salaries were fairly rigid, most of the inputs came from land and, secondarily, from a greater or lesser use of labour. Since the latter factor is very difficult to measure, surely it is likely that land rent, the measure of the contribution from land, will function as the only indicator worth bothering to locate (Béaur, 2000: 159), according to the well-known adage: 'if the land is worth more this is no doubt because it produces more' (Levasseur, 1893). We have seen how Le Goff and Sutherland made free use of rent as a measure of agricultural progress based on hospital accounts (2000) and what results they drew from it to reinterpret agricultural development during the Revolution (Le Goff & Sutherland, 1999).

In any case there is no point in asking more from TFP than it is capable of giving. By focusing on revenues, it provides a good approximation of the evolution of agricultural productivity and accounts for growth in economic terms, but it is not able to deliver a real explanation for that growth. And if there is one nagging question in economic history, it is why growth started in the course of the eighteenth century. TFP is very valuable in the context of our deliberations but it needs to be completed by a close study of land and labour productivity that can only be obtained by using records of farmers (accounts, memoranda books, and diaries), agricultural accounts, as Afton, Beckett and Turner did with such success to measure the development of production over the long term in England (Afton, Beckett & Turner, 2001). All of these data would need to be completed with elements drawn from other sources, such as agricultural treatises. It is only by reconstructing a picture of labour at this level that it will be possible to understand labour productivity in the agricultural sector.

There are other possible approaches. It is tempting to suggest trying another tool, less flexible but detached from the value of products, such as the PEM (*Prélèvement des Eléments Minéraux*), suggested by Jean-Michel Chevet, or any other instrument capable of dealing with productivity in a way that is neutral in terms of the market. The PEM is certainly more difficult to use but has the immense advantage of being an indicator intrinsic to the agronomic sector. It consists of calculating the amount of different mineral elements taken from the soil in the course of a harvest cycle, and reducing them to a yearly time unit. Although this necessitates some approximations the index has the advantage of emphasising soil enrichment (Chevet, 1999b).

III.3. Using an experimental approach

In this volume each author has chosen one or another of these methods and, most often, has tried several of them. Each author made this choice as a function of individual scientific approaches but also according to the archival resources available. Each author knows that these results are necessarily open to caution and criticism and that the indicators are imperfect by their very nature, as indeed are all statistical constructions. Wisdom lies in being conscious of this fact and not asking more of them than they can provide. To state the obvious, if you do not know the surface of land cultivated it is useless to try and calculate productivity by hectare. However, putting aside these persistent gaps in documentation and concentrating on agricultural accounts, we must remember that there were rarely real account books before the end of the eighteenth century, except for odd specimens in certain favoured regions where the merchant model was adopted very early.[5] As Annie Antoine shows, in sharecropping areas they were compiled by owners who were interested in things other than satisfying the curiosity of historians, or even than creating a correct accounting system. In these regions it may only be possible to work from the archives of the great landowners who had self-managed farms or operated part of their estate as such (Antoine, 1998). What these landowners wanted was an account of the profits they were going to receive and what their sharecroppers would get, so the data are only present on their books in a contingent form. As a result, the accounts were inconsistent, unpredictable and irregular. We might even go so far as to say that nothing that historians care about was of prime interest to the owner or the tenant. The authors show that the question that obsessed the person in charge of the holding was the income it would earn. But here again the historian is faced with doubts. Was it gross revenue or net? In the latter case, the ideal one, the costs and expenses that weighed down the farmer's resources have to be subtracted from the revenue, and this is extremely hard to calculate.

---

[5] As was the case in Italy and England, for example.

Such gaps are many, inevitable and without remedy unless one is lucky enough to have external sources to make up for them. This is why Annie Antoine is reluctant to use these account books to try to recreate ideal accounts (Antoine, 2000). She sees them rather as a way of studying a management strategy, that of the owner or possibly of his tenant, and understanding the logic behind it. Generally it was the owners who kept these books, only rarely the farmers themselves. This means that the accounts were the work of the great landowners and it is inevitable that small landowners remain largely unknown. These were large landowners, then, but this did not necessarily mean large holdings. In fact, in all the examples we have, the land was broken up into a vast number of medium-sized farms, from a few hectares to a few tens of hectares at the most.

To escape their dilemma, the authors, who are aware of the gaps and biases in their sources, have used many devices. Sometimes they sought to create stable and usable samples by using only a small part of the data and abandoning the rest, like Tim Le Goff (this volume); sometimes, like Bruce Campbell, they avoid the difficulties by using data that is more neutral and representative on a larger scale (Campbell, this volume); sometimes they found the elements they needed elsewhere, in the case of Donald Sutherland or Jean-Michel Chevet for example (Chevet, Sutherland, this volume). One might think that the testimony of contemporaries would be a useful addition. The exemplary case referred to by Paul Brassley shows that this is not necessarily so (Brassley, this volume). The lamentations of those affected by the depression of the inter-war years show the unreliability of opinions which are only representations and nothing else. When contemporaries intuitively felt that their production profits and revenues were continually falling, it was because the frequent recurrence of bad years gave them that impression, even though the levels reached just before the Second World War do not justify this belief. The choice of period of reference arbitrarily accentuates the difference, as the euphoric levels reached immediately after World War I set a starting point in the collective memory that was artificially high in relation to output at the beginning of the century. This does not mean that we should not inquire how farmers felt about price movements and how this could influence their decisions. All that needs to be done is to compare the level at moment t, then at another moment t +1, with that of the ten previous years of which the farmers would still have a clear recollection (José Miguel Lana Berasain, 2011). It is then possible to see how they experienced the changing times and better understand their actions, even if, once again, their opinions did not correspond to reality.

Operations at 'micro' level, particularly in farm accounts, make it possible to compensate for some of the inconveniences that arise from lumping together heterogeneous data, and to propose some models. It is nonetheless true that there could be a vast range of products from one farm to another and considerable differences in production between them, even when they were managed by the same owner. Jean Duma, working with data from Garaison, in south-west France, shows the wide range of products and the shifting instability of production levels over the years that made it very difficult to measure long-term trends, and also the tendency of the owner to specialise on each unit according to the suitability of the soil and his own needs (Duma, this volume). Here, as no doubt in many other places, production strategies seem to have reflected the constraints of nature rather than being a clear economic choice on the basis of anticipated profit.

IV. Lessons learned

IV.1. Farm productivity questioned

We have seen how in this book the authors' hypotheses have involved us in old, but still hotly disputed, questions. Keeping in mind the continuing opposition between the agricultures on either side of the Channel, Jean-Michel Chevet questions the difference in labour productivity, which is supposed to be much greater in England than France (Chevet, this volume). The almost total absence of sources needed to measure labour productivity in agriculture may be overcome by using farm accounts when these become more precise than commonplace books (*livres de raison*), as they do in the eighteenth and, especially, the nineteenth centuries. It is all too clear that these accounts, particularly in sharecropping areas, cannot provide these data unless we take the risk of relying on other sources and making some assumptions, which historians are frequently reluctant to do, preferring to refrain from making an estimate rather than to approximate. Here we come to an essential difference between economists and historians, for problems of sources and methods are not the only matters at issue: there are also the big questions on the growth of western economies that belong to economists and in which historians are frequently reluctant to engage. History tends to hide behind a convenient empiricism which consists of putting some order into the boxes of documents found in archives. But what is the use of describing the introduction of machines in agriculture if we are not told how this affected agricultural productivity? What is the use of talking about artificial meadows and fertilisers if we are not given explanations for growth?

Jean-Michel Chevet takes the big farms in the Paris Basin as an example and has constructed a theoretical model for measuring the growth of labour productivity in agriculture in the eighteenth and nineteenth centuries, which is fortunately the period when it began to change. After close analysis he shows that the progress achieved, both with stronger and faster horses and with the introduction of efficient new equipment, such as diggers and grubbers, and improvements in existing machines like the new ploughs that dug deeper and cut the earth more cleanly, necessarily led to gains in productivity (Chevet, this volume). This progress made up for most of the extra work required to grow new crops such as sugar beets and accentuated the albeit limited labour savings that came from the introduction of artificial fodder (Chevet, 1994). What Jean-Michel Chevet has done in this volume for the plough should be done for all the aspects of a farm: harvest, seeds, stock-rearing, etc. Then these findings should be cross-checked with those derived from the farm accounts. This would make it possible to get some idea of the differences in production levels between one country and another, or, even better, one region and another.

It can be seen that this excursion into the cost and availability of labour is an argument for a serious re-examination of the accepted and superficial conclusions on the gap between English and French agriculture and on the gap with other countries which, in nineteenth-century English representations, seem even more exotic than France. For after all, if growth originated because English enclosures dispossessed those who worked the land themselves, that process should be visible in the documentation. If those who favour this thesis do not want to be viewed as practicing the philosophy of history, they should show how the disappearance of the peasants in England led to economies of scale on the large farms. As there was no technical progress in ploughing equipment in the seventeenth and eighteenth centuries one feels intuitively that the evidence for it must be very fragile (Allen, 1992; Chevet, 1997). Moreover, there is already evidence, if we follow Jean-Michel Chevet's calculations, that technical progress followed similar paths on both sides of the Channel (Chevet, 2010). In that case, evicting those who worked their own land would not have helped reduce labour on English farms any more than feudalism would have delayed progress in France.

IV.2. The myth of negligent owners

Another myth that has been seriously damaged is that landowners were absent from their properties and always inactive in managing them, only waiting placidly to receive their rent. This is obviously the opposite image to that of the English landlord, agriculturally informed and eagerly advocating new techniques. Donald Sutherland and Tim Le Goff have shown, with figures to back them, that this is a caricature (Le Goff, Sutherland, this volume).

By comparing accounts from hospitals, tax and notarial records, and archives of local agricultural societies in the region of Le Mans, in an analysis that covers three centuries, Donald Sutherland shows that this assumptionis false (Sutherland, this volume). He shows that growth took off in the second half of the eighteenth century after a long period of stagnation. The TFP increased to 40% before the Revolution and tripled in the course of the nineteenth century. But there is more to be learnt from this study. It shows that, far from neglecting their land the owners made considerable investments, perhaps as much as the English owners, even though the farmers paid for the essentials. Most of it was spent on constructing, repairing, extending or improving the buildings, while the farmers bought equipment and fertilisers. This was also true around Dijon as Tim Le Goff found when he worked on the accounts of a sample taken from the farms belonging to the Hôpital Géneral of Dijon and the Hôpital Saint Anne (Le Goff, this volume). His long-term analysis also showed that owners were strongly involved, particularly in repairing and constructing buildings. Although these could be classed as investments in buildings, they must also have improved farming conditions. The attitude of the farmers confirms this impression of progress. Up until the eighteenth century they had been forced to sublet through intermediaries, Dijon merchants or bourgeois, but from the end of the old regime they were able to arrange contracts directly with the owner, often in association with other members of their family.

Spanish owners were not absentees either, according to José Miguel Lana Bersain and Maria Teresa Pérez-Picazo, who worked on two very different regions, at the opposite ends of Spain – Navarre in the far north and the typically Mediterranean region of Murcia – each enjoying completely different pedological, climatic, economic and social contexts, during the nineteenth century (Pérez-Picazo, 2000). In both cases the owners sought to improve productivity as best they could. In spite of the great differences between the two areas, agricultural development showed two opposing tendencies at the same time. One was a mainly extensive type of growth, characterised by increase in the cultivated surface. The other was intensive growth, marked by the substitution for existing crops of more speculative products intended for the market, more resistant to economic fluctuations: market gardens and orchards in Murcia, vineyards and olive plantations in Navarre. All of this calls into question James Simpson's 'long siesta' of Spanish agriculture (Simpson, 1995).

IV.3. The solution of specialised crops

According to José Miguel Lana Berasain, even though cereal production went up in Navarre it had difficult keeping up with population growth, and the increase was mainly the result of more intense labour and improved seeds and methods, rather than of more deliberate use of fertilisers. Nevertheless, the six estates studied in detail in this article showed overall progress in growing vines and olives, with increased productivity of the surface unit but only selective progress when labour productivity is taken into consideration. The reason that productivity in olive output did not improve was that for that particular crop, greater productivity required more trees per hectare and therefore more work – which shows that stable labour productivity does not necessarily imply economic backwardness.

Maria Teresa Pérez-Picazo found the same was true in Murcia (Pérez-Picazo, this volume). To be sure, at the present stage of research it is very hard to say whether labour productivity improved; however, there were clear advances in production. Geographic conditions meant that the English model was completely unsuitable, and though there were big landowners, the holdings were very small. Progress was slow because of the small amount of technical change; the main improvements came about by changes in crops. Barley replaced wheat and rye, commercial plants like vines, olives and almond trees replaced subsistence crops. This specialisation was greater in irrigated areas, where mulberry trees were replaced by more profitable fruit trees; but there were still several other products for the farmer to grow on the side, as Annie Antoine and Jean Duma have shown in other areas (Antoine, Duma, this volume). Specialisation never degenerated into monoculture thus avoiding the risk from natural disasters and delays in changeable markets.

It is not surprising that the owners took a large part in these changes. There was no absenteeism, no indifference, no lack of interest but, on the contrary, a permanent search for profit by investment, by extending the cultivated surface, by putting more pressure on gross product. To this was added a strongly rational choice in the way the farm was worked, and the use of sharecropping as a way to reduce risks in a vulnerable region and to keep down the costs of overseeing a system dominated by smallholders. This is far from the traditional image of the inefficient, parasitic, uninvolved, latifundia owner.

Yields measured by surface unit or by seed remained low as lack of water and the inability to grow artificial fodder in such climatic conditions were recurring handicaps. Productivity grew little, no doubt because skilled labour for work in the fields was hard to come by, and demand for labour outside agriculture was low, with the result that the rural population remained high. However, there were some positive developments, such as the fall in cost of labour with the first introduction of mechanisation in cereal production, and greater selectivity of vines. Geographic constraints persisted at the same time as the difficulties of the general economic context discouraged attempts to develop agriculture. There is no need to adopt such explanations as the intrinsic inferiority of the agricultural sector, and to pay worship to a bogus English model that was neither transposable nor vastly impressive.

V. Conclusion

Although this book cannot hope to do more than take a few soundings to try and increase our understanding of the thousand faces of agriculture and the thousand aspects of agricultural progress, it has certainly allowed us to focus on some evident facts, to work out some unexpected breakthroughs and to write off some outdated myths. Let us set out some of the things we have learnt.

The papers offer a variety of solutions to get round the lack of sources or difficulties in quantifying them. There are discussions of land productivity and labour productivity but also proposals of more general estimations: PTF, WAGY/WACY, unit of value (Donald Sutherland, Bruce Campbell, this volume) which open the way for wider comparisons. They use accounts (Annie Antoine, Jean Duma, Tim Le Goff, Donald Sutherland, this volume) or macroeconomic data (Paul Brassley, this volume), they have put both of these together (Jean-Michel Chevet, this volume) and they have shown that contemporaries' perception of events may be biased (Paul Brassley, this volume).

We must always be aware of the difference between large estates and large holdings. Though great landowners might keep one set of accounts, the estate might be made up of many small farms. Large estates had therefore no intrinsic advantage in comparison with the small ones. It is also not relevant to class types of landholding on a single scale. There was a rationale behind the way the land was worked. Sharecropping, which has long been vilified, was not the juridical monster that most authors have described and sharecroppers were not necessarily the poor wretches depicted by a prejudiced literature. Sharecropping could have advantages in areas where production was vulnerable and where it was difficult to oversee large numbers of smallholders. The owners made this choice, not because they had no interest in making a profit, but because they wanted to reduce risk and also keep down the cost of supervision. After all, sharecropping emerged in Norfolk at the beginning of the seventeenth century in the particular circumstances of that time, and historians, irony of ironies, have seen it as proof of a remarkable adaptability (Griffiths, 2003).

Contributors have shown that the reputation of the great landowners, and particularly Spanish landlords, for absenteeism and indifference was nothing but a legend. Clearly they were moved by a desire for income; clearly, persistent myth to the contrary, they had no hesitation about investing to obtain it, preferring that to extending the cultivable surface or taking a larger cut of gross product. Given the slow advance of technological change, many of them chose to specialise and gradually to substitute commercial crops for subsistence ones. This specialisation, in vines, in olive, almond and fruit trees and other more profitable and better adapted crops than cereals, spread widely in irrigated areas, where mulberry trees were replaced by fruit trees, sometimes on the owners' initiative. However, specialisation was never the same thing as monoculture. Everywhere, or almost everywhere, subsistence crops carried on alongside the speculative crops. The fact that a region was devoted to stock-rearing did not mean that wheat growing was neglected there; Annie Antoine shows how far this was from the case (Antoine, 1994). And the fact that mixed farming persisted, where the soil was suitable, did not mean that the products were not commercialised. This confusion has to be avoided.

The calculations, some would say the strategies, of the owners, their farmers and share-croppers were obviously at the heart of these changes and these efforts. In some places the owners played a large role in improving the conditions of cultivation by various means: developing irrigation or even bringing in new machines just as much as they might do so by extending the cultivable surface or taking a larger cut of the gross product. In other situations, they used some of their profits to construct, repair and extend buildings to benefit the farms. In still others, they helped farmers invest by agreeing to reduce rents. They adapted to market possibilities; for what was the point of engaging in speculation if there were no clients waiting to consume the goods they produced and if they could not be delivered in good condition? These factors may have been decisive, but no doubt they partly masked the preponderance of the geographic conditions, whatever producers did. The type of soil, the constraints of the climate, played a role that historians often neglect. In some zones, it would have been as useless to try and grow artificial fodder as it was to expect miracles from enclosures or yields on the Norfolk scale. The English model was not adopted everywhere and in fact it existed almost nowhere else but England, simply because it was not adapted to conditions elsewhere.

The race to productivity is itself an ambiguous term because productivity does not necessarily have to keep pace with the progress of production. The interplay between the two elements: production and productivity, is complex and an increased yield was quite often accompanied by lower labour productivity. This was the case in the Roman countryside at the beginning of the early modern period when every effort to increase yield required more labour, thus decreasing productivity, while every attempt to economise on labour brought about lower soil productivity (Revel, 1982). This incompatibility is not self-evident but was no doubt very common. On the other hand we must beware of the ambiguous effects of improved productivity. It is certain that the people producing the crops, whether working their own land or as tenants, in their attempts to reduce the labour costs, turned to early mechanisation or selection of vines. But these efforts were often counterbalanced by the introduction of more labour-intensive crops and also by the need to maintain a large rural population when there was little demand for non-agricultural labour unless these peasants were pushed into the towns to swell the ranks of the *lumpenproletariat* or outward to join the flow of emigrants abroad. If rising productivity could have a beneficial effect at the micro-economic level by increasing farmers' profits, it could also be harmful at the macro-economic level if alternative jobs in other economic sectors did not keep pace and chronic underemployment resulted. When the price of strong productivity was rural underemployment or massive urban unemployment, economic success could bring with it an exorbitant social cost.

Bibliography

Abad, Reynald (2002) *Le Grand marché: l'approvisionnement alimentaire de Paris sous l'Ancien Régime*, Paris, Fayard.

Afton, Bethany (2000) 'Investigating Agricultural Production and Land Productivity', *Histoire & Mesure*, XV, 3/4, pp. 233–245.

Afton, Bethany, Beckett, John V. & Turner, Michael E. (2001) *Farm Production in England 1700–1914*, Oxford, Oxford University Press.

Allen, Robert C. (1992) *Enclosure and the Yeoman. The Agricultural Development of the South Midlands 1450–1850*, Oxford, Clarendon Press.

Allen, Robert C. (2004) 'Agriculture during the Industrial Revolution', in Roderick Floud and Paul A. Johnson (eds), *The Cambridge Economic History of Modern Britain, Volume I: Industrialisation, 1700–1860*, Cambridge University Press, pp. 96–116.

Antoine, Annie (1994) *Fiefs et villages du Bas-Maine au* XVIII*e siècle*, Mayenne, Éditions Regionales de l'Ouest.

Antoine, Annie (1998) *Les Comptes ordinaires de Pierre Duchemin du Tertre, marchand de toile et seigneur dans la première moitié du* XVIII*e siècle*, Mayenne, Société d'Archéologie et d'Histoire de la Mayenne.

Antoine, Annie (2000) 'Entre macro et micro: les comptabilités agricoles du XVIIIe siécle', in 'Productivité et Croissance agricole', *Histoire et Mesure*, vol. XV, 3/4, pp. 247–270.

van Bavel, Bas J.P. & Thoen, Erik (eds) (1999) *Land Productivity and Agro-systems in the North Sea Area, Middle Ages-20th century. Elements for Comparison*, Corn Publication series 2, Turnhout, Brepols.

Béaur, Gérard (ed.) (1996) 'Prix, Production, Productivité agricoles', *Histoire et Mesure*, 1996, XI-n°3/4, see Introduction, pp. 201–211.

Béaur, Gérard (1999) 'From the North Sea Area to Berry and Lorraine: Land Productivity in Northern France 13th-19th centuries' in Bas van Bavel & Erik Thoen (eds), *Land Productivity and Agro-systems in the North Sea Area, Middle Ages–20th Century. Elements for Comparison*, Turnhout, Brepols, CORN Publication series 2, pp. 136–167.

Béaur, Gérard (2000) *Histoire agraire de la France au* XVIII*e siècle. Inerties et changements dans les campagnes françaises à la fin de l'époque moderne (jusqu'en 1815)*, Paris, SEDES.

Béaur, Gérard (2006) 'En un débat douteux. Les communaux, quels enjeux dans la France des XVIIIe-XIXe siècles?' *Revue d'Histoire Moderne et Contemporaine*, 53–1, pp. 89–201.

Béaur, Gérard, (2009) 'Alternative Agriculture or Agricultural Specialization in Early Modern France', *Agricultural History Review*, suppl. *England-France A Common Agricultural Heritage*, pp. 121–137.

Béaur, Gérard & Chevet, Jean-Michel (eds) (2000) 'Productivité et croissance agricole', *Histoire & Mesure*, 2000, XV-n° 3 / 4, see Introduction pp. 187–201.

Béaur, Gérard & Chevet, Jean-Michel (2013) 'Institutional Change and Agricultural Growth' in Gérard Béaur, Phillipp Schofield, Jean-Michel Chevet & Maria-Teresa Pérez-Picazo (eds), *Property Rights, Land Markets and Economic Growth in the European Countryside (13th–20th Centuries)*, Turnhout, Brepols, pp. 19–68.

Béaur, Gérard, Schofield, Phillipp, Chevet, Jean-Michel & Pérez-Picazo, Maria-Teresa (eds) (2013) *Property Rights, Land Markets and Economic Growth in the European Countryside (13th–20th Centuries)*, Turnhout, Brepols, Rural History in Europe 1.

Bennezon, Hervé (2009) *Montreuil sous le règne de Louis XIV*, Paris, Les Indes Savantes.

Bloch Marc, *Les Caractères originaux de l'histoire rurale française*, Paris, Armand Colin, 1931.

Campbell, B.M.S. (2002) *English Seigniorial Agriculture*, Cambridge, Cambridge University Press.

Campbell, B.M.S., and Overton, Mark (eds) (1991) *Land, Labour and Livestock. Historical Studies in European Agricultural Productivity*, Manchester, Manchester University Press.

Chevet, Jean-Michel (1984) *Le Marquisat d'Ormesson, essai d'analyse économique, 1700–1850*, thèse de 3° cycle, E.H.E.S.S., Paris.

Chevet, Jean-Michel (1994) 'Production et productivité: un modèle de développement économique des campagnes de la région parisienne aux XVIIIe et XIXe siècles', *Histoire & Mesure*, IX, 1/2, pp. 101–145.

Chevet, Jean-Michel (1997) 'Quelle 'révolution agricole' en Angleterre? A propos de deux livres récents sur l'agriculture anglaise du Moyen Âge au milieu du XIXe siècle', *Histoire & Mesure*, XI-3/4, pp. 389–410.

Chevet, Jean-Michel (1998, 1999a) *La Terre et les paysans en France et en Grande-Bretagne. Du début du XVIIe siècle à la fin du XVIIIe siècle. Volume I: Les hommes et les structures foncières, Volume II: Les hommes et la production*, Paris, Messenne.

Chevet, Jean-Michel (1999b) 'A few arguments to begin the discussion on the measurement of agricultural production and soil productivity', in Bas J. P. van Bavel & Erik Thoen, *Land Productivity and Agro-systems in the North Sea Area. Middle Ages–20th Century*. Turnhout, Brepols, CORN Publications Series 2, pp. 339–356.

Chevet, Jean-Michel (2010) 'Reconsidering a Rural Myth: Peasant France and Capitalist Britain', in John Broad (ed.), *Revising French and British Rural Divergence. A Common Agricultural Heritage?*, Agricultural History Review, Supplement Series 5, pp. 37–54.

Clark, Gregory (2007) *A Farewell to Alms: A Brief Economic History*, Princeton, Princeton University Press.

Congost, Rosa (2003) 'Property Rights and Historical Analysis. What rights? What history?', *Past & Present*, 181, pp. 73–106.

Congost, Rosa & Santos, Rui (eds) (2010) *Contexts of Property. The Social Embeddedness of Property Rights to Land in Europe in a Historical Perspective*, Turnhout, Brepols, series Rural History in Europe 5, see introduction pp. 15–38.

Dejongh, Guy & Thoen, Erik (1999) 'Arable Productivity in Flanders and the Former Territory of Belgium in a Long-term Perspective (from the Middle Ages to the End of the Ancien Régime)', in Bas J. P. van Bavel & Erik Thoen (eds), *Land Productivity and Agro-systems in the North Sea Area. Middle Ages–20th Century*, Turnhout, Brepols, CORN Publications Series 2, pp. 30–65.

de Vries, Jan & van der Woude, Ad (1997) *The First Modern Economy: Success, Failure, and Perseverance of the Dutch Economy, 1500–1815*, Cambridge University Press.

Goy, Joseph & Le Roy Ladurie, Emmanuel (eds) (1972) *Les Fluctuations du produit de la dîme. Conjoncture décimale et domaniale de la fin du Moyen Âge au XVIIIe siècle*, Paris-La Haye, Mouton.

Goy, Joseph & Le Roy Ladurie, Emmanuel (eds) (1982) *Prestations paysannes, dîmes, rente foncière et mouvement de la production agricole à l'époque moderne*, Paris-La Haye-New York, Mouton.

Grantham, George (1991) 'The Growth of Labour Productivity in the Production of Wheat in the Cinq Grosses Fermes of France, 1750–1929', in Bruce M. S. Campbell & Mark Overton (eds) (1991), *Land, Labour and Livestock. Historical Studies in European Agricultural Productivity*, Manchester, pp. 340–363.

Griffiths, Elisabeth (2003) 'Contrats de métayage et métayers dans le Norfolk à la fin du XVIIe siècle', in Gérard Béaur, Mathieu Arnoux & Anne Varet-Vitu (eds), *Exploiter la terre. Les contrats agraires de l'Antiquité à nos jours*, Rennes, Association d'Histoire des Sociétés Rurales, BHR 3, pp. 447–456.

Gurvil, Clément, (2010) *Les Paysans de Paris du milieu du xve au début du xviie siècle*, Paris, Honoré Champion.

Herment, Laurent (2012a) *Les Fruits du partage. Petits paysans du Bassin parisien au xixe siècle*, Rennes, Presses Universitaires de Rennes.

Herment, Laurent (2012b) 'Mesurer les performances 'céréalières' des petites exploitations du Bassin parisien durant le premier xixe siècle', *Histoire et Sociétés Rurales*, n°36, pp. 97–136.

Hoffman, Philip (1996) *Growth in a Traditional Society. The French Countryside 1450–1815*, Princeton University Press.

Hoyle, Richard W. (1990) 'Tenure and the Land Market in Early Modern England: or a Late Contribution to the Brenner Debate', *Economic History Review*, 43, pp. 1–20.

Hoyle, Richard W. (2003) 'Estate Management, Tenurial Change and Capitalist Farming in Sixteenth-century England', in Simonetta Cavaciocchi (ed.) (2004), *Il mercato della terra*, Acti delle 35 'Settimane di Studi' e altri Convegni, Istituto Internazionale di Storia Economica 'F. Datini', Prato, Le Monnier, pp. 353–82.

Jacquart, Jean (1974) *La Crise rurale en Île-de-France (1550–1670)*, Paris, Armand Colin.

Kander, Astrid & Warde, Paul, (2011) 'Energy Availability from Livestock and Agricultural Productivity in Europe, 1815–1913: a New Comparison', *Economic History Review*, vol. 64, n°1, pp. 1–29.

Kelly, Morgan & O'Grada, Cormac (2012) 'Population et niveau de vie dans la longue durée: l'histoire quantitative se mesure à Malthus', in Jean-Claude Daumas (ed.), *L'Histoire économique en mouvement entre héritages et renouvellements*, Villeneuve d'Ascq, Presses Universitaires du Septentrion, pp. 389–405.

Keyder, Caglar & O'Brien, Patrick (1978) *Economic Growth in Britain and France 1780–1914: Two Paths to the Twentieth Century*, London, George Allen & Unwin.

Lachiver, Marcel (1982) *Vin, vigne et vignerons en région parisienne du xviie au xixe siècle*, Pontoise, Société Historique et Archéologique de Pontoise, du Val d'Oise et du Vexin.

Lana Berasain, José Miguel (2011) 'Dealing with Deflation in Turbulent Times. Agricultural Markets and Rural Management in Southern Navarre (Spain), 1817–1833', *Histoire & Mesure*, XXVI, 1, pp. 75–104.

Laslett, Peter (1965) *The World We Have Lost*, London, Methuen.

Le Goff, T.J.A. & Sutherland, D. M.G. (1999) 'La Révolution française et l'économie rurale', *Histoire & Mesure*, XIV, 1/2, pp. 79–120.

Le Goff, T.J.A. & Sutherland, D.M. G. (2000) 'What Can We Learn from Leases? A Preliminary View', *Histoire & Mesure*, XV, 3/4, pp. 289–320.

Le Roy Ladurie, Emmanuel (1966) *Les Paysans de Languedoc*, Paris, SEVPEN.

Le Roy Ladurie, Emmanuel (1973) 'Anthropologie de la jeunesse masculine en France au niveau d'une cartographie cantonale (1819–1830)', in Emmanuel Le Roy Ladurie, *Le territoire de l'historien*, vol. 1, Paris, Gallimard.

Le Roy Ladurie, Emmanuel (1978) 'Les Paysans français au xvie siècle', in Emmanuel Le Roy Ladurie, *Le Territoire de l'Historien*, vol 2, Paris, Gallimard.

Levasseur, Emile (1893) 'Des Progrès de l'agriculture française dans la seconde moitié du xviiie siècle', *Revue d'Economie Politique*, t. XII, n°1, pp. 1–29.

Lévy-Leboyer, Maurice & Bourguignon, François (1985) *L'Economie française au* XIX*e siècle. Analyse Macroéconomique*, Paris, Economica.

Marchand, Olivier & Thélot, Claude (1991) *Deux siècles de travail en France*. Paris, INSEE.

Marx, Karl, *Capital. A Critique of Political Economy*, 1867 (English translation, 1887) Chapters 27 and 29, 'Expropriation of the Agricultural Population from the Land' and 'Genesis of the Capitalist Farmer'.

Mathias, Peter (2001) *The First Industrial Nation: The Economic History of Britain 1700–1914*, Routledge, London & New York.

Mérot, Florent (2007) 'Un Paysage rural à l'ombre de Paris. La vallée de Montmorency aux XVIIe et XVIIIe siècles', *Bulletin de la Société Historique de Montmorency et de sa Région*, vol. 25, pp. 14–36.

Mérot, Florent (2010) *L'Homme et son milieu en vallée de Montmorency sous l'Ancien Régime. Un paysage original aux portes de Paris (vers 1640-vers 1800)*, Thèse Université Paris XIII-Villetaneuse.

Meuvret, Jean (1977 & 1988) *Le Problème des subsistances à l'époque Louis XIV*, vol. I : *La production des céréales dans la France du* XVII*e et du* XVIII*e siècle*, Paris/La Haye, EHESS/Mouton, 2 vol. ; vol. II : *La production des céréales et la société rurale*, Paris, EHESS, 1987, 2 vol.

Moriceau Jean.-Marc & Postel-Vinay Gilles (1992) *Ferme, Entreprise, Famille, Grande exploitation et changements agricoles,* XVII*e*-XIX*e siècles*, Paris, Éditions de l'École des Hautes Études en Sciences Sociales.

Morineau, Michel (1971) *Les Faux-semblants d'un démarrage économique : agriculture et démographie en France au* XVIII*e siècle*, Paris, Armand Colin, *Cahiers des Annales*, 30.

Morineau, Michel (1991) 'Ruralia', *Revue Historique*, 1991, 2, pp. 359–384, and in Gérard Béaur (ed.), *La Terre et les hommes: France et Grande-Bretagne (*XVII*e*-XVIII*e siècles)*, Paris, Hachette, 1998, pp. 174–183.

Neeson, Jeanette M. (1993) *Commoners: Common Right, Enclosure and Social Change in England, 1700–1820*, Cambridge University Press.

O'Brien, Patrick (1996) 'Path Dependency, or Why Britain Became an Industrialized and Urbanized Economy Long Before France', *Economic History Review*, 49 (2), pp. 213–249.

Olsson, Mats & Svensson, Patrick (eds) (2011) *Growth and Stagnation in European Historical Agriculture*, Turnhout, Brepols, Rural History in Europe series 6.

Orwell, G. (1967) *The Road to Wigan Pier*, London, Penguin Books.

Overton, Mark (1979) 'Estimating Crop Yields from Probate Inventories: An Example from East Anglia, 1585–1735', *Journal of Economic History*, vol. 39, 1979, pp. 363–378.

Overton, Mark (1980) 'English Probate Inventories as a Source for Research in Economic and Social History', *AAG Bijdragen*, 23, pp. 205–216.

Overton, Mark (1996) *Agricultural Revolution in England: the Transformation of the Agrarian Economy 1500–1800*, Cambridge University Press.

Overton, Mark (2005) 'Inventaires après décès et mesure du changement agricole en Angleterre, 1550–1750', in Nadine Vivier (ed), *Ruralité française et britannique,* XIII*e*-XX*e siècles: approches comparées*, Rennes, Presses Universitaires de Rennes, pp. 229–244.

Overton, Mark & Campbell, Bruce M. S. (1991) 'Productivity Change in European Agricultural Development', in Bruce M.S. Campbell & Mark Overton (eds), *Land, Labour and Livestock: Historical Studies in European Agricultural Productivity*, Manchester University Press, pp. 1–50.

Overton, Mark & Campbell, Bruce M. S. (1992) 'Norfolk Livestock Farming 1250–1740: a comparative study of manorial accounts and probate inventories', *Journal of Historical Geography*, 18, pp. 377–96.

Overton, Mark & Campbell, Bruce M. S. (1996) 'Production et productivité dans l'agriculture anglais, 1086–1871', *Histoire et Mesure*, XI-3/4, pp. 255–297.

Pérez-Picazo, Maria Teresa (2000) 'Essor de la production et gains de productivité agricole dans une región meditérranéenne au XIXe siècle. Le cas de Murcie', *Histoire & Mesure*, XI, 3/4, pp. 217–312.

Pinilla, Vicente (ed.) (2009) *Markets and Agricultural Change in Europe from the 13th to the 20th century*, Turnhout, Brepols, Rural History in Europe series 2.

Poussou, Jean-Pierre (1999) 'L'"Alternative agriculture". A propos d'un livre récent de Joan Thirsk', *Histoire & Sociétés Rurales*, n°12, pp. 131–148.

Revel, Jacques (1982) 'Rendements, production et productivité: les grands domaines de la Campagne romaine aux XVIIe et XVIIIe siècles', in Joseph Goy & Emmanuel Le Roy Ladurie (eds), *Prestations paysannes, dîmes, rente foncière et mouvement de la production agricole à l'époque préindustrielle*, Paris, EHESS, vol. 1, pp. 226–236.

Rostow, Walt Whitman (1960) *The Stages of Economic Growth: A Non-Communist Manifesto,* Cambridge University Press.

Simpson, James (1995) *Spanish Agriculture. The Long Siesta, 1765–1965*, Cambridge University Press.

Thirsk, Joan (2000) *Alternative Agriculture: A History from the Black Death to the Present Day*, Oxford University Press.

Thoen, Erik (2001) 'A "Commercial Survival Economy" in Evolution. The Flemish Countryside and the Cransition to Capitalism (Middle Ages–19th century)', in Peter Hoppenbrouwers and Jan Luiten van Zanden, (eds*), Peasants Into Farmers? The Transformation of Rural Economy and Society in the Low Countries (Middle Ages–19th Century*) *in Light of the Brenner Debate*, Turnhout, Brepols, CORN Publication Series 4, pp. 102–157.

Thoen, Erik (2004) '"Social agrosystems" as an Economic Concept to Explain Regional Differences. An Essay Taking the Former County of Flanders as an Example (Middle Ages–19th century)', in Bas J. P. van Bavel and Peter Hoppenbrouwers (eds), *Landholding and Land Transfer in the North Sea Area (Late Middle Ages–19th Century),* Turnhout, Brepols, CORN Publication Series 5, pp. 47–66.

Toutain, Jean-Claude (1961) 'Le Produit de l'agriculture française de 1700 à 1958', *Cahiers de l'ISEA*, AF n° 1 et 2.

Traversat, Michel (2001) *Etude sur les jardins français et sur les jardiniers et les pépiniéristes*, Thèse EHESS.

Verdon, Nicola (2002) *Rural Women Workers in Nineteenth-Century England: Gender, Workers and Wages*, Boydell, Woodbridge.

Verley, Patrick (1997) *La Révolution industrielle*, Paris, Gallimard.

Wrigley, Edward A. (1989) 'Urban Growth and Agricultural Change: England and Continent in the Early Modern Period', in Edward A. Wrigley, *People, Cities and Wealth, Oxford*, Blackwell Publ., pp. 157–193.

van Zanden, Jan Luiten (1994) *The Transformation of European Agriculture in the 19th century. The Case of Netherlands*, Amsterdam, VU Uitgeverij.

van Zanden, Jan Luiten (2009) *The Long Road to the Industrial Revolution. The European Economy in a Global Perspective, 1000–1800*, Leiden-Boston, Brill.

2 Unit land values as a guide to agricultural land productivity in medieval England*

Bruce M. S. Campbell, The Queen's University of Belfast

I. Introduction. Alternative measures of yields and land productivity

There are several different land productivities (Overton, 1996: 70–74; Overton and Campbell, 1996: 256–60, 288–89). The most difficult to measure from the historical record, especially for relatively early periods, is total agricultural output per unit area of farmland. One reason is that complete information on the full range of agricultural outputs – field and horticultural crops; hay, straw, grass and other sources of fodder; timber and wood products; and animals and animal products – is in practice never available. Another is that the total area of all farmland is seldom recorded and often included grazing and other hard-to-quantify rights in common pastures and wastes. A third is that problems attach to the conversion of very different commodities into standard units of measurement. This is most obviously and easily done using prices, but rarely is a sufficient range of accurate price information available. For these reasons historians generally rely upon more limited measures of land productivity.

Crop yields per unit area devoted to that crop are the single most specific, readily available, and widely used measure of land productivity. Even so, they are rarely truly representative of productivity in general for they are invariably limited in availability to certain types of farm, periods of time, and geographical contexts. They can also be misleading, for, at constant yields, the more frequently that land was cropped, the higher its productivity. Indeed, some producers accepted lower yields per *grain* or *cropped* acre in order to secure higher yields per *arable* acre. Usually that meant replacing fallows with courses of legumes and expending more labour on manuring, ploughing and weeding. Weighted Aggregate Crop Yields (WACY) per unit area of arable (weighted by the relative price and sown area of each crop) therefore represent a superior measure of the true productivity of the arable sector. Calculating this measure naturally makes more exacting demands upon the evidence since it requires documents that either record the area fallowed and/or left uncultivated or allow that area to be estimated via the reconstruction of rotations.

Table 2.1 summarises the composite seeding rates, individual crop yields, Weighted Aggregate Grain Yields (WAGY) yields per seed and per grain acre, and WACY yields per seed and per arable acre, calculated for six well documented demesnes operating contrasting cropping and rotational systems over the period *c.* 1280 to *c.* 1360 (Thornton,

* Adapted from Bruce M. S. Campbell (2000), Chapter 7: 'Arable productivity', and Bruce M. S. Campbell and Ken Bartley (2006), Chapter 10: 'The demesne: unit land values'.

Table 2.1 Alternative measures of arable productivity on six demesnes, *c.* 1300–1349[1]

Manor	Cropping Type	Grain area as % arable	Seeding rate	Gross yield per seed			Grain area		Arable area	
				Wheat/ (Rye)	Barley	Oats	Relative value	WAGY per seed (gross)	Relative value	WACY per seed (gross)
Index: 100 =		050.1		003.4	002.8	001.9	064.1	002.1	034.8	001.1
Martham	1	**148**	**312**	168	114	147	**123**	152	**200**	241
Cuxham	5	122	175	**188**	**207**	163	119	**214**	144	**261**
Brightwell	4	*100*	200	132	196	142	**123**	177	118	173
Rimpton	5	122	*100*	165	175	**184**	117	187	140	227
Bircham	2	108	190	(135)	129	168	*100*	121	*100*	124
Cheriton	5	*100*	163	*100*	*100*	*100*	110	*100*	108	*100*

[1] Cheriton was also out-performed by all five of the Taunton demesnes of the bishop of Winchester and the Westminster Abbey demesne at Kinsbourne in Hertfordshire (Thornton, 2003). These demesnes, like Cheriton, grew mainly wheat and oats but gained part of their productivity edge by doing so in three-course rather than two-course rotations.

Table 2.1 Alternative measures of arable productivity on six demesnes, *c.* 1300–1349[1]

Manor	Cropping	Grain	Seeding	Gross yield per seed			Grain area		Arable area	
	type	as % arable	rate	Wheat/ (Rye)	Barley	Oats	Relative value	WAGY per acre (net)	Relative value	WACY per acre (net)
Index: 100 =		052.7		005.1	007.3	003.8	064.1	003.7	034.8	002.0
Martham	1	**174**	**312**	**353**	211	**437**	**123**	**344**	**200**	**521**
Cuxham	5	127	175	282	271	242	119	288	144	349
Brightwell	4	*100*	200	135	**299**	255	**123**	236	118	229
Rimpton	5	126	*100*	137	162	192	117	144	140	177
Bircham	2	103	190	*(100)*	162	261	*100*	158	*100*	159
Cheriton	5	102	163	104	*100*	*100*	110	*100*	108	*100*

Source: Campbell, 1983: 390–4; Thornton, 1991: 191–3; Titow, 1962: 17–18, 67; Titow, 1972; National accounts database; FTC1 accounts database; Table 5.07.

Note: Gross and net yields are both net of tithe.

WAGY = weighted aggregate grain yield; WACY = weighted aggregate crop yield. **bold** = maximum; *italics* = minimum

[1] Cheriton was also out-performed by all five of the Taunton demesnes of the bishop of Winchester and the Westminster Abbey demesne at Kinsbourne in Hertfordshire (Thornton, 2003). These demesnes, like Cheriton, grew mainly wheat and oats but gained part of their productivity edge by doing so in three-course rather than two-course rotations.

2003: 118,120).[2] Martham (Norfolk), the only one of the six to have employed virtually continuous cultivation, is an example of cropping-type one – the most intensive of all cropping types – and was one of the most valued possessions of Norwich Cathedral Priory. Bircham, also in Norfolk, is on intrinsically poorer light land and hence was cultivated using a convertible regime whereby the arable was sown for three or four years and then fallowed for an equivalent period. It belonged to the de Clares, earls of Gloucester and Hertford, and is an example of cropping-type two. Cuxham in Oxfordshire, a property of Merton College Oxford, and Rimpton in Somerset, part of the estate of the bishops of Winchester, both operated regular three-course rotations devoted mostly to the cultivation of wheat and oats and, as such, are examples of cropping-type five.[3] Cheriton on the southern edge of the Hampshire Downs and Brightwell in Berkshire's Vale of the White Horse also belonged to the bishops of Winchester. The former is a third example of cropping-type five whereas the latter is an example of cropping-type four, cultivating wheat and oats in conjunction with significant areas with barley and legumes. Both operated two-course rotations.

How great was the differential between the most and least productive of these six demesnes? As Table 2.1 reveals, the verdict depends to a great extent upon the choice of productivity measure. For instance, on the evidence of the gross yield per seed of individual crops the maximum productivity differential was barely twofold between the maximum yields obtained for wheat and barley by Cuxham and oats by Rimpton and the minimum yields for all three crops obtained by Cheriton. WAGY yields calculated on those yield ratios widen the gap slightly to a little more than two-fold and WACY yields, which take account of the frequency of cropping, widen it further to over two-and-a-half-fold. Both measures identify Cuxham as the highest- and Cheriton as the lowest-yielding demesnes. Gross yields per seed nevertheless understate the contrast. Thus, net yields per acre (which, unlike yields per seed, take account of variations in seeding rates) reveal a three- to four-fold difference in the output per unit area of the individual crops, the differential being greatest for oats and least for barley. Collectively, WAGY yields confirm a three-and-a-half-fold difference in the net output of grains, with Martham now eclipsing Cuxham as the most productive demesne while Cheriton is confirmed as the least productive. Yet even WAGY yields understate the true productivity gap, which WACY yields per arable acre show to have been in excess of fivefold between Martham and Cheriton (twice the maximum differential between these two demesnes indicated by WACY gross yields per seed). Underpinning this contrast lay differences in the crops being cultivated and their respective values, differences in the rates at which seed was sown, and differences in the proportions of the arable that were cropped. Plainly, by themselves individual crop yields are a very partial and inadequate measure of land productivity.

Nor is this the whole story, for how productivity is measured also affects the verdicts passed on the respective performances of individual demesnes. Yield ratios suggest that

---

[2] C. Thornton has calculated WACY net yields per acre for the five demesnes of the bishop of Winchester at Taunton in Somerset plus the demesne at Kinsbourne in Hertfordshire belonging to Westminster Abbey. All six of these demesnes operated three-course rotations and employed variants of cropping-type five. Their indexed WACY yields are as follows: Taunton Hull 203; Taunton Holway 202; Taunton Staplegrove 159; Kinsbourne 141; Taunton Nailsbourne 133; Taunton Poundisford 117.

[3] For detailed analysis and discussion of these two demesnes (Harvey, 1976; Thornton, 1991: 183–210).

Cuxham was the most productive, by a narrow margin, of these six demesnes. WACY yields put it 14% ahead of Rimpton and WAGY yields just 8% ahead of Martham. Net yields per acre, on the other hand, leave no doubt of Martham's superiority. Although barley, its main crop, yielded 22% lower than at Cuxham and 29% lower than at Brightwell, its wheat and oats yields were respectively 25% and 67% better than those of its nearest rivals. WAGY yields per acre put it 19% ahead of Cuxham and WACY yields widen this advantage to an impressive 50%. Acre for acre, the monks of Norwich obtained half as much again from their demesne arable at Martham as did the fellows of Merton College Oxford from theirs at Cuxham. Notwithstanding consistently inferior yield ratios, Martham emerges as by far the more productive demesne.

Similarly, whereas yield ratios suggest that three-course Rimpton out-performed two-course Brightwell by a substantial margin, net yields per acre reverse that advantage and put Brightwell 30% ahead of Rimpton. The latter may have sown more of its arable and secured better returns on the seed sown, but Brightwell sowed its arable twice as thickly and thereby obtained significantly higher net yields per acre. Both productivity measures do, however, concur in placing Bircham consistently ahead of Cheriton. Neither had the benefit of good soils, with the result that both regularly sowed only half of their arable. Yet whereas Cheriton employed biennial fallowing, Bircham practised a form of convertible husbandry. Probably it was this, a function of its more flexible field system, which gave Bircham its productivity edge. Its WACY yields per seed and per acre were respectively 24% and 59% higher than those at Cheriton.

On the evidence of these six demesnes, provided that land quality and economic opportunities were propitious, increasing the proportion of the arable under crops, substituting high-value for low-value crops (e.g. wheat for rye and barley for oats), adopting more flexible rotations, and raising seeding rates provided medieval demesne managers with their best prospects of improving land productivity. Improving yield ratios *per se* was harder to achieve and, paradoxically, did not necessarily guarantee higher net returns per acre of arable, since lengthening fallows and lowering yield ratios were the strategies most likely to deliver this result. Any demesne that matched the standard of arable productivity attained and sustained at Martham during the first half of the fourteenth century was doing outstandingly well. The neighbouring demesne of Hemsby, also in the possession of the prior of Norwich, may just have had the edge on Martham, but no more. Both cropped practically their entire arable area and in each case the arable was expected to yield an annual net income or 'profit' of at least 28d an acre.[4] Valuations as high or higher do occur elsewhere but, on the evidence of *IPM* valuations, are exceptionally rare (Table 2.2 and Figure 2.1).[5] They are confined to a few equally distinctive localities – the

---

[4] The arable was actually valued at 36d per customary acre measured according to a perch of 18½ feet; i.e. each customary acre was equivalent to 1¼ statute acres: B.L., Stowe MS 936 fol. 37. At about this time the actual purchase price of small parcels of arable in this fertile and densely populated district often exceeded £2 per acre. In 1284–5 the prior of Norwich paid £1 10s 0d per acre at Plumstead, £2 7s 1d at Hemsby, and £3 3s 4d at Scratby, but only 7s 6d at Hindolveston: N.R.O., DCN 1/1/8.

[5] In 1915 H. L. Gray drew attention to 'the somewhat numerous Kentish manors on which in the middle of the fourteenth century all the acres of the demesne were sown yearly [...] under these conditions the value of an acre often became 12d'. Notable examples include the lands of John Crul (1271–2) and Thomas de Morton (1293), and the demesnes at Ivychurch (1308–9), Westgate

Table 2.2 Frequency distribution of mean value per (sown) acre of arable, England south of the Trent, 1300–1349

Mean value per acre of (sown) arable pence	Number of places
<1	5
1 – <2	76
2 – <3	495
3 – <4	829
4 – <5	1,148
5 – <6	133
6 – <7	548
7 – <8	28
8 – <9	111
9 – <10	24
10 – <11	24
11 – <12	4
12 – <15	126
15 – <18	10
18 – <21	19
21 – <24	2
24 – <30	22
30 – <36	3
36<	6
N	3,613
Mean = 4.64d	

Source: Campbell 2000: 348.

silt fens of Lincolnshire and Norfolk, and the Isle of Thanet and Romney Marsh in Kent. Common denominators in each case include deep, naturally fertile and easily cultivated soils, freedom from communal rotations, an abundant labour force, and convenient access

in Thanet, and Elmstone (both 1309–10) – all valued at 24–29d an acre: P.R.O., C132 File 41(16); C133 File 64(14); C134 Files 10(14), 17(7); the demesnes at Flete (1263–4) and Wickham (1330) – valued at 30–35d an acre: P.R.O., C132 File 31(1); C135 File 23; and the demesnes at Preston and Overland (1309–10) – both valued at 36d an acre: P.R.O., C134 File 17(7) (Gray, 1915: 302).

to major markets both locally and at a distance. While it is conceivable that Martham's standard of land productivity may have been exceeded by demesnes in these rival localities, it is inconceivable that it can have been by a significant margin. Certainly West Walton, the one relatively well-documented demesne in the Norfolk Fenland, secured WAGY net yields per acre that were a third lower than Martham's. Nor does Canterbury Cathedral Priory's Romney Marsh demesne of Appledore appear to have yielded any better. On the available evidence Martham and Hemsby win the laurels for the most productive arable demesnes currently known in early fourteenth-century England.

Outside these few economically and environmentally privileged areas land productivity and arable valuations were both lower. Here there can be little doubt that poor as was Cheriton's productivity performance, there were many demesnes whose land productivity was even lower. Conspicuous among them were those light-land demesnes whose soils repaid only the lightest seeding rates and admitted little more than infrequent cultivation of the hardier grains, particularly rye and oats. Under these environmental constraints low yields per arable acre were practically unavoidable. The bishop of Ely's demesne at Brandon in the Suffolk Breckland and bishop of Winchester's demesne at Esher in Surrey are good examples of this type of low-yielding demesne.[6] Many upland areas in the north and west imposed equivalent constraints, limiting the range of crops that could be grown and the intensity of their cultivation, as, for example, in the case of the predominantly oats-growing demesnes of Bolton Priory in the Pennine valleys of the Wharfe and Aire (Kershaw, 1973: 71–78; Miller, 1975: 1–16). The maximum differential in arable land-productivity between the most and least productive demesnes is therefore likely to have been considerably greater than the five-fold differential between Martham and Cheriton. On the poorest soils of west Norfolk, for instance, arable valuations fell to 2d an acre or less, in contrast to the princely 28d commanded by Martham. Valuations as low or lower occur in many other parts of the country, especially in the poorer areas of the Welsh borderland and the south-west, where low levels of land productivity were presumably the norm (Figure 2.1).

II. Unit land values

At the end of the day, what mattered to producers was less the physical output of crops from the land than whether costs were covered, a net surplus produced, and a profit made. The rent or profit to be obtained from any given acre of arable was a function of the crop that it yielded times the price of that crop less production costs. It follows that a close association must therefore have existed between the rate at which arable yielded and the value placed upon it. Systematic statistical comparison of yields and valuations confirms such an association. Between 1295 and 1341 Norwich Cathedral Priory maintained a central record of both yields and unit land values on 14 of its demesnes.[7] Statistical analysis of the relationship between the value per sown acre and the WAGY

[6] See M. Bailey for an account of Breckland cropping systems (Bailey, 1989: 56–65).

[7] Norfolk Record Office (hereafter N.R.O.), DCN 66/1; DCN R236A. See E. Stone for a discussion of these profit calculations and their significance (Stone, 1962), and also Postles (1986).

net yield per acre on these 14 demesnes yields a clear positive correlation of +0.79.[8] The strength of this correlation is all the more remarkable given the approximate nature of the valuations, the evidential shortcomings of the WAGY yields, and the differing unit production costs of these 14 demesnes, with their contrasting soils, varying ploughing technologies, and differing labour processes. Perhaps that is why sown arable at Martham commanded a value over three times that at Sedgeford even though Martham's WAGY yields were barely 50% better. A positive correlation between the productivity and value of arable was by no means confined to the Norfolk demesnes of Norwich Cathedral Priory. Within the county as a whole a correlation of WAGY net yields per acre on 36 demesnes against the mean value per acre of arable at those self same locations, as estimated from *inquistiones post mortem* (*IPM*s), yields a positive correlation coefficient of +0.56. Extending this exercise to include the 50 demesnes belonging to the bishop of Winchester produces a marginally higher positive correlation coefficient of +0.58. On this evidence values per acre as recorded by *IPM* extents can be used as a surrogate guide to variations in land productivity.[9]

Few valuations made for the royal escheators were as scrupulously estimated as those calculated on behalf of Norwich Cathedral Priory.[10] Most represent generalised values for a notionally 'average' year. Some bear all the hallmarks of careful estimation, others are patently much more impressionistic. Many are stated explicitly but some have to be calculated from the information provided separately of the total value and total amount of land. The strength of the *IPM*s therefore lies less in their precision than their quantity, for they are the single greatest available compendium of information on the unit value of land at the climax of medieval agrarian expansion in the early fourteenth century. These valuations represent not the total capital value of the land but the anticipated net profit or 'rent' that it was capable of yielding, depending upon whether it was managed directly or farmed out (Raftis, 1974: 16–17). They are representative of a far wider cross-section of estates than accounts (albeit, all of them in lay ownership) and are incomparably fuller in their geographical coverage, with over 3,750 separate locations represented in the counties south of the Trent. For all their inadequacies, they are arguably the best available *indirect* guide to spatial variations in the productivity of arable in the half century or so before the Black Death (Campbell, 2000: 37–40; Campbell and Bartley, 2006). Significantly, they were not fixed and immutable but varied over time as output and prices rose and fell (Campbell, 2000: 345–64). Between 1270 and 1349 they reveal a chronology in which short term variations were superimposed upon a long-term tendency for unit values to decline. Irrespective of land-use type, the unit values recorded in the 1340s were substantially below those returned when values were at their peak in the late 1270s and the

[8] The demesnes emesnes are Eaton, Gateley, Gnatingdon, Hemsby, Hindolveston, Hindringham, Martham, Monks Granges, Newton-by-Norwich, North Elmham, Plumstead, Sedgeford, Taverham and Thornham. The WAGY yields are calculated from the yields recorded in the *Proficuum maneriorum* (N.R.O., DCN R236A) augmented by relevant manorial accounts.

[9] On the same reasoning R. Allen has used rents as an index of productivity differences (Allen, 1992: 176–9).

[10] These values pertain to an average type of grain (and price) on an average piece of land in a typical year. Allowance was sometimes made for different qualities of land and possibly even for the particular crops sown in the rotation course in the year of the extent.

early 1290s. Combining unit values from the entire 50-year period 1300–49 to produce a single map therefore leads to some unavoidable loss of precision.

The relationship between unit value and unit output was nevertheless indirect rather than direct due to the mediating effect of production costs, which varied in their own right according to the nature of the prevailing husbandry system, wage rates, and the physical attributes of the land. The most important of these costs were labour, draught power, and capital inputs, notably seed and fertiliser. Their sum total per acre could be considerable. Walter of Henley reckoned that it required at least a threefold yield to defray the costs of cultivation, on which estimate many arable demesnes can barely have broken even (Oschinsky, 1971: 272–273, 325). Whether Walter's estimate is high or low there is no doubt that cultivation costs were invariably several times the annual rental value of the land being cultivated. The margin between profit and loss was consequently a very narrow one and likely to vary a good deal from year to year.

Labour was an intrinsic component of the costs of manuring and marling, ploughing, harrowing, sowing, weeding, reaping and stacking, carting, threshing and winnowing. The mid-thirteenth-century *Fleta* reckoned that it cost 25½d per acre to prepare and harvest a crop, exclusive of the cost of seed (Langdon, 1986: 267). Walter of Henley endorses this figure, on the basis that three ploughings cost 6d each, one harrowing 1d, weeding ½d., reaping 5d, and carriage 1d per acre (Oschinsky, 1971: 325). Kosminsky, however, has argued that many demesnes could manage with half this level of expenditure (Kosminsky 1956: 288–9). Nevertheless, Walter's estimate is remarkably close to the actual level of expenditure per sown acre on Merton College's manor of Cuxham in Oxfordshire before 1348, where total labour costs were approximately 22d per sown acre.[11] As has been seen, Cuxham obtained above average yields from a regular three-course rotation. On more intensively worked demesnes, with more frequent ploughings, greater attention to manuring and weeding, and a heavier harvest to reap, cart, stack, and thresh, labour costs would have been correspondingly higher, especially in regions of above average wage rates. Thus, agricultural wages were consistently higher in the vicinity of London than those in the provinces (Farmer, 1988: 734). As a general rule, wages were highest where prices were highest and vice versa, with the result that they partially offset the tendency of prices to inflate or deflate land values.

After labour, the single greatest production cost was draught power, primarily for ploughing and harrowing but also for haulage. Certainly, the direct costs of maintaining demesne draught animals, ploughs and carts could be considerable. Animals had to be managed, fed, and shod, ploughs and carts to be repaired and maintained. All three were subject to depreciation and required regular replacement. At Cuxham, *c.*1300, John Langdon has estimated that maintaining the demesne's ploughs, plough beasts, carts, and cart-horses will have added a further 13d per sown acre per year (Langdon, 1982: 32–38; Harvey, 1965: 57–61). Such costs naturally varied a good deal from demesne to demesne, depending upon the type of plough, size and composition of team, speed of ploughing, and physical wear and tear on ploughs and carts (Campbell, 2000: 120–134). In this, light-land farmers enjoyed a real cost advantage over their heavy-land counterparts. By

[11] Calculated from P. D. A. Harvey (Harvey, 1965: 75–86, 164–71), using mean national prices for the period 1290–1347 calculated from D. L. Farmer (Farmer, 1988: 734).

the second quarter of the fourteenth-century unit ploughing costs at light-soil Sedgeford, in the extreme north-east of Norfolk, were only a quarter those of heavy-soil Thorpe Abbotts on the boulder clays of south Norfolk.[12] Such charges obviously bit deep into the net profit that could be made from arable land and ensured that stiff and heavy clay soils were rarely valued in the *IPM*s at more than 6d an acre.

The other main costs involved in arable production were seed and fertiliser. Commercial incentives had to be strong before demesnes would commit themselves to a policy of heavy seeding rates and labour-intensive manuring. For instance, during the first half of the fourteenth century it would have cost on average 18d to sow an acre of wheat at a rate of 2 bushels, but 36d to sow it at a maximum rate of 4 bushels. There was therefore a positive relationship between costs and prices which meant that one tended to compensate for the other in the determination of land values. Certain other costs were yield dependent. Larger harvests required more labour to reap, stack, and thresh the grain (Clarck, 1991: 221–231). Improving net yields per unit area by shortening fallows and lengthening rotations raised the work-loads of man and beast and, other things being equal, thereby added substantially to unit costs. Because high rates of output were contingent upon high rates of input, high-yielding demesnes were not necessarily profitable. Nor, for that matter, were low productivity systems necessarily loss making, as Mark Bailey's analysis of demesne husbandry in Breckland has amply demonstrated (Bailey, 1989). Low-yielding demesnes could generate worthwhile profits provided that unit costs were kept down. Yield-dependent costs thus had the opposite effect from price-dependent costs upon the capacity of unit land values to reflect variations in land productivity.

Price variations provided some cushion against temporal fluctuations in physical yield, since low yields tended to be compensated by high prices and *vice versa*. Indeed, seigniorial producers reliant upon the market for the disposal of much of their output had far more to fear from glut than they had from dearth. Prices also varied spatially and this, too, could make a difference to the unit value of land. Other things being equal, high prices could inflate and low prices deflate the value of land independently of any real difference in physical productivity. Moreover, the spatial range in prices could be considerable. In a low-price region such as the east midlands mean wheat prices were on average 26% below the national average *c.*1300, whereas in the high-price region of south Hampshire they were 18% above that average (Farmer, 1988: 744). On David Farmer's figures, prices were lowest in inland areas at some remove from major markets and, often, with no cheap means of getting their grain to them, as in the case of the east midland counties of Leicestershire and Northamptonshire and the Cotswolds of Oxfordshire and Gloucestershire. More surprisingly, low prices were a feature of Cambridgeshire and the lower Severn valley, both of which, and especially the latter, enjoyed good riverine communications and were involved in the wider grain trade (Gras, 1915: 171–6; Pelham, 1936: 301; Farmer, 1991: 356, 372). Low prices were probably a precondition of participation in that trade since they were necessary to defray high transport costs. The influence of transport costs upon local prices is clearly to be seen within the wheat-supply zone of London, where the difference between the local and the London wheat price was commonly the cost of transporting the grain to that city (Campbell, Galloway, Keene and Murphy, 1993: 63–69,

[12] N.R.O., L'Estrange IB 1/4, 3/4; WAL 274 × 6/479–95.

193–198). Nevertheless, there were also areas within these counties where the price was generally too high to admit of profitable sale in London and others where prices were so low that they appear to have been beyond the capital's influence (Campbell and al., 1993: 66–67). This differential was of a sufficient magnitude to have had a real impact on relative land values.

Far greater distortions arise from the concurrent use of statute and non-statute acres. Only in eastern and south-eastern England had the acre become the ubiquitous unit of land measurement. Yet even here the statute acre measured with a perch of 16½ feet was far from universally employed. Some customary acres were smaller, others could be as much as twice as large. Arable valuations of 3d, 4d, and 6d an acre might thus simply reflect differences in the sizes of the acres being valued. This naturally creates the greatest problems wherever it was the norm to employ customary rather than statute acres, especially when the size discrepancy between customary and statute acres was pronounced. Both conditions prevailed in much of England north of the Trent. In Cheshire, Lancashire, and the Border counties customary acres were typically more than twice the size of statute acres. Mean per acre values calculated for these areas will thus appear inflated when set against those calculated for areas employing smaller customary acres or statute acres. Unfortunately, there is no simple or reliable way of removing this distortion. In fact, abnormally low or high per acre valuations are themselves a useful clue to the possible existence of under-size or out-size customary acres.

Unit land values were also affected by variations in property rights. Whether or not rights of common grazing applied to fallow arable and mown meadows could make a modest but material difference to their respective unit values. Sometimes, too, the arable could gain added value from the common rights in meadows, pastures, and 'wastes' that were appurtenant to it. In the north of England this may in part be why so much arable was valued so highly and why pasturage was seemingly so scarce (i.e. the value of the latter is subsumed in the former). Scarcity could similarly result in the transfer of value from one land use to another. As Adam Smith explained,

> [...] In an open country [...] of which the principal produce is corn, a well-inclosed piece of grass will frequently rent higher than any corn field in its neighbourhood. It is convenient for the maintenance of the cattle employed in the cultivation of the corn, and its high rent is, in this case, not so properly paid from the values of its own produce, as from that of the corn lands which are cultivated by means of it (Smith, 1872: 69).

Arable, meadow, and pasture did not exist in isolation of each other; whichever was in most limited supply may have gained transferred value from that which was most abundant. In many lowland arable-husbandry contexts it is likely to have been the meadow whose unit value, as Smith points out, was most prone to inflation in this way. Conversely, in upland pastoral-husbandry contexts the rental value of the arable may have been enhanced by its vital role in supplying the larger pastoral sector with the fodder crops and straw necessary to sustain animals through the winter. The unit values of individual land uses should therefore be analysed in combination as well on their own (Table 2.4 and Figure 2.3). It is also desirable to combine temporal with spatial analysis, analysis of mean unit values with analysis of extreme unit values, and analysis of any given land-use type's unit value with analysis of its absolute quantity. Only a range of different approaches can bring out all the attributes and imperfections inherent within the data. As much care needs to be exercised in the interpretation of the results thereby obtained.

III. The unit value of arable and other land-uses, 1300–1349

Demesne arable valuations ranged from 1d to 36d per acre, with a modal value of 4d and a mean of 4.8d (Table 2.2 and Figure 2.1). The tendency for valuations to cluster at multiples of 3d and 4d – i.e. 6d, 8d, 12d, 18d, 24d, and 36d – is very pronounced and highlights the notional nature of these valuations. The vast majority of arable land was, however, valued at 6d an acre or less. The same clustering is even more marked in the valuation of meadow land, since it commanded valuations which ranged from 3d to as much as 80d (i.e. half a mark). Nevertheless, 12d, 18d, and 24d an acre were the per acre values most commonly returned by the jurors who supplied the information. Meadow, on most manors the most highly values land-use, had a modal value of 12d and a mean value of 18.6d. Pasture was the least highly valued land use. Valuations ranged from a fraction of a penny to 24d per acre, with a modal value of less than 2d and a mean value of 3.4d.

Selective mapping of arable worth less than 3d or at least 8d – the highest and lowest of these unit valuations – highlights a clear spatial dichotomy between that part of the country which lay to the south and west of a line running from London to Chester and that which lay to the north and east (Figure 2.1). The former area is characterised by large numbers of exceptionally low and, apart from coastal Sussex, no significant concentrations of high per acre valuations. The latter area, in contrast, contains the bulkof the highest per acre valuations with a strong tendency for those valuations to occur in distinctive sub-regional groupings: the Hull Valley of East Yorkshire, coastal Lincolnshire, the East Anglian silt fens, central and eastern Norfolk, s outh Cambridgeshire, northern and eastern Kent, and the coastal plain of south-west Sussex. In every case, the highest valuations of all are supported by numbers of valuations that are well above the national average. They also occur within a relatively short distance of some correspondingly low valuations: on the Lincolnshire Wolds, on the poor sands of west Norfolk, on the heavy boulder-clay soils of north-east Suffolk, and on the infertile sands and heavy clays of western and central Kent and interior Sussex. Significantly, high and low valuations were returned within the same sub-escheatries. North of the Trent the pattern is strikingly different. Here there are almost no low valuations to counterbalance the significant numbers of high valuations, many of which occur in relatively remote locations that were far from propitious for arable husbandry. There is a clear implication, therefore, that in this instance a bias towards high per acre valuations reflects the prevalence throughout much of the north of an outsize customary acre. Conceivably, too, the concentrations of exceptionally low valuations in some parts of the west midlands, the south and the south-west may represent an equivalent reliance upon an undersize customary acre.

Shifting analysis from extreme values to mean values provides a further perspective on these configurations. Setting aside England north of the Trent with its scanty data coverage and problematic acre sizes, a strong east-west gradient is apparent (Figure 2.2). The most highly valued arable of all – worth at least 12d an acre and accounting for barely 2% of the total area south of the Trent – was restricted to a few privileged locations on

Table 2.3 Mean unit land values, percentage of national classified area, 1300–1349

Arable		Meadow	
Unit value (d)	*% of area*	Unit value (d.)	*% of area*
12+	*03.4*	28+	*03.0*
10 – <12	*01.8*	24 – <28	*08.2*
8 – <10	*06.7*	20 – <24	*16.7*
6 – <8	*14.2*	16 – <20	*35.0*
4 – <6	*33.5*	12 – <16	*25.2*
2 – <4	*38.7*	8 – <12	*08.6*
<2	*01.7*	<8	*03.4*
Mean N Trent	6.7d	Mean N Trent	17.8d
Mean S Trent	4.6d	Mean S Trent	18.7d
Mean England	4.8d	Mean England	18.6d
Pasture		**Grassland**	
Unit value (d)	*% of area*	Unit value (d.)	*% of area*
18+	*00.7*	28+	*01.6*
15 – <18	*01.0*	24 – <28	*03.7*
12 – <15	*04.9*	20 – <24	*09.3*
9 – <12	*14.3*	16 – <20	*27.2*
6 – <9	*33.0*	12 – <16	*33.9*
3 – <6	*29.4*	8 – <12	*15.6*
<3	*16.9*	<8	*08.7*
Mean N Trent	0.8d	Mean N Trent	17.3d
Mean S Trent	3.8d	Mean S Trent	16.0d
Mean England	3.4d	Mean England	15.7d

Source: Campbell and Bartley 2006.

Figure 2.1 High and low unit valuations of arable: England south of the Trent, 1300

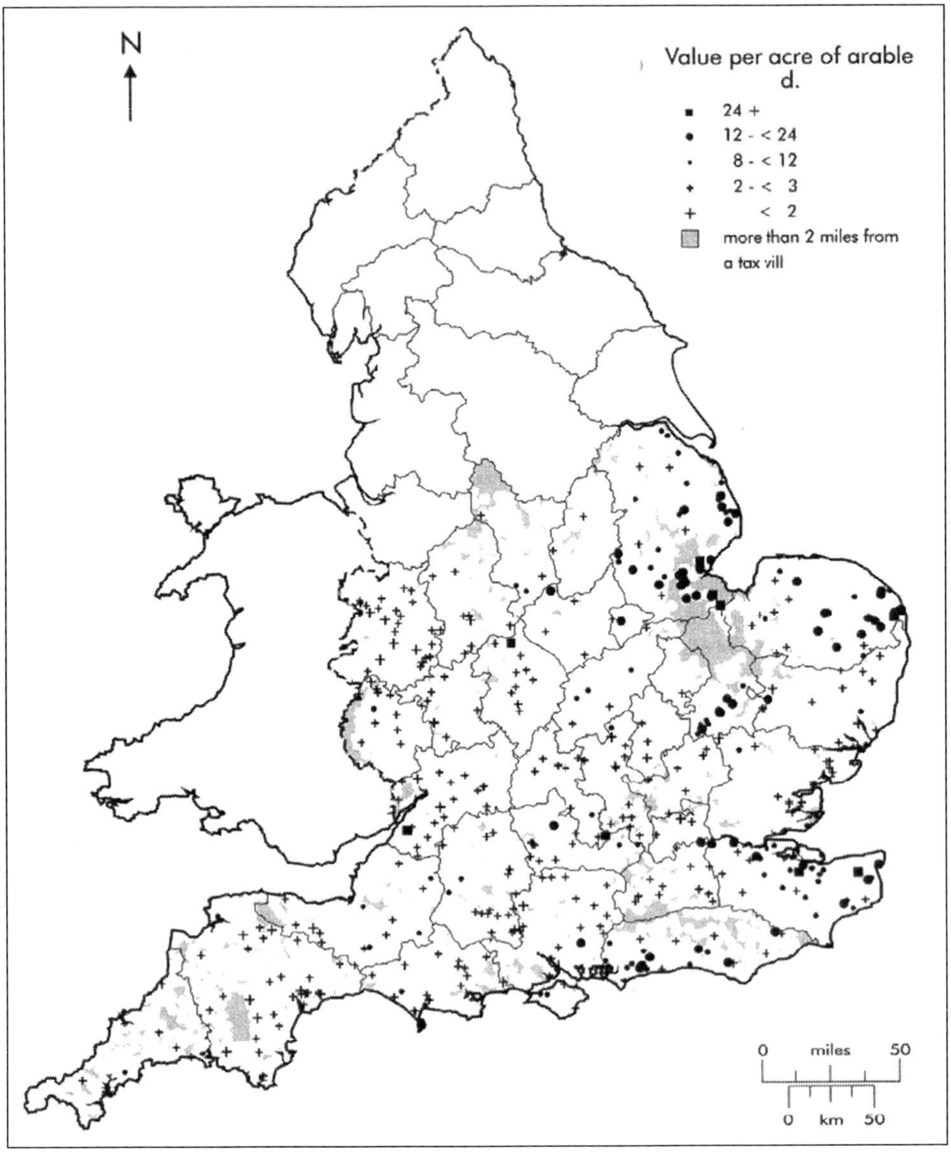

Source: Campbell, 2000: 349.

Figure 2.2 Mean unit value of arable, England south of the Trent, 1300–1349

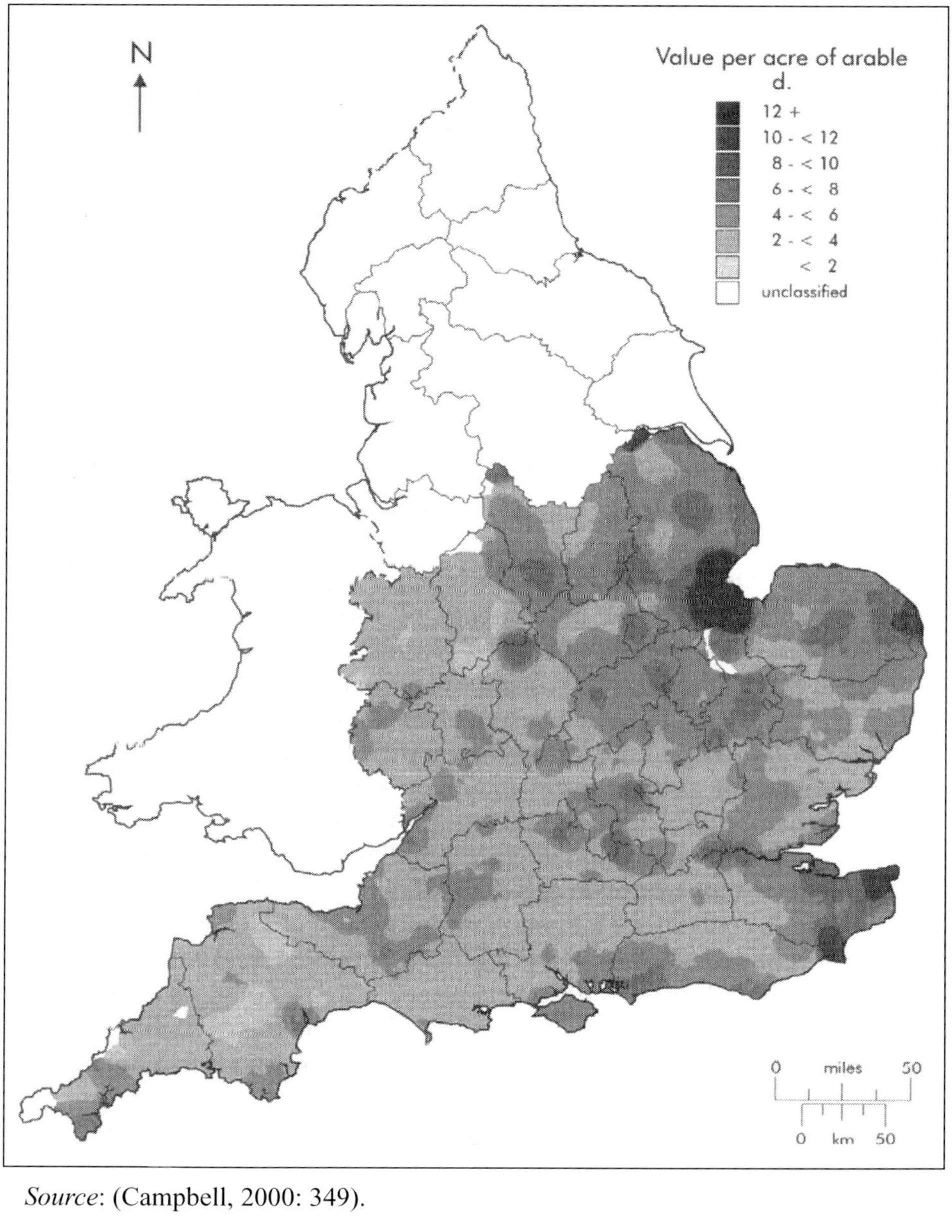

Source: (Campbell, 2000: 349).

the east and south-east coasts.[13] It was complemented in distribution by arable with an above average valuation of at least 6d an acre, the bulk of which was likewise largely concentrated in the eastern half of England, at a scatter of environmentally, commercially, and institutionally favoured locations. Arable land south of the Trent had an average value of 4.6d an acre. Over a third of the country had arable valued within a penny's range of this figure and the bulk of that was likewise located east of a line from the Mersey to the Solent. The concentration of such valuations in much of East Anglia, the east midlands, the mid-Thames Valley, Kent, and coastal Sussex is especially striking. Significantly, this is the very area where the earliest reliable national yield statistics – the agricultural statistics of the late nineteenth century – show that yields of wheat and barley were highest (Overton, 1986: 51–52).[14] In the west and south-west of England, in contrast, arable thus valued was more the exception than the rule, showing up in such environmentally and commercially advantaged areas as the lower Severn Valley, the Avon Valley around Trowbridge in Wiltshire, central Somerset inland from the port of Bridgewater, and the lower Exe Valley in Devon.

Collectively, just over half of all demesne arable was valued at less than 4d an acre and therefore well below average. Striking as the high-value arable may be, there is no escaping the fact that low unit values and by implication low arable productivity were the norm throughout the greater part of lowland England in the first half of the fourteenth century (Table 2.2). Arable thus valued shows up in several parts of the east and south-east – the East Anglian Breckland, eastern Essex, the Chiltern Hills, the Weald of Surrey, Sussex, and Kent – where soils either yielded poorly or were expensive to cultivate. West of a line from the Mersey to the Solent, however, arable valuations of less than 4d an acre were the norm rather than the exception. Here, too, was concentrated that 2 percent of the country with arable worth less than a meagre 2d an acre. None of the localities thus valued – Dartmoor and Exmoor in Devon, Cannock Chase in southern Staffordshire, the Long Mynd in central Shropshire, and the Black Mountains of south-east Wales – was kindly to the cultivator and all were land-locked and therefore at a serious disadvantage commercially.

It is possible that the unit value of any given land use was in part a function of its absolute supply. If so, arable ought to have been worth most where it was scarcest and *vice versa* (Postan 1996: 544). This has been be tested by measuring and mapping the relationship between the quantity and the unit value of arable land. The results show that scarcity was no more likely to drive the unit value of arable (or meadow) up than abundance was to drive it down. Areas existed which combined, first, low unit values with limited recorded acreages (thus inevitably giving rise to low aggregate values); second, high unit values with limited recorded acreages; third, low unit values with substantial recorded acreages; fourth, high unit values with substantial recorded acreages (thus inevitably giving rise to high aggregate values); and, fifth, the greater part of the country which lay midway between these four alternative extremes. The distribution of the extremes is nonetheless revealing.

[13] In both Norfolk and Kent arable valued at 12d an acre was described as being capable of being sown every year: Public Record Office, C134 File 83; C135 File 56(1). Raftis thought that valuations of 10d or higher resulted from a different system of evaluation; while this was sometimes the case it was clearly not so in these particular instances (Raftis, 1974).

[14] This remained the case a century later (Coppock, 1964: 70–80).

In the case of arable, large demesnes (i.e. with at least 160 arable acres) with low unit values (i.e. worth less than 3½d an acre) were strongly represented in the southern half of the country. Small demesnes (i.e. with less than 72 arable acres) with low unit values were more circumscribed in distribution and were mostly confined to the north-west midlands, especially Staffordshire and Shropshire, the south-western counties of Devon and Cornwall, and a few other localities – the New Forest of southern Hampshire and the Surrey and Sussex Weald – which were physically unrewarding for arable husbandry. Large demesnes with high unit values (i.e. worth at least 6d an acre) were yet more restricted in scale and were mostly confined to the eastern half of the country, especially wherever there were strong commercial incentives to reclaim potentially fertile alluvial marshlands, as most conspicuously in the case of the coastal marshes of Sussex, Kent and Essex, and the East Anglian Fens. Small demesnes with high unit values were also, but more rarely, a feature of coastal areas of fertile alluvial and loam soil, as in the case of the Flegg district of east Norfolk, coastal Lincolnshire, and Holderness. Demesnes with this combination of characteristics were, however, much more widely distributed north of the Trent where they provide tell tale evidence of large customary acres.

To suppose that scarcity alone drove up unit land-values is consequently far too crude. This is because land uses that were limited in supply were often also poor in quality. The inherent physical quality and productivity of any given land type was therefore an important determinant of its unit value. So, too, were the uses to which it was put and the productivity and profitability of those uses. Where husbandry systems were intensive and productive and their products commanded a high price, unit land-values – whether of arable or grassland – tended to be comparatively high. Variations in unit land-values were thus in part a function of variations in farm enterprise and thereby of the economic factors by which they, in their turn, were in part determined. Unit land-values were also, to a lesser extent, a function of property rights. Producers could not realise the full value of their land when others were entitled to rights of common grazing on it. Other things being equal, arable held in severalty was always worth more to the owner than arable held in common, except when rights of common grazing appurtenant to that land were incorporated in its valuation.

IV. Ratios between the unit values of arable and grassland

Nationally, grassland had on average a unit value 4.1 times that of arable but this ratio was far from consistent across space. For instance, in several distinctive localities within eastern and south-eastern England – the East Anglian silt fens, the Flegg district of eastern Norfolk, northern and eastern Kent including the Isle of Thanet, and the Walland and Romney Marshes in south-east Kent – the unit values of arable and grassland approached parity. There are even a few extreme instances in which the arable actually exceeded the meadow in unit value.[15] In all of these locations this exceptional state of affairs arose from

[15] Kosminsky believed that the value of meadow land 'is always higher than that of the arable'(Kosminsky, 1956: 50). Yet the opposite could and did occur in areas of rich coastal alluvium, where highly fertile arable land existed in close juxtaposition with a relative abundance of meadow and pasture.

the conjunction of very highly valued arable with more modestly valued grassland. The high arable values reflected its quality, productivity, and profitability; the modest grassland values, either its unusual abundance or inferior quality. A similar juxtaposition of high arable values and low grassland values also applied in the north-west and north of England, possibly due to the relative scarcity of arable, the unimproved quality of much grassland, and the fact that arable values may have been inflated by grazing rights appurtenant to the arable. In Cornwall, in contrast, a correspondingly narrow differential between the unit values of arable and grassland arose because arable and grassland were both low in value.

Each of these distinctive localities formed part of a territorially far wider area within which the differential between the unit values of grassland and arable was narrower than that within the country as a whole. Outside of the south-west, arable of above average value was the common denominator of each. In most of Kent, away from the coastal marshlands, highly valued arable co-existed with a relative abundance of grassland whose low unit value reflected its poor quality. A similar relative abundance of grassland in conjunction with arable of above average value also pertained in much of Lincolnshire but with the difference that here the grassland was generally of much better quality. In most of Norfolk and Cambridgeshire, however, grassland was in exceptionally limited supply. Its quality, moreover, was often indifferent. Scarcity of grassland, therefore, did not translate into high unit values. Arable, in contrast, was generally of superior productivity, with the result that only a relatively narrow differential prevailed between the unit values of arable and grassland. Indeed, but for the scarcity of the grassland it would doubtless have been narrower still. On the boulder-clay soils of neighbouring Suffolk, Essex and Hertfordshire, in contrast, this qualitative differential between arable and grassland tended if anything to be reversed. Arable existed in quantity but was of indifferent quality; grassland was much more circumscribed in supply, but evidently highly productive and correspondingly highly valued. Suffolk boasted the highest-valued meadowland in the country, indicative of a highly developed pastoral sector. Here, therefore, a wide differential existed between the unit values of arable and grassland.

Much the same differential applied on heavy land throughout the interior counties of lowland England. High costs of cultivation, in conjunction with prices that were low by comparison with other parts of England, kept arable unit values down: at the same time, for the reasons stated by Adam Smith, scarce grassland of quality commanded a disproportionately high rent. This applied particularly to meadow. In parts of Staffordshire, Shropshire, Worcestershire, Warwickshire, Gloucestershire, Oxfordshire, Wiltshire, Hampshire, and Dorset, meadow was worth at least nine times more per acre than arable. Consequently, it was on these poorer soils of the land-locked, ox-ploughing and commonfield west and south-west midlands that the differential between the unit values of arable and grassland was widest.

To the immediate north-west, however, the differential between the unit values of arable and grassland narrowed once again, as befitted a predominantly pastoral region where scarce but relatively valuable arable coexisted with abundant but relatively poor grassland. A similar explanation would appear to fit South Wales, parts of Devon and much of Cornwall. Here, but for very different reasons, the narrow differential between the unit values of arable and grassland echoes that of the profitable arable-husbandry districts on the opposite side of the country. Moreover, within the grassland sector, the differential between the unit values of meadow and pasture was far wider in most of the north and north-west, the south-west, and much of the extreme south and south-east than it was in the rest of the country. This, quite clearly, was a function of differences in the nature and provision of grassland, reinforced, perhaps, by different administrative approaches to the respective valuation and recording of meadow and pasture. This contrast shows up most strikingly in Yorkshire and Lincolnshire: within some parts of these counties (including, significantly, the separate sub-escheatry of Holderness) meadow was no more than twice the value of pasture, in others, it was worth at least six times as much.

V. Unit land values: an overall classification

Given the complex relationships that existed between the unit values of different land uses there is merit in analysing the unit values of arable, meadow, pasture and grassland in combination. Accordingly, Table 2.4 and Figure 2.3 offer a national classification of the unit value of demesne land-use. The classification has been derived using cluster analysis (Campbell, 2000: 41–46). It is based on four key variables. Three express the relationship between the unit value of one land use and the unit value of another, i.e. the ratio of grassland to arable (with a weighting of 2.0) and the ratios of meadow to arable and meadow to pasture (both with a weighting of 1.5). The fourth – the value per acre of arable (with a weighting of 1.2) – relates to the single most important land use and serves as an absolute control upon the three relative variables. By weighting the classification towards relative rather than absolute measures of value the distorting effect of customary acres is minimised. Applying cluster analysis to the first seven principal component scores calculated from these four variables identifies four 'core' land types, which together account for half of England south of the Trent and east of the Tamar (36% of the country as a whole). The rest of the country is apportioned among twelve 'non-core' land types. These have been defined using discriminant functions to establish which of the 'core' land-use types these areas most resemble on both a first- and second-choice basis. The result is the four primary and sixteen secondary land types whose mean attributes are summarised in Table 2.4.

For convenience, the four 'core' land-use types can be termed 'land with a very high unit value of arable', 'land with a high unit value of arable', 'land with an average unit value of arable', and 'land with a low unit value of arable'. Each is very unequal in area, their respective land-use shares increasing as the mean unit value of arable falls (Table 2.4 and Figure 2.3). Thus, whereas only 2% of the classified area rated as 'very high', 42% rated as 'low'. Moreover, as the mean unit value of each 'core' land-use type falls, so the differentials between the unit values of arable, grassland, meadow, and pasture progressively widen. Areas where the unit value of arable was low both absolutely and relatively were therefore far more extensive than those where it was high. Consequently, on many a seigniorial demesne some combination of low productivity, low prices, low profits and rents, and high production costs must have been the order of the day.

In their configuration these four 'core' land-use types and their respective sub-types display a high degree of spatial differentiation at national, regional and local scales (Figure 2.3). Four counties alone – Lincolnshire, Cambridgeshire, Norfolk, and Kent – contain exam

Table 2.4 National typology of land types classified according to unit value

Definition: Land category	*% classified area*	Mean unit value of arable (d./ac.)	Mean ratio (unit value: unit value) of: Grassland to arable	Meadow to arable	Meadow to pasture
Very high	*02.2*	16.2	1.1	1.3	2.9
High	*23.2*	07.0	2.2	2.8	3.3
Average	*32.7*	04.3	3.6	4.3	3.9
Low	*41.8*	02.6	5.7	6.5	5.3
All	*100.0*	03.9	4.5	5.3	4.5

Variables: (unit value grassland: unit value arable) x 2.0; (unit value meadow: unit value arable) x 1.5; (unit value meadow: unit value pasture) x 1.5; (unit value arable) x 1.2
Source: Campbell, 1998: 31.

ples of all four 'core' land-use types. All are on the eastern side of England, had selective access to coastal ports and navigable rivers, contained a variety of physical land and soil types, were diverse in their agrarian institutions, and were characterised in parts by exceptionally high population densities. Economic, environmental, and institutional factors therefore combined to generate the marked differentiation of unit values by which these four counties were characterised. As such they serve as a microcosm of the country at large.

In each case the limited areas falling within the 'very high' category of land use – in north Lincolnshire at the mouth of the River Trent, the Fenland of Lincolnshire, Cambridgeshire, and Norfolk, the Isle of Thanet and associated Ash Levels in east Kent, and, at a secondary level, the Isle of Flegg and associated Broadland of east Norfolk, and the Romney and Walland Marshes in south-eastern Kent – were confined to coastal areas of easily worked loam soil or reclaimed alluvial silt and fen peat. These, therefore, were areas of intrinsically fertile soil, with an abundance of well-watered grassland (which depressed the value of grassland relative to that of arable and inflated the value of pasture relative to that of meadow), capable of sustaining the most intensive forms of cultivation. Field systems and other related agrarian institutions were flexible and population densities were high. Strong local demand therefore reinforced the external demand to which these localities enjoyed privileged access via the coastal trade. Many of these attributes were shared to a less pronounced degree by the areas with 'high' unit values, which complemented these areas with 'high values' in location and exceeded them in extent. Land of this type, with a mean value per acre well above the national average and a narrower than average differential between the unit values of different land uses, dominated the low-lying alluvial soils of coastal Lincolnshire and the countryside immediately to the east of Lincoln, the East Anglian Fen edge and Isle of Ely, the mid-Trent Valley around Newark, the better soils of south Cambridgeshire, the good loam soils of mid-Norfolk and east Norfolk (close to Norwich and unencumbered by restrictive

Figure 2.3 Unit value of agricultural land, England south of the Trent, 1300–1349

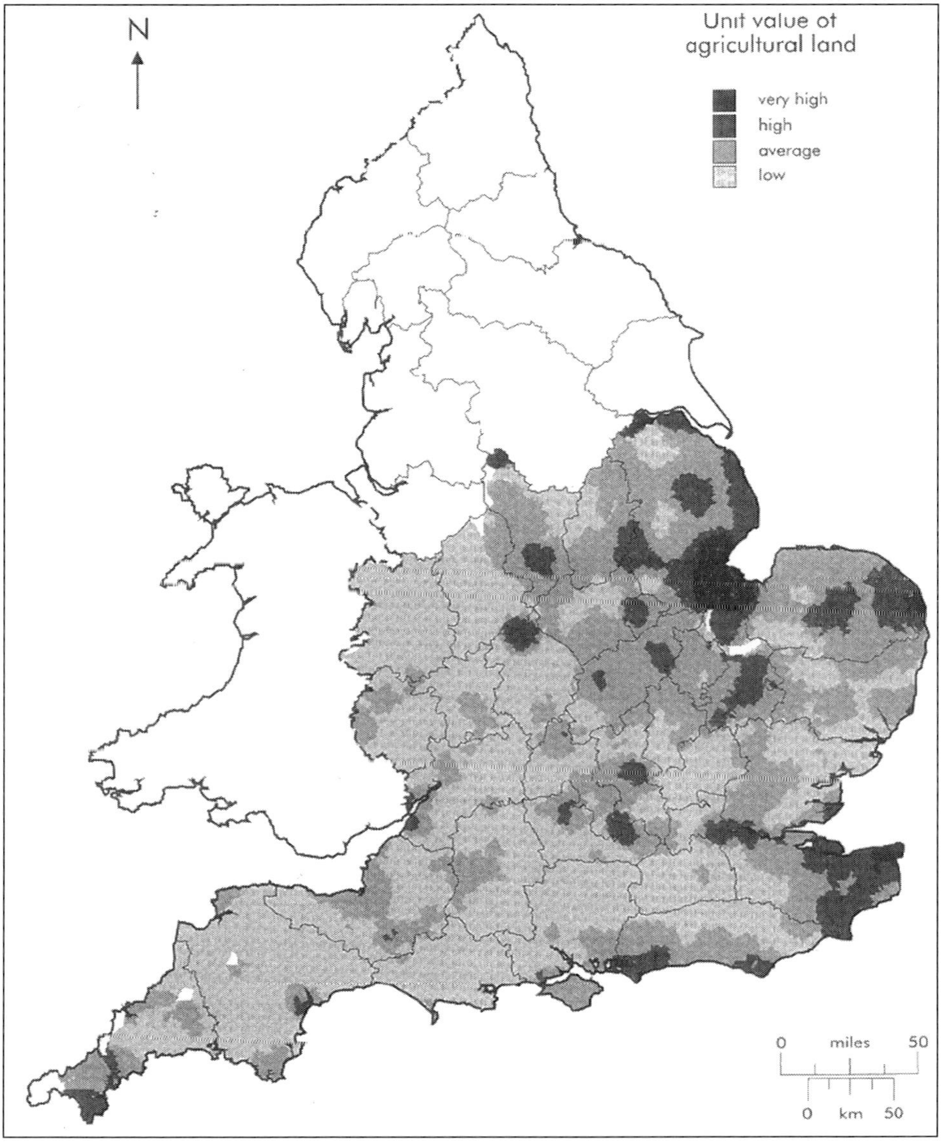

Source: Campbell, 1998: 30.

agrarian institutions), that part of north-western Kent bordering the Thames estuary, north-eastern Kent around Canterbury, and the upland margins of Romney Marsh. These were all areas whose distinctive conjunction of economic, environmental and institutional circumstances was evidently conducive to above average profits and rents. Cognate areas show up in several other similarly advantaged parts of the country: in the immediate vicinity of London and that city's principal up-river entrepot of Henley, in the Vale of Oxford, in the broad, fertile coastal plain of West Sussex around Chichester, and at the mouth of the Severn in Gloucestershire and mouth of the Exe in Devon.

Within the country at large land with 'high' and 'very high' unit values accounted for about a quarter of the total area. Although the proportion was significantly higher in Lincolnshire, Cambridgeshire, Norfolk, and Kent, these four counties nevertheless contained much land that was of only 'average' value and some land that was of below-average or 'low' value (Figure 2.3). Within these counties 'average' unit values were characteristic both of light, free-draining soils incapable of sustaining the more intensive forms of cultivation and of heavy soils with associated high costs of cultivation. Light-soil areas include the Lincolnshire Wolds, the 'good sands' of northern and north-western Norfolk, the poor sands in the immediate neighbourhood of Norwich, and the downlands of south-east Cambridgeshire, and heavy-soil areas, the lower Trent Valley of Lincolnshire, the lower Ouse and Waveney Valleys of Norfolk, south-west Cambridgeshire, and the upper Medway Valley of Kent. The scarcity of quality grassland in these light-soil areas and the critical importance of hay meadows on the heavy soils where ox ploughing prevailed also tended to widen the differential between the unit values of arable and meadow and meadow and pasture. Field systems in several of these areas were more closely regulated and less flexible than those in areas with higher unit values. Indeed, but for a favourable location, either within the immediate provisioning hinterland of a major city or close to ports actively engaged in the coastal grain trade and the navigable rivers by which they were served, unit values in several of these areas would undoubtedly have been lower. Certainly, elsewhere in the country areas of 'average' unit values were generally characterised by an above average exposure to commercial opportunities both internal and external to the localities in question. This was true of much of those parts of the east midlands penetrated by the navigable rivers Trent, Welland, Nene, and Ouse; the Waveney and Deben Valleys of Suffolk; the western half of Essex served in part by the navigable River Lea; the greater part of the middle Thames Valley from Staines to Oxford together with much of the Vale of Oxford; coastal Sussex and the Isle of Wight; substantial portions of the lower Severn Valley from Worcester to Gloucester and thence the sea; the upper Avon Valley of Wiltshire; the hinterland of Bridgwater (a port which drove a considerable trade in grain) and the Yeo Valley in Somerset; and the immediate hinterlands of Barnstaple and Exeter in north and south Devon.

Most areas with 'low' unit values either lacked such a strong commercial stimulus, especially to arable husbandry, or laboured under a real environmental disadvantage. Much of the thin-soiled Lincoln Edge in Lincolnshire was thus valued, as were the poor sands of west Norfolk, the dry and barren Breckland of south-west Norfolk and north-west Suffolk, the heavy-soiled Stour Valley of Suffolk, the infertile Tendring Peninsula of north-east Essex, the stiff boulder-clay soils of northern and eastern Essex, and the even heavier clay soils of the Wealden interior of south-west Kent. 'Low' unit values were similarly characteristic of many equivalent areas of light land and heavy land, wold land and vale land, particularly in the land-locked interior of England and west of the Solent where the commercial pulse beat least strongly. The Chiltern Hills of Hertfordshire and Buckinghamshire stand out in this respect, as do the Surrey and Sussex Weald, the Hampshire, Berkshire and Marlborough Downs, Salisbury Plain, the North and South Dorset Downs, the Mendip, Brendon and Blackdown Hills of Somerset, a great deal of Devon, the Cotswolds, substantial portions of lowland Herefordshire, Worcestershire, and Warwickshire, and the western edge of Sherwood Forest in Nottinghamshire and the neighbouring hill country of north-east Derbyshire. Within all these areas the rental value of grassland was significantly better than that of arable since pastoral husbandry tended to offer better commercial prospects than did tillage. The capacity of concentrated commercial demand to differentiate unit land values shows up most clearly in three main areas. First, those parts of eastern Kent most strongly exposed to the urban demand of the great Flemish and northern French cities. Second, those portions of the upper and lower Thames Valley most actively engaged in provisioning London. Third, the wide hinterland that supplied Kings Lynn with the provisions the port traded up and down the east coast and across the North Sea.

VI. Conclusion

Unit land values measure the financial rather than the physical yield of the land. They are recorded in far greater quantity than crop yields and consequently allow a far more detailed exploration of spatial variations in 'productivity' than would otherwise be possible. Grain prices and production costs together interacted with yields in a variety of ways, sometimes inflating and sometimes deflating the effect of the latter upon unit land values. The net outcome in large measure determined the market rent which the land commanded. This helps explain why the Crown's escheators were more interested in recording the financial than the physical yield of the land (Raftis, 1974: 16–17.[16] Prior Henry de Lakenham of Norwich was unusual among landlords in taking the trouble to calculate and record both the profit and yield of his arable. He had a good reason for doing so: the precise combination of yields, prices, and production costs prevailing on his estate meant that he could anticipate a healthy profit of at least 8d an acre from all 17 of his properties. Yet such a high rate of return was characteristic of only 4% of England south of the Trent. A further 45% of the country could enjoy a moderate return of 4d to 8d an acre but fully 51% of the country could expect no more than a low return of less than 4d an acre (Table 2.3). On this evidence the vast majority of English demesnes in the period 1300–49 were low profit-making and by implication low yielding (Figure 2.2 and Figure 2.3).

These respective proportions – representative of high, moderate, and low rates of return – are remarkably close to those predicted by Thünen's land-use model of a closed economy dependent upon animate sources of power and engaged in provisioning a single central city. In such an economy Thünen reckoned that 6% of the arable area

[16] Raftis cites Oschinsky's observation that 'By value was then understood the annual income from the estate not its capital value' (Oschinsky, 1971: 69).

would be devoted to the most productive forms of manure-intensive arable husbandry, a further 54% to moderately intensive and productive regimes, and 40% to low-yielding, extensive cropping systems (Campbell, 2000: 5–7). Artificial though this model may be it suggests that the predominantly low productivity performance of fourteenth-century English demesnes was an essentially rational response to prevailing levels of economic rent which themselves were consistent with the small size of the capital and limited extent of its provisioning hinterland. Across large parts of the country the economic incentives do not yet appear to have been strong enough to have encouraged demesne managers to adopt the measures necessary to secure higher levels of land productivity (Campbell, 1997). When, in the post-medieval centuries, the productivity of arable land eventually rose, that rise was principally achieved by improving the performance of these low-productivity regimes under the twin stimuli of higher prices and lower capital costs so that productivity differentials were progressively narrowed. This in turn was contingent upon a trade-based expansion and concentration of market demand (Wrigley, 1970, 1985; Overton and Campbell, 1991: 41–42).

Bibliography

Allen, R.C. (1992) *Enclosure and the Yeoman: the Agricultural Development of the South Midlands 1450–1850*, Oxford: Clarenton Press.

Astill, G.G. and Langdon, J.L. (eds) (1997) *Medieval farming and technology: the impact of agricultural change in north-west Europe in the Middle Ages*, Leiden: Brill.

Bailey, M. (1989) *A marginal economy? East Anglian Breckland in the later Middle Ages*, Cambridge: Cambridge University Press.

Campbell, B. (1983) 'Arable Productivity in Medieval England: some Evidence from Norfolk', *Journal of Economic History*, xliii, pp. 390–394.

Campbell, B.M.S., Galloway, J.A., Keene, D.J. and Murphy, M. (1993) *A Medieval Capital and its Grain Supply: agrarian Production and Distribution in the London Region c.1300*, Historical Geography Research Series 30.

Campbell, B.M.S. (1997) 'Economic Rent and the Intensification of English agriculture, 1086–1350', in G.G. Astill, and J.L. Langdon, (eds), *Medieval Farming and Technology: the Impact of Agricultural Change in North-West Europe in the Middle Ages*, Leiden: Brill, pp. 225–250.

Campbell, B.M.S. (1998) 'Constraint or Constrained? Changing Perspectives on Medieval English Agriculture', *Neha-Jaarboek voor economische, bedrijfs-en techniek-geschiedenis*, 61.

Campbell, B.M.S. (2000) *English Seigniorial Agriculture 1250–1450*, Cambridge: Cambridge University Press.

Campbell, B.M.S. and Bartley, K. (2006), *England on the Eve of the Black Death: an Atlas of Lay Wealth, Land Ownership, and Lordship 1300–49*, Manchester: Manchester University Press.

Clark, G. (1991) 'Labour Productivity in English Agriculture, 1300–1860', in B.M.S. Campbell and M. Overton, (eds), *Land, Labour and Livestock: Historical Studies in European Agricultural Productivity*, Manchester: Manchester University Press, pp. 211–235.

Coppock, J.T. (1964) *An Agricultural Atlas of England and Wales*, London: Faber and Faber.

Farmer, D.L. (1988) 'Prices and wages', in H.A. Hallam, (ed.), *The Agrarian History of England and Wales, ii, 1042–1350*, Cambridge: Cambridge University Press, pp. 716–817.

Farmer, D.L. (1991) 'Marketing the Produce of the Countryside 1200–1500', in E. Miller, (ed.), *The Agrarian History of England and Wales, iii, 1348–1500*, Cambridge: Cambridge University Press, pp. 324–430.

Gras, N.S.B. (1915) *The Evolution of the English Corn Market from the twelfth to the eighteenth Century*, Cambridge: Mass.

Gray, H. (1915) *English Field Systems*, Cambridge: Mass.

Harvey, P.D.A. (1965) *A Medieval Oxfordshire Village: Cuxhaam 1240–1400*, Oxford: Oxford University Press.

Harvey, P.D.A. (ed.) (1976) *Manorial Records of Cuxham, Oxfordshire circa 1200–1359*, London: Oxfordshire Record Society 50.

Kershaw, I. (1973) *Bolton Priory: the Economy of a Northern Monastery 1286–1325*, Oxford: Oxford University Press.

Kosminsky, E.A. (1956) *Studies in the Agrarian History of England in the thirteenth Century*, trans. R. Kisch and R.H. Hilton, (eds), Oxford: Basil Blackwell.

Langdon, J.L. (1982) 'The economics of Horses and Oxen in Medieval England', *Agricultural History Review*, 30, pp. 31–40.

Langton, J.L. and Morris, R. (eds) (1986) *Atlas of Industrialising Britain 1780–1914*, London: Routledge.

Langdon, J.L. (1986) *Horses, Oxen and Technological Innovation: the Use of Draught Animals in English Farming from 1066–1500*, Cambridge: Cambridge University Press.

Miller E. (1975) 'Farming in Northern England', *Northern History*, 11, pp. 1–16.

Oschinsky, D. (ed.) (1971) *Walter of Henley and other Treatises on Estate Management and Accounting*, Oxford: Oxford University Press.

Overton, M. (1986) 'Agriculture', in J. Langton and R.J. Morris, (eds), *Atlas of Industrialising Britain 1780–1914*, London: Routledge, pp. 34–53.

Overton, M. and Campbell, B.M.S. (1991) 'Productivity Change in European Agricultural Development', in B.M.S. Campbell and M. Overton, (eds), *Land, Labour and Livestock: Historical Studies in European Agricultural Productivity*, Manchester: Manchester University Press, pp. 1–50.

Overton, M. (1996) *Agricultural Revolution in England: the Transformation of the Agrarian Economy 1500–1850*, Cambridge: Cambridge University Press.

Overton, M. and Campbell, B.M.S. (1996) 'Production et productivité dans l'agriculture anglaise, 1086–1871', *Histoire et Mesure*, 11c, pp. 255–297.

Pelham, R.A. (1936) 'Medieval foreign Trade: eastern Ports', in H.C. Darby, (ed.), *A Historical Geography of England before A.D. 1800*, Cambridge: Cambridge University Press.

Postan, M.M. (ed.) (1966) *The Cambridge Economic History of Europe, I, The agrarian Life of the Middle Ages*, Cambridge: Cambridge University Press, 2nd edn.

Postles, D. (1986) 'The Perception of Profit before the Leasing of Demesnes', *Agricultural History Review*, 34, pp. 12–28.

Raftis, J.A. (1974) *Assart Data and Land Values: two Studies in the East Midlands 1200–1350*, Toronto: Pontifical Inst. of Medieval.

Smith, A. (1872) *The Wealth of Nations*, Book I, Edinburgh: new edn.

Stone, E. (1962) 'Profit and Loss Accountancy at Norwich Cathedral Priory', *Transactions of the Royal Historical Society*, 5th series, 12, pp. 25–48.

Thornton, C. (1991) 'The Determinants of Land Productivity on the Bishop of Winchester's Demesne of Rimpton, 1208 to 1403', in B.M.S. Campbell and M. Overton, (eds), *Land, Labour and Livestock: Historical Studies in European Agricultural Productivity*, Manchester: Manchester University Press, pp. 183–210.

Thornton, C. (2003) 'The Level of Arable Productivity on the Bishopric of Winchester's Manor of Taunton, 1283–1348', in R.H. Britnell, (ed.), *The Winchester Pipe Rolls and Medieval English Society*, Woodbridge: The Boydell Press, pp. 109–38.

Titow, J.W. (1962) *Land and Population on the Bishop of Winchester's Estates 1209–1350*, unpublished PhD thesis, University of Cambridge.

Titow, J.W. (1972) *Winchester Yields: a Study in Medieval Agricultural Productivity*, Cambridge: Cambridge University Press.

Wrigley, E.A. (1967) 'A simple Model of London's Importance in Changing English Society and Economy, 1650–1750', *Past and Present*, 37, pp. 44–70.

Wrigley, E.A. (1985) 'Urban Growth and Agricultural Change: England and the Continent in the Early Modern Period', *Journal of Interdisciplinary History*, 15, pp. 683–728.

3 The dubious delights of farm accounts*

Annie ANTOINE, University of Rennes II

I. Introduction

Farm accounts from a pre-statistical era cannot be seen as a set of accountant's books (Hubsher, 1981; Garnier and Hubsher, 1984). They may appear to be so because they are made up of columns of figures, but in fact they have more in common with family journals (Perrot, 1978). Whether they are diaries kept by the landowner himself or accounts submitted by his steward, these documents were not created according to the principles of accountancy and suffer greatly from being treated as if they were (Antoine, 2000).

In the eighteenth and nineteenth centuries, farm accounts could take the form of an annual statement or of a chronological list of the farm's activities but, in either case, only those areas that had an immediate monetary value to the landlord were concerned. This means that all the aspects of the farm that involve only the farmer are invisible. The accounts are those of the landlord, not those of the holding. This is one of the principal characteristics (or limitations?) of this type of document. There are thus a host of questions of interest to historians for which these documents are of very little use. To seek information from farm accounts on agricultural productivity, or, worse, on the evolution of productivity, implies bringing in external data that was not relevant to the concerns of those who drew them up (the area of cultivation – but how much of it was effectively tilled each year? The value of farm implements – an inventory would be needed for that –, the amount of capital invested etc.).

The statement of accounts at the end of each year always involved showing the money spent and the money received. This document met the needs of the landlord who needed to know every year if he had earned more or less money than he had spent. In the first half of the eighteenth century Pierre Duchemin du Tertre, who kept the accounts for a great many farms in Maine (Antoine, 1998), always marked the end of the accounting year (between February and March) by the following formula: *j'en retire quitte et libre* ('accounts cleared') and in most cases *libre* would be followed by the difference between the receipts (*le revenant bon*) and the expenses. For him the only criterion was whether he put more money into his pocket than he had taken out of it. He needed to know every year whether he had made a profit or a loss: he much preferred to make a profit but was ready to accept a loss, if, for example, a building had to be renovated, justifying this in his own journal.

In order to have the best chance of finding signs of agricultural progress it is necessary to have accounts for a period when there was progress, or at least change (Clout, 1979). But of course there is always a risk of coming across farms where there was no progress, even in the nineteenth century (Cocaud, 1999). The accounts used here are those of a small estate made up of seven to ten farms, held for a period of 25 years (1828–1853). This

* Translated by Judith Le Goff.

Figure 3.1 Location of the Saint-Mirel estate

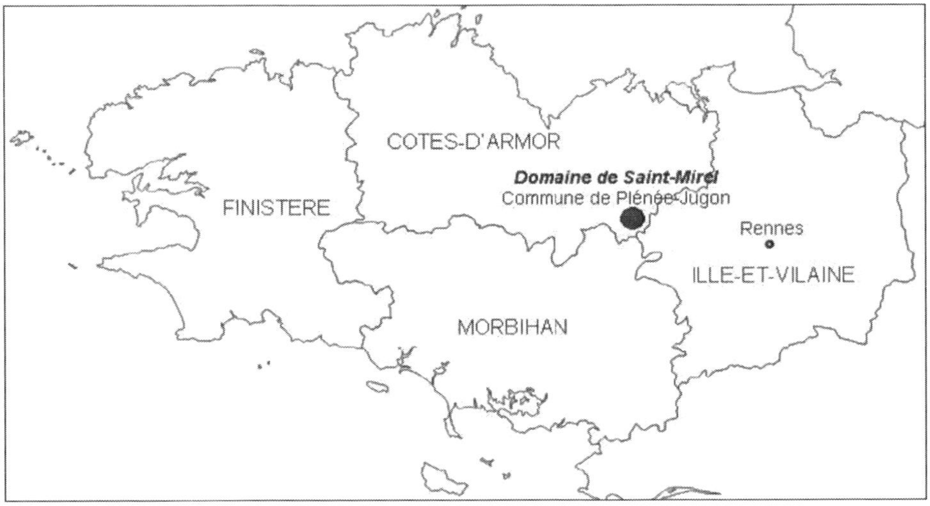

estate was at Plenée-Jugon, in the south of the present département of the Côtes-d'Armor, close to the boundary with Ille-et-Vilaine.[1] The aim of this paper is to show what can be done (and also what cannot be done) with farm accounts of this kind.

II. Description of the document

There is no common formula for farm accounts from the eighteenth and nineteenth centuries because they are always set up according to the individual wishes of the landlord, without reference (other than implicit) to a model (Revel, 1996). The accounting rules to which they conform are those of the landlord (or steward) of the holding. In theory they can be grouped into different types:

- according to what they dealt with: whether accounts for single holdings, or for estates (several farms, perhaps demesne lands, some woods, everything pertaining to a fine landed property): in each of these cases, the question of profitability was presented in different terms.

- according to the way they were drawn up: whether a journal was kept daily, or at least regularly, so that a calendar of the activities mentioned can be constructed, or a statement of accounts was drawn up at the end of the year giving the landlord the incomings and outgoings.

[1] Archives départementales d'Ille-et-Vilaine, 39 J. Fonds Urvoy de St-Mirel à Plénée Jugon. Côtes d'Armor.

But beyond these classifications all accounts are different because they are closely linked to the conditions of the lease that define the reciprocal obligations of the landlord and the farmer. Those for properties held in *fermage* (tenant farming) do not include the same information as those for properties held in *métayage* (share-cropping). The first type is likely to be limited to the annual rent of the land and the landlord's expenses; the second may be much richer and contain evidence of almost all the farmer's activity, since he owed the landlord half of his profits. But contrary to some too hasty claims, eighteenth-century leases, and even nineteenth-century ones, at least in the West of France, cannot be simply assigned to one of these categories; there are only intermediate cases; payment in cash for certain products, payment in kind for others, payment in proportion to the harvest in some cases, fixed payment in others. It is obvious that these choices made by the landlord when leasing make accounts more or less useful for understanding how the farm operated (Mayaud, 1999).

II.1. An estate consisting of several holdings

The accounts used in this article were made up of statements of account (*un livre de marque*) presented by the steward to the landlord every year. This balance sheet dealt with the whole estate. Its composition varied over the course of 25 years (1828–1853); the same seven *métairies* were always included and others were added in certain years. The total for most of the period was seven to eight *métairies*, and 10 between 1829 and 1834. As the aim of this study is to look at the whole estate and find out how profitable it was for its owner (and not how profitable one holding was for its farmer) all have been included in the calculation.

The area of eight of these holdings is specified in the document. They range from 6 to 20 hectares, 13.5 on average. These were quite small farms (Sée, 1919 and Cocaud, 1999), still typical of the area at the beginning of the nineteenth century. It can be assumed that the area for which the steward had responsibility and which is covered by the accounts varies between 100 and 130/140 hectares according to the year. The livestock on these holdings is also known as *l'ensouchement* – that is, the basic stock, excluding the births, purchases and annual sales. These were small herds (cows, horses, sheep and pigs). These *métairies* had cows which produced milk, pigs and a few sheep. Horses did the draught work. There was a mixed livestock and the document enables their different functions to be studied.

Details of the *ensouchement* on the seven *métairies* of the Saint Mirel estate:

La Porte: 4 horses, 7 cows, 12 sheep, 4 pigs.
La Fontaine: 4 horses, 7 cows, 4 heifers, 12 sheep, 4 pigs.
La Maison Neuve: 4 horses, 7 cows, 16 sheep, 4 pigs.
Le Pallouais: 3 horses, 6 cows, 12 sheep, 3 pigs.
La Grande Villanée: 3 horses, 6 cows, 12 sheep, 3 pigs.
La Petite Villanée: 7 cows, 9 sheep, 2 pigs.
Le Chef des Clos 12 ha. : 4 cows, 6 sheep, 2 pigs.

II.2. The steward's lease

The information contained in the steward's account book relates both to his contract with the landlord and to the leases of the different tenants on the *métairies* which he managed.

The steward of the Saint Mirel estate had a non-notarised lease which is now in the Urvoy de Saint Mirel collection.[2] At the beginning of the period the steward was Sieur Berest; after 1840 the accounts were submitted by François Moysan but the conditions of the lease were probably not altered as the way the accounts were drawn up was the same from 1827 to 1853. In the lease of 1835, which survives, Madame de Saint Mirel rented to her steward, Sieur Berest, the *retenue* of Saint Mirel[3] as well as a watermill and some outbuildings. He was to benefit from all the produce, harvests and profits which he could make there; he could prune the trees; he was to make the repairs to the buildings incumbent on the tenant and sow the land 'according to the customs of the place', and for that he paid a rent of 625 francs a year. This part of the holding was thus held on a typical tenant-farming lease concluded between a landlord and farmer. But in this case the farmer was also the steward of the other holdings on the estate. In the same document he also agreed to manage the dependent properties of the land at Saint Mirel (he was paid 5% of the total revenues for doing this). For the other *métairies* on the estate he had to perform all the duties incumbent on a landlord in that region:

- measure and divide the grains after the harvest, divide the pigs at the end of the autumn, take the landlord's share from livestock deals, divide the apples and hemp etc.

- sell all that made up the landlord's share: animals, grains, apples, butter, wool, hemp etc., and record the amounts in the *livre de marque*, the account books which have survived.

Excerpt from the 1835 lease between Madame de Saint Mirel and the estate steward, Berest:

> Consequently, he [the steward] is required to divide up the grains from the *métairies*, to store them in the regular granaries, to look after them, turn and winnow them so they do not spoil, to take them to the market at Lamballe when the landlord requires, to divide the pigs and other animals which he shall sell at the ordinary fairs; to divide the apples and sell them at the current price for the year; to go to the market at Lamballe at the beginning of Lent to sell the butter which the *métayers* must transport there and if there is any unwrapped butter, to pay cash or put it in pots to be sold with the rest; to sell the hemp standing and the pruned wood by branch; to have the sheep and ewes shorn, to divide the wool, have it carded in the usual way, to have it ready to be sold when instructed; to keep a *livre de marque* of what each *métairie* has produced separately and to submit this book to Madame the lessor, who will make a copy, to calculate the net profit and make a summary of the yield, to account for the receipts to the landlord whenever required to do so; to attend to repairs and to see that no

[2] Archives Départementales de Ille-et-Vilaine. 39 J 11 non-notarised lease, 17 February 1835. In 1835 the lease was signed with Sieur Berest who stated he was the current steward of the estate.
[3] The term 'retenue' refers to the main *métarie* on the estate, which formed its centre, and where the landlord lived if he was resident.

damage is done to the said property, to buy all the material needed for the repairs to the said *métairies*, and generally to do everything necessary for the administration of the said property as a good and diligent father of a family would do. Madame de Saint Mirel gives him full authority to this end.

The leases of the *métayers* on the different holdings on the estate managed by Berest have not been found. It is very likely that they were verbal leases (a tenant on a *métairie* belonging to Madame de Saint-Mirel was expelled in 1830 by a judicial decision and it appears that he had a verbal lease). However the steward's lease shows that the grains, pigs, the profit from the other livestock, the hemp, the wool, the apples,[4] were all divided in half, which was typical of share-cropping leases in this region.

To sum up, there was a steward who lived on and worked the principle *métairie* on the Saint-Mirel estate. On the other holdings he performed all the duties of supervision and management that were incumbent on a landlord under a sharecropping system. He received 5% of the total profits of the estate for his pains.

II.3. The steward's *livre de marque*

The accounts are set out by year. For each year they show the gross profit, the expenses and the net profit. The figures always agree: the steward did not make mistakes in his sums.

The 'gross profit' (*produit brut*) was composed of the following items:

- the result of the sale of cereals in the previous year, by volume and value (this was the landlord's share only).
- the 'subsides'; that is, the annual payments made by each holding in value or kind (from sales of animals, butter, hemp, wood, apples, potatoes, money collected for the tax on doors and windows) and the total value of these payments.
- the revenues from some detached fields which were rented separately and from the home farm (*retenue*) of Saint-Mirel which was rented directly to the steward for cash; a mill was sometimes included as well.
- the profit of the sale of wood (that which belonged to the landlord).[5]
- sometimes the profit from the sale of wool (or a note that it had been delivered to the landlord's house in Dinan).

The steward also listed and noted the cost of the expenditures borne by the landlord, general expenses for the management of the estate and the expenses peculiar to each

[4] Butter is the only product where it has not been possible to find out if the tenants gave a fixed quantity or a proportion of the amount produced. This makes it difficult to estimate the share of butter in the production of the holdings.

[5] The principle was that unpruned trees and the trunks of trees that were trimmed belonged to the landlord. The tenant had the branches of hedgerow trees when they were pruned.

métairie, (mostly repairs),[6] the landlord's contribution to the purchase of livestock, to the expense of breeding and to buying fertilisers (marl, lime, bone meal).[7] The list of expenses also included taxes, sometimes the rental of additional parcels of land, and the management fee (about 5% of the gross profit) paid to the steward.

The difference between the 'gross profit' and the 'expenses and taxes' was then calculated and appears as 'net profit'. There are never any mistakes in the calculations. Some partial accounts are then added in support of the annual statement of accounts: a summary for that year of the harvest of each type of grain by volume for each *métairie*,[8] the statement of the value of the apple crop (but this was redundant because of the record of annual payments and the steward quickly ceased to note it) and, most important, the summary of all the expenses, first generally and then by holding.

On the whole this document is as precise as accounts for a half-share lease can be (Antoine, 2000). However those who wish to work in detail on the crops must remember that the question of seed is not dealt with at all in this document. It was taken from the common pile before the division between landlord and tenant was made and so the landlord's share was not half of the total crop. There were also sometimes arrangements between the landlord and the steward or the tenant by which the tenant kept more of one kind of grain and less of another (Antoine, 1998).[9] It is impossible to know the total volume of the crop: it is thus not possible to calculate the profitability of grains in relation to the seed or the acreage. Finally, it is uncertain what proportion of the butter produced appears in these accounts: the figures vary from year to year but it is not known whether this is because of variability of production or variations in the landlord's demands. This is why these accounts can only be used to calculate the profitability of the estate to its owner, not the profitability of the land or seeds or capital. Introducing a hypothesis would create a theoretical model which no longer represented the real holding, whose logic was not necessarily that which the present-day scholar may be tempted to attribute to it (Perrot, 1978).

III. An analysis of the accounts

The material analysed included all of the summarised data, in the form of receipts and expenses, and the details on the sale of grain, crops, *subsides* and sales of wood and wool. This gives us information, from the landlord's point of view, on the overall balance sheet of the estate, on cereal production (as the landlord received a share every year which he

[6] The buildings were maintained jointly by the tenant (tenant repairs) and the landlord. The latter bore the greater share because he was responsible for all the major work on the buildings.

[7] The sharing of all the expenses of the holding is a consequence of the *métayage* lease. It is for this reason that regions where this type of lease is common provide historians with much richer farm accounts than regions with regular tenant-farmer leases.

[8] The sale of grains took place in winter and spring and only appeared in the landlord's profits the following year. In practice the revenues for 1830, for example, comprise all the revenues of livestock, apples, butter etc. for 1830 and the profit of the grains harvested in 1829. This way of accounting has been kept for in this paper since it is the landlord's accounts that are being studied.

[9] See 'comptes avec Chatelier'.

Figure 3.2 Revenue of the Saint Mirel estate. Receipts and expenditure, 1828–1853

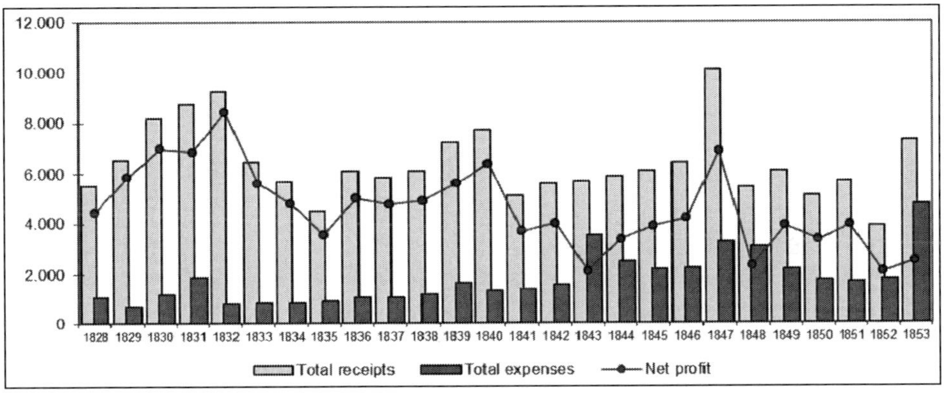

Source: Stewart's accounts (*Livres de marque*) of the estate of Saint-Michel, 1828–1853. Archives départmentales d'Ille-et-Vilaine, 39 J. Fonds Urvoy de Saint-Mirel à Plénée Jugon, départment des Côtes d'Armor.

then sold) and on all the other products which seem to have been divided in half, and which made up what are termed *subsides* in the document.

III.1. An overall balance sheet of the estate revenue

Over twenty-five years the total incomings were 166,076 fr., an average of 6,643 fr. a year, and the outgoings 46,670 fr., or 1,866 fr. a year. The landlord's profit was therefore 46,670 fr. in 25 years, 4,776 fr. a year on average.

Figure 3.2, which illustrates the yearly receipts, expenditures and profits of the landlord, shows that the balance sheet was always positive. However, the landlord's annual profit oscillated considerably, between a minimum of 2,000 fr. and a maximum of 8,000 fr. The receipts varied, over cycles of five to six years, from 5,000 fr. to 9,000 fr. The expenditures were more regular, and can be split into two periods: until 1841 they were on average 1,145 fr. a year (1828–1841: 16,026.97 over a period of 14 years), and from 1842 to 1853 they were 2553 fr. a year (1842–1853: 30,643.07 over a period of 12 years). From the 1840s onward the cost of fertilisers increased greatly, but profits were not increased thereby. The landlord's profits therefore tended to shrink.

In this balance sheet the outgoings ('expenses') are made up of four categories:

- general expenses on the estate and on each holding (repairs to buildings, purchase of animals, contributions to the purchase of fertiliser and, more broadly, to all the investments made in the estate)
- sometimes the cost of renting extra parcels of land, a few land purchases and notaries' fees (this last item has not been included in the calculations)
- taxes (on doors and windows, which were very low and paid with the *subsides*)
- the cost of management (5% of receipts) paid to the steward.

The receipts were also made up of several categories (see Figure 3.3).

A large part of the revenue was paid directly or delivered by the *métayers*. The grains were delivered in kind and the steward was responsible for their sale. The *subsides* which the *métayers* owed made up roughly half of all their other revenues: the profit made on livestock, wool, hemp, apples, cider, poultry, butter etc. They were either paid in cash or delivered in kind and sold by the métayer. In addition to these revenues from the various holdings on the estate there were those from the rental of detached parcels of land, the mill and the home farm (*retenue*) of Saint Mirel (rented to the steward), the sale of wood (from the standing trees, the profits of which were not shared with the *métayer*).

As has already been shown in Figure 3.2, the cash receipts underwent annual fluctuations. The sale of grains, which made up 56% of revenue, was the main cause of the rise or fall of the total (see Figure 3.4); the *subsides* (mainly the revenues from livestock, butter and apples) were more regular. The same result was found in a study of several sets of accounts from Maine in the eighteenth century; livestock rearing constituted an element of stability in the landlord's revenues while large crops of cereals brought large profits (Antoine, 1994).

III.2. Cereal production

Cereal production was considerable, comprising 56% of the landlord's revenues. The document shows this clearly as it is mentioned twice each year; each set of accounts closes with the list of the landlord's share of the grains by volume and in the following year, these grains were sold and the value of their earnings estimated. These holdings produced mainly buckwheat (50% of the total volume of the crop) and rye (30%). The remainder was made up of oats, of maslin (*métay*, a mixture of rye and wheat) and of pure wheat in very small quantities (see Figure 3.5). Thus in the first half of the nineteenth century the model of cereal production was still that of the Old Regime.

In the course of the 25 years being studied there was very little change (see Figure 3.6) (Letaconnoux, 1908 and Le Nevanic, 1909). Buckwheat maintained its position, and even increased slightly; there was a slight decline of rye after 1830 and a very slight increase in maslin and wheat at the end of the period. Certainly this has to be considered in relation to the purchase of fertiliser, particularly bone meal (Sée, 1919 and Cocaud, 1999), but it cannot be denied that the growth is not in line with the sacrifices made by the landlord, whose expenses increased considerably after 1840.

III.3. Other productions

Productions other than grain made up 26% of the landlord's cash receipts. These items appear in the accounts under the heading 'subsides'. Here the term refers to that share of all the various productions that the *métayer* had to pay to the landlord. In many cases it is almost certain that this was half of the crop (or of the profit from its sale). This is the case for apples, potatoes, hemp, faggots, etc. It is also the case for livestock: when the animals were sold, half of the profit went to the landlord; when animals were bought the landlord paid half of the purchase price. On the other hand it is more difficult to say what the sums from the sale or the production of butter represent: half the produce, or a fixed sum? The document does not allow us to say.

Figure 3.3 Revenue of the Saint Mirel estate. Composition of receipts, 1828–1853

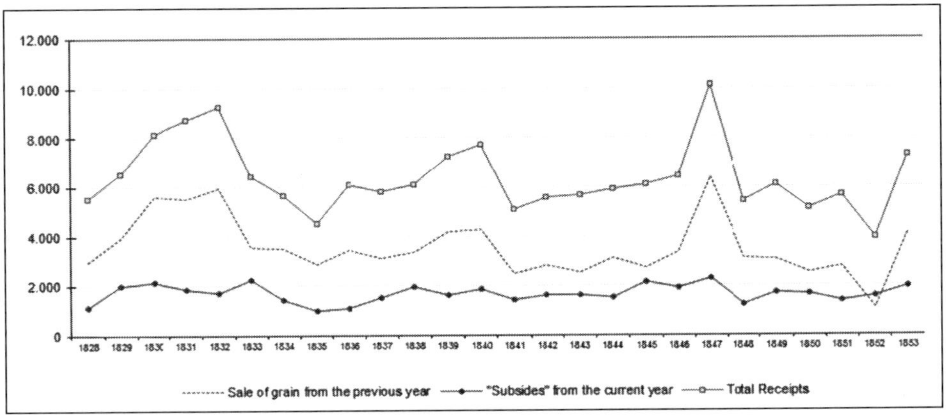

Source: See figure 3.2.

Figure 3.4 Revenue of the Saint Mirel estate. The proportion of cereals and other sources of revenue in the receipts, 1826–1853

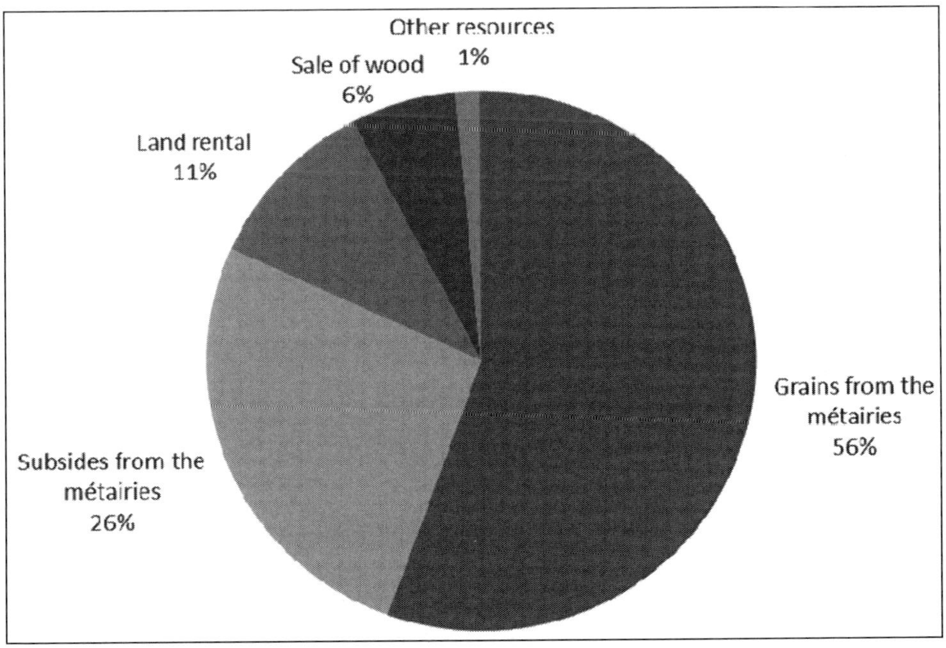

Source: See figure 3.2.

Figure 3.5 Revenue of the Saint Mirel estate. The proportion of different cereals in the landlord's revenue, 1828–1853

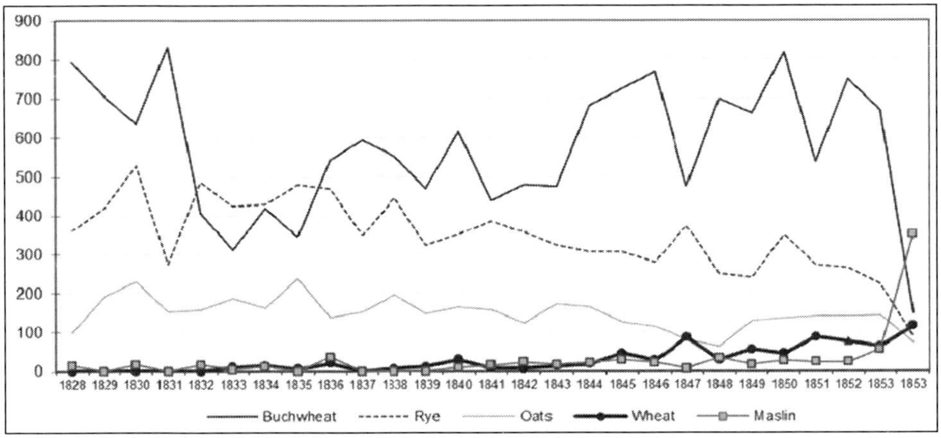

Source: See figure 3.2.

Figure 3.6 Revenue of the Saint Mirel estate. Changes in the proportions of different cereals in the total crop, 1828–1853

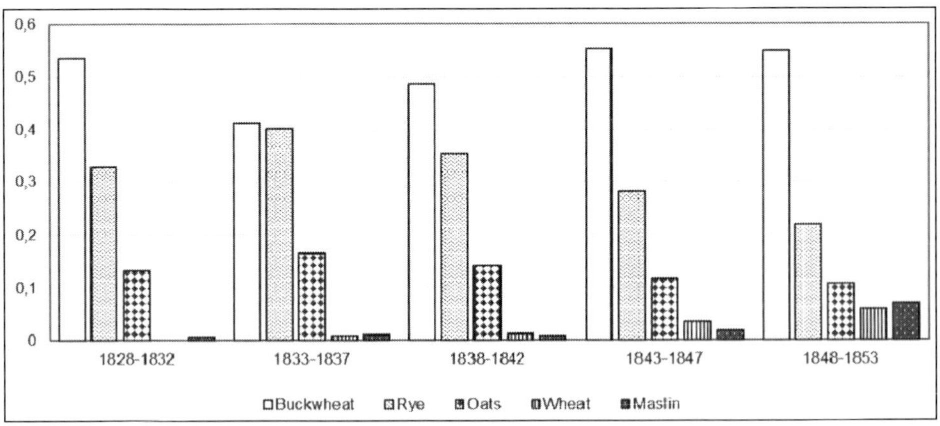

Source: See figure 3.2.

The graph below (Figure 3.7) shows both the diversity of these productions (this really was mixed farming) and the predominance of three of them: butter, pigs and apples.

Calculations were made by five-year periods to try and identify changes but the results were not significant enough to be worth reproducing here. Perhaps there was a slight decline in butter (but that may be because the *métayers* were not asked for so much), poultry and potatoes may have become a little more important after 1835 (Sée, 1919).

Figure 3.7 Revenue of the Saint Mirel estate. Components of the 'subsides', 1828–1853

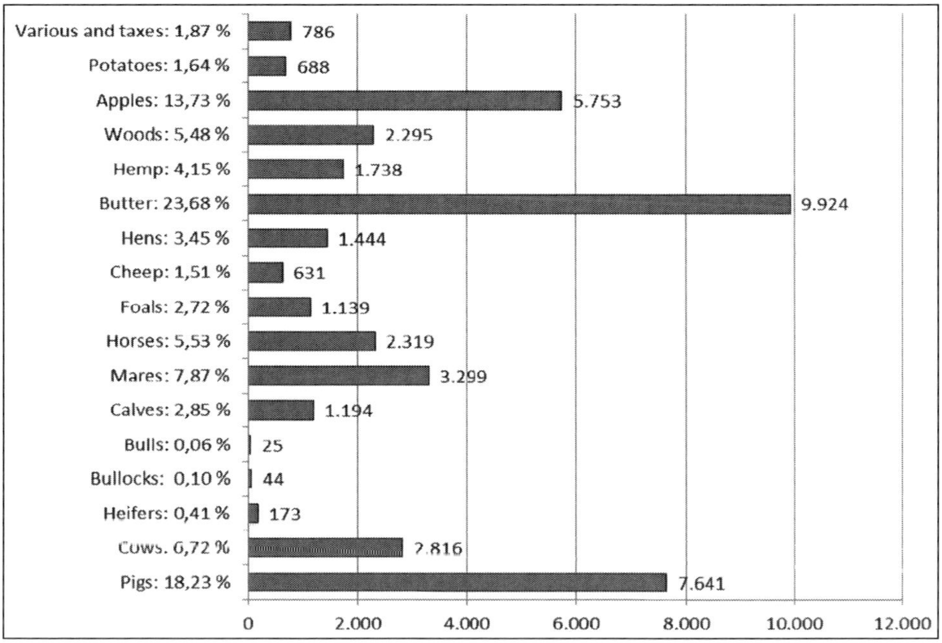

Source: See figure 3.2.

But these changes were minimal and the differences between one period and the next are not clear enough to show any real trends.

IV. The limitations of the analysis

At the end of this study it appears that two things are known in some detail: the evolution of the landlord's revenue and its composition. It can be shown, with little chance of error, what an estate with ten or so holdings brought in to its landlord. Is it possible to go beyond this?

IV.1. Can the grain yield be calculated?

In order to calculate the cereal yield in a satisfactory way we would have to know precisely the area sown, the quantity of seed and the total production. These figures are all lacking. Of course it is possible to extrapolate, to put forward hypotheses and then base calculations on them. This would produce a set of figures that would not be completely wrong. If one were working on periods for which so little is known, that any approximation would be better than nothing, this would make sense; but this is not the case for the first half of the nineteenth century. And, if small changes are being calculated, approximations are dangerous if they frequently concern values higher than those being measured (Antoine, 2000).

The yearly crop of cereals by volume is certainly known for the Saint Mirel estate. But it is only known for the landlord's share, not for the total crop. Studies of other sets of accounts (Antoine, 1998) have shown that the landlord's share is not half of the crop either in value or, more important, in kind. It is often mentioned in passing that the mare ate so many quarts of oats before the division, that the tenant, in a certain year, kept the whole crop of one grain for seed (in some other accounts we see him in the end selling part of the grain he kept for seed). Thus simply multiplying by two does not give the total crop. On the other hand, these accounts show that the volume of grain sold is often less than what is noted as harvested. The difference lies in the fact that the grain was cleaned after being divided. This is explained for the year 1850.[10] The proportion of waste varied according to the year and the crop but it was far from negligible (for buckwheat it could be up to one-tenth of the harvest).

Buckwheat, as has already been noted, did not seem to have lost ground, apart from its large annual fluctuations. On the other hand, wheat made a temporary appearance during the 1830s and then more definitely after 1840. It can be seen that the landlord was regularly buying lime and, above all, bone meal, from the middle of the 1830s. Clearly, these two developments are linked. But should every possible effort be made to calculate the possible increase in productivity of the land? Not necessarily. The production figures available are too imprecise (as we have seen above) to measure changes concerning only very small quantities. The potential errors in the data available (production, area, quantity of seeds) are much greater than the values to be estimated (the increase in productivity): this makes the calculation impossible or, at the very least, gives misleading results. The document provides a qualitative measure of agricultural change (the use of bone meal, hens appearing in much greater numbers in the *subsides* at the end of the thirties, the cultivation of wheat and potatoes, the slight decline of rye etc.) but it is difficult to translate this into figures. It is even difficult to say if this really was progress: while these changes were occurring the landlord's profit margin was tending to decrease (see Figure 3.2). The same comments can be made on the expenditure for the repair of buildings. In the absence of additional information (an inspection of the buildings for example), it would be rash to interpret this as an unambiguous sign of progress: does it indicate a landlord who had a programme of modernisation for the buildings on his property? Or is it a rather a sign of a landlord losing money while trying to patch up worn-out buildings?

IV.2. And all the other things that cannot be known

Although this is such a rich and detailed document, the productivity of the land is not the only thing that cannot be learned from it. Nothing is known for example of the turnover of the animals on the holding. The steward's accounts only give the financial balance sheet for the livestock. Since there is no day-to-day record of purchases and sales, it is impossible to know what strategies for profit were followed (if any), or what criteria were

[10] 1850: 364 quarts of rye harvested, 3 quarts waste; 824 quarts of buckwheat harvested, 97 quarts waste; 44 quarts of wheat harvested, 1 quart waste; 37 quarts of maslin harvested, 1 quart waste; 173 quarts of oats harvested, 4 quarts waste.

used in managing the herd. A daily, or at least monthly, journal of activities would be needed to show what types of animal were sold, what they were replaced with, and why. Here there is only the final total. But it seems that the large animals were not essential on these farms; they made up only a quarter of the *subsides*, which were in turn only a quarter of the landlord's profits.

Finally, there is one thing seen in almost all the accounts available: next to nothing is known of the farmer's activities, neither where he found money nor what he did with his share of the crop. It seems from reading the document that some farmers had trouble in making the cash payments owed as part of the *subsides*. Certain payments were sometimes put off for more than a year. This shows both the financial difficulties of the farmer and the landlord's role as a lender. By accepting a delay in payment he left the cash in the hands of the *métayer*. This was one of the characteristics of social relations in sharecropping regions. This has been shown in the eighteenth century, particularly in the case of the tenant of La Pagerie, a very small farm on the outskirts of Laval, whose volume of activity (measured by grain produced and livestock sold) was so small that he only seemed to hang on thanks to these deferred payments (Antoine, 1996). But apart from the assistance the landlord gave his tenant, which has often been noted, nothing more is known from this document about the activities of the farmer.

IV.3. Agricultural specialisation

Even though it is not realistic to expect eighteenth and nineteenth-century farm accounts to provide precise figures for analysing productivity and its evolution, they are still of great use in distinguishing different models of agricultural production (Hubsher, 1981). They contradict the idea that all older types of agriculture were equally unimpressive, and they show that within the mixed farming economies typical of the old agriculture there were many specialisations.

In the old economics all the holdings had to produce enough cereal to feed the farmer and his family. This can be seen in the accounts in the large amounts of buckwheat produced, which remain steady throughout the period studied. Where specialisation is found it is in the other produce, not the basic essentials. For the farms in Lower Maine, eighteenth-century accounts show a general tendency towards speculative cattle rearing, with some local variations: either choosing to keep the maximum number of females to sell when they were ready to have a first calf, or keeping many of the males to sell when fully or partially fattened, and therefore sending the female calves to market early, or choosing (or being forced?) to sell all the calves, male and female, as early as possible to bring in a quick but small cash revenue (Antoine, 1995).

The accounts of Saint Mirel were not kept from day to day so it is not possible to be so precise about the livestock rearing strategies used there. They do, however, show the type of agriculture practiced and the choices and constraints of the landlords and tenants. The extreme diversity of productions has been mentioned already. This should not be labelled with the disparaging term 'mixed subsistence farming' (Mayaud, 1999). It was a type of specialisation in butter, apples and pigs. Within the specialisation there was a proportion conceded to the farmer's subsistence needs (buckwheat) and a part for commercial production. After these four main productions came wood and horses. When all the information in the accounts concerning the livestock is examined in detail the most noticeable fact is the importance given to fattening the pigs. Each farm produced two to four a year and seemed to have a sow all the time. The piglets were sold if there were too many or bought if there were not enough to be fattened. On the other hand these farms did not specialise in cattle rearing as the ones in Maine did at that time. They did not keep the males (oxen, bullocks or bulls). They only had cows that calved and gave milk for butter. These cows left the farm when they were old and were replaced by heifers. Some were sold and replaced by others, younger and cheaper. The same practice can be seen here with the heifers as with the cattle in Maine, which changed hand several times in the course of being fattened. These exchanges were designed to produce profits spread over several years: the sale of a more expensive animal, the purchase of a cheaper one, the profits of the deal being divided between the landlord and the farmer (it is this division which is noted in the accounts and makes it possible to understand this practice).

The sale of mares also brought in large sums. They were there for both work and profit, playing the same role that oxen played in neighbouring Maine. And again as in Maine sheep do not seem to have been the object of any special care or strategy. On the whole, in the farms of the Saint Mirel estate, animals were sold when they were young, not when they were worth the most (except perhaps for a few mares); this is a sign of a type of agriculture in which the farmer is forced to look for small profits to obtain cash quickly. This suggests that the farmers were less comfortable than those who were able to speculate over longer periods with larger sums of money.

V. Conclusion

Eventually, it seems quite vain to try asking to the farms accounts questions that they can't answer. In the nineteenth century, it went the same way than in the previous century, there wasn't any model for accounts' books. They were kept under different principles following the type of contract that bound the tenant to the landlord (or his/her steward). It is thus reasonable to only ask to each farm account information that they contain. In the case study presented here, we see that it is impossible to calculate the grain yield: on one hand we don't know the quantity of seed used each year and on the other hand we don't know if the seed was bought outside the estate or sampled on the crop before its sharing out. We know the yearly profit of the grain culture but we don't know the sown area, nor the quantity of seed used, nor the exact volume of the crop.

Now, if we turn ourselves towards the questions that might receive answers: we can firstly talk about the landlord's profit. We notice that for the 25 years studied the landlord has always a profit balance and he seems even to be making some investments on his estates (buying fertilisers at the end of the period, probably to increase the production of wheat). But can we determine that these investments are profitable for him? It can't be ascertained when looking at the graph of the landlord's profit (Figure 3.2). Can we also raise the question of the tenant's profit? Can we say that his profit is the same as the landlord's profit because they are in a sharecropping system? Theoretically: yes, practically: no, because the landlord has several estates while the tenant works only on one tenure and he has to live and makes his family and servants live.

Finally if we accept to let this farm account tell us only what it can truly teach us, the result is not less interesting. We see how estates that practice both subsistence farming and commercialised farming work. Like in the previous century, the choice of a massive production of various cereals is not challenged as it is the highest money entrance for the estates. But still in the mid-nineteenth century, it is a variable entry, the sums gained from selling grains can vary by three times as much (Figure 3.3).

This grain production is only one part of the farm's activity that produces also apples, wood from pruned hedges, fattened pigs and a hosts of other things. Reading Figure 3.6 which gives all these productions could lead to conclude hastily to what is often called in disparaging terms 'mixed farming of subsistence'. The reality is more complex than that because it is a production system that offers the possibility to both feed the tenant and for him to sell his products. The pattern 'buckwheat-butter-apples-pigs' which has been identified in this farm account plays this role. It is very close to similar patterns that have been brought out for the previous century, except that the pattern has grown richer with potatoes. The whole is intrinsically bound together: the inhabitants eat buckwheat, the apple trees meadows provide milk; the milk is transformed into butter while the whey and potatoes feed the pigs. We have also seen that the sharecropper seems sometimes to have difficulties to pay the landlord's part and that he asks for payment facilities. He trades several times his cows during their time of growth to replace them with younger cows which are less expensive; this gives the evidence that an immediate need for money forces the sharecropper to prefer a small immediate profit to a more important but more distant profit. Ultimately, what a farm account of this kind shows us is less figures calculating productivity than strategies between subsistence and profit.

Bibliography

Antoine, A. (1994) *Fiefs et villages du Bas-Maine au XVIIIe siècle*, Mayenne: Éditions Régionales de l'Ouest.

Antoine, A. (1995) 'Les Bovins du Bas-Maine, un modèle économique pour les campagnes de l'Ouest? (1720–1820)', *Histoire et Sociétés Rurales*, 4: 2, pp. 105–136.

Antoine, A. (1996) 'Une Petite exploitation agricole au milieu du XVIIIe siècle : la closerie de la Pagerie' (c. Arquenay, dép. de la Mayenne), *L'Oribus*, 40, pp. 3–19.

Antoine, A. (1998) *Les Comptes ordinaires de Pierre Duchemin du Tertre, marchand de toile et seigneur dans la première moitié du XVIIIe siècle*, Mayenne: Société d'Archéologie et d'Histoire de la Mayenne.

Antoine, A. (2000) 'Entre macro et micro : les comptabilités agricoles du XVIIIe siècle', in G. Béaur and J.-M. Chevet, (eds), *Productivité et Croissance agricole*, *Histoire et Mesure*, vol. XV, 3–4, pp. 247–270.

Clout, H. (1979) 'Land use change in Finistère during the eighteenth and nineteenth centuries', *Études Rurales*, 73, pp. 69–96.

Cocaud, M. (1999) 'Une Approche de la modernisation agricole de l'Ouest au XIXe siècle: des statistiques aux comptabilités d'exploitation', *Ruralia*, 1999/5. URL : <http://ruralia.revues.org/108>.

Garnier, B. and Hubscher, R. (1984) 'Recherches sur une présentation quantifiée des revenus agricoles', *Histoire, économie et société*, 1984, 3, pp. 427–452.

Hubscher, R. (1985) 'La Petite exploitation en France : reproduction et compétitivité (fin XIXe siècle-début XXe siècle)', *Annales, Économies, Sociétés, Civilisations*, 40, pp. 3–34.

Hubsher, R. (1981) 'Modèles d'exploitation et comptabilité agricole : l'exemple du Pas-de-Calais au début du XIXe siècle', *Études Rurales*, pp. 31–48.

Le Névanic, A. (1909) 'L'Agriculture en Ille-et-Vilaine de 1815 à 1870', *Annales de Bretagne et des Pays de l'Ouest*, 25, 4, pp. 624–629.

Letaconnoux, J. (1908) 'L'Agriculture dans le département d'Ille-et-Vilaine en 1816', *Annales de Bretagne et des Pays de l'Ouest*, 24, 4, pp. 599–618.

Mayaud, J.-L. (1999) *La Petite exploitation rurale triomphante. France, XIXe siècle*, Paris: Éditions Belin, 278 p.

Perrot, J.-C. (1978) 'La Comptabilité des entreprises agricoles dans l'économie physiocratique', *Annales, Économie, Sociétés, Civilisations*, 1978, 3, pp. 559–579.

Revel, J. (1996) 'Micro-analyse et construction du social', in: Revel, J. (ed.), *Jeux d'échelles. La micro-analyse à l'expérience*, Paris: Gallimard-Le Seuil, pp. 15–36.

Sée, H. (1919) 'L'Agriculture dans les Côtes-du-Nord en 1844', *Annales de Bretagne et des Pays de l'Ouest*, 34, 2, pp. 111–128.

4 Land and growth in the eighteenth century: the *métairies* of Garaison and their accounts, or the uncertainties of growth*

Jean Duma, University of Paris X-Nanterre

I. Introduction

This paper is a micro-study based on the accounts of properties held by a community of chaplains established in the sanctuary of Garaison, in South West France, near the Pyrenees (the present department of Haute-Pyrénées). It attempts to reconstitute how a group of basic economic units functioned in the rural world of the Old Regime. It provides some data on the difficulties of agricultural production in a little-studied transitional region, part of the diocese of Auch and the Pays des Quatre Vallées (a medieval entity situated between France and Spain, Bigorre and Comminges) (Barifouse, 1874; Dumoret, 1869; Sarramon, 1954). It is part of a work in progress, and therefore concentrates on methodological problems and the questions raised by them rather than presenting complete and definitive results. This is a specific and limited case that may serve as an example for other such studies; it is rich in information on the resources and limitations of this type of accounting material.

First the setting of this study, the chapel of Garaison, its estate and accounts, will be described in more detail, then the land holdings and system of production of one part of the estate, the *métairies* of Garaison, will be examined more closely, and finally, some attempt will be made to estimate the changes in production over short term (1782–1789) and medium-term fluctuations (1738–1789).

II. The estate and accounts of Garaison

II.1. The chapel of Garaison

The Val de Garaison is a small valley, mostly heath, at the point where the Lannemezan plateau meets the plain of Magnoac. It would have seemed a complete wasteland at the beginning of the sixteenth century; there was only a hamlet, which came under the town of Montléon-Magnoac, and a small chapel. The hamlet was a typical example of the overlapping authorities of old regime France. The town had been under the authority of the kings of France since the end of the fifteenth century and its consuls administered the revenues of the parish church and its annex, the chapel of Garaison, according to the customs of the Pays des Quatre Vallées. In 1511, Bernard d'Antin, younger son of an old family of Bigorre, was the seigneur of the hamlet. In the sixteenth century there were about fifteen inhabitants settled around the chapel.

---

* Translated by Judith Le Goff.

Figure 4.1 Map by Cassini (eighteenth century)

Figure 4.2 Road map, *c.* 1930

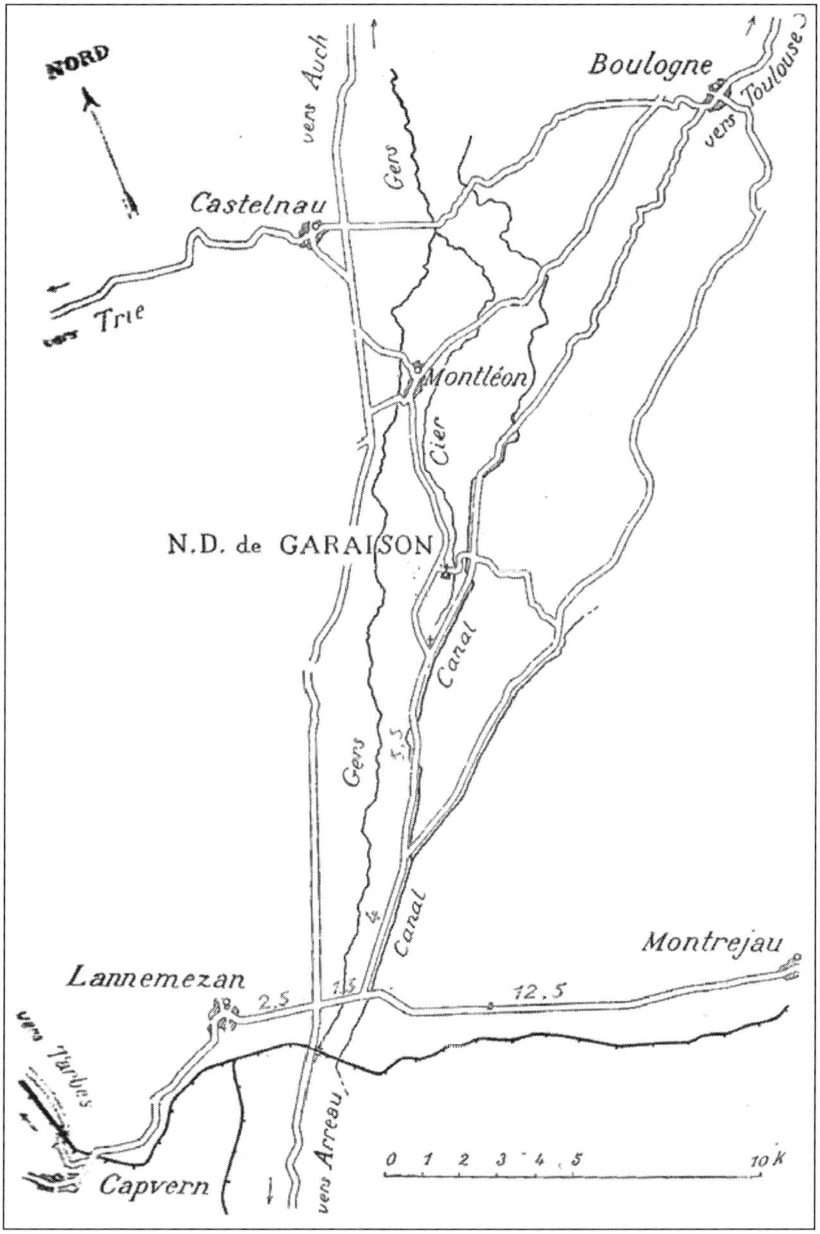

Source: Notre-Dame de Garaison 1510–1515 1836 1936, Édition abrégée et illustrée de la Petite Histoire de N.-D. de Garaison par le P. Antoine Larrouy. Paris. J. David & E. Vallois, 1936.

As it was on one of the routes to Compostela many pilgrims stopped there on the way to Notre Dame de Monserrat. The chapel illustrates the deep roots of the Marian cult in the region, with its strong tradition of miracles and other marvellous happenings. Appearances of the Virgin were quite frequent. It was there that in 1520, a young shepherdess named Anglèze de Sagasan, whose father seems to have been the head of one of the households in the hamlet, saw the Virgin Mary appear and order her to 'go and tell the Consuls of the town of Montléon that they should have a cross erected by the spring and when that is done there will be enough donations to build a church there' (Decroix, 1983). The chapel was rebuilt and, from the beginning of the seventeenth century, through the efforts of Pierre Geoffroy, an associate of the Bishop of Auch, who was then responsible for the chapel, the sanctuary grew, and eventually was made an independent benefice.

A relatively stable community was set up to take care of the sanctuary, made up of about twenty priests. Its core was a group of twelve chaplains, and their numbers remained stable throughout the seventeenth and eighteenth centuries. Six or seven priests, depending on the period, were authorised to assist them and new chaplains were chosen from them when a place became vacant. In addition about forty people were involved with the sanctuary ranging from the choirboys to the various staff in charge of the upkeep of the sanctuary and the management of the estate.

An estate had fairly quickly formed around the chapel to enable its members to live and carry out their missions. Pierre Geoffroy bought about fifteen hectares on which buildings were reconstructed and enlarged. Some thirteen *métairies* were added to the whole. This came about largely through mass foundations, land purchase and bequests. As a result, by the end of the eighteenth century the chapel had relatively large landholdings and income (more than 30,000 livres in revenue).

It is situated in a region with very distinctive characteristics. Though the seigneurial system existed there it was above all a group of four valleys, those of the Aure, the Barouste, the Neste and the Magnoac, where the influence of peasant communities (communautés) was particularly great, thus giving the peasantry some autonomy (Soulet, 2006; René Souriac, 1978, or, in a wider perspective, Zink, 1997). The valley of the Magnoac, where Garaison was situated, was made up of 35 communities and the métaries that were dependent on Garaison were within the territory of the communities. This was a mountain economy, based on stock rearing and, as the region was on the border of the two countries, a good deal of trade with Spain. Magnoac, however, was situated on the Lannemezan plateau, separate from the three other valleys and had more agriculture than stock rearing. The economic evolution of the region was in step with the general trends of the early modern period, with some significant divergences. It was relatively distant from the theatres of the Wars of Religion and from the economic hardships of the seventeenth century so the situation there was rather better.

On the other hand, the eighteenth century was more difficult, with continuing famines, noticeable price fluctuations and increased fiscal pressure from the monarchy (For the regional context, see Frêche, 1974; Minovez, 1997; Zink, 1969). Various records, including the accounts, survive, and make it possible to study the economy of the sanctuary.[1]

[1] This article is based on the Notre Dame de Garaison papers in series G of the Archives départementales des Hautes-Pyrénées (G 1057 to G 1109).

In the remainder of this paper one part of the sanctuary's possessions, the core group of thirteen *métairies*, of varying size, will be studied.

II.2. The nature of the accounts

Among the sources available for this study there are almost no documents giving the overall extent and description of the estate or of its component parts. There are not many contracts and only a few acts of *boriage* (the term for sharecropping used in Gascony) have been kept at the end of the period. Thus there are practically no clues as to the area of the *métairies*. On the other hand some accounts were kept for the chapel of Garaison, between 1738 and 1789.

These accounts are not uniform. They are not continuous over time and some data are missing. For the fifty-one years studied there is information on only nineteen. The accounts were preserved for 1738–1747 (eight years), 1756–1767 (six years) and finally, 1782–1789 (five years). These groups of records, which happened to survive the vagaries of archival conservation, are, however, interesting because they correspond to the three main periods Ernest Labrousse discerned in the eighteenth-century economy (Labrousse, 1933). The first corresponds to the slow take-off, the second covers the growth spurt of the 1760s when the economy flourished. The third period coincides with the levelling-off at the end of the century.

The accounts are also not kept and presented in a uniform way. They are the account books of the *syndicat* responsible for the chapel, and thus give the viewpoint of the landlord and manager, but they are not in an identical format for the three periods. Moreover, the documents are in varying states of preservation.

In the first period the accounts appear to be exhaustive.[2] All the receipts of the chapel were listed chronologically, for the estate lands as well as for the religious activities, in a journal where expenses and receipts were entered on a daily basis (there were more receipts than expenses). At the end of each book there are summary statements of sheaves, grains, seed, and grapes harvested. However the results of animal husbandry appear in a much more uneven and haphazard way, the variety and differing forms in which the material is presented on a yearly basis make it hard to construct series from the data available.

In the 1760s the accounts are mainly concerned with the landed property.[3] The accounts were set out by *métairie*; those of Arné, Villemur and Garaison were sometimes missing. These were much briefer than the preceding set and included only one or two pages for each *métairie*, shown as a summary. The *syndic* drew up a balance sheet of the situation of each one, showing whatever was owed by the *bordier* and what he had repaid during the year. It usually included a reminder of what was owed from previous years and mentioned delays in payment, which existed, and generally accumulated. Payments in kind are often mentioned but the precise amount is rarely given. Sometimes there are references to the contract of *boriage*, but as these contracts were rarely preserved we can say little about them. An inventory of the animals was given for each *métairie*. These were more complete and show the relative importance of livestock rearing. The accounts

[2] Archives départementales des Hautes-Pyrénées, G 1098 and 1099.
[3] Archives départementales des Hautes-Pyrénées, G 1100 and 1101.

end with inventories of sheaves, grains, seed and grapes harvested, bringing together in one account the contributions and results of all the *métairies*.

The accounts for 1780 show, for each *métairie*, all transactions that concerned the *syndicat*.[4] The remaining documents are more uniform and make up a set of overall balance sheets. However they are briefer and provide less information than the earlier ones; they no longer resemble a farm journal (*livre de raison*). The accounts show a cash equivalent for the payments in kind but the actual nature of the payments made by the *bordier* is not always clear. It seems that they may not always have been made in kind but were sometimes paid in cash.

This brief description of the sources highlights their diversity. In general those responsible for managing the estates seem to have had a good knowledge of the situation and to have followed developments closely. However, with such diverse sources it is impossible to make a precise quantitative study of production, with rigorous series. On the other hand, the documents contain very valuable information on the changes in the holding, the qualitative as well as the quantitative. The rhythm and methods of the management of an estate can be seen on the daily level and show how the relations between the landlord and his tenants were built up. That is material for a future work.

Now that questions of methodology have been discussed, the next section will deal with some of the material obtained from studying these accounts. It concerns the nature of the estate and the holdings of which it was composed, and some of the results that can be obtained.

III. The overall income of the estate

III.1. What the revenues included

The accounts of the last period, from 1782 to 1789, make it possible to discern the extent and make-up of the estate and to estimate its size. It had a large income. The chaplains of Garaison had been able to build up an estate that gave them the means to carry out their religious functions and to take their place among the local *notables*. It was equal, if not superior, to the possessions of the Marquis of Lons in nearby Béarn. He owned at least fifteen mills, six châteaux and five *métairies* in the Jurançon vineyards, which brought in about the same revenue (Desplats, 1992: 578).

Because there are no contracts it is impossible to know the exact area of the different *métairies*. For the same reason the exact conditions of the leases are not known, although it seems that they were typical sharecropping (*métayage*) leases (Brumont, 2003; Féral, 1987; Brumont, 1999). The accounts however emphasise one very important finding – the extremely large range of results, which, according to the year, could be as great as 25%. This is a direct consequence of sharecropping. A good harvest could mean a fall in prices and thus in the revenues of the chapel. Two of the crops on the *métairie* of Arné may serve as an example. In 1783 the *bordier* brought in eleven sacks of rye which, that

[4] Archives départementales des Hautes-Pyrénées, G 1102.

Table 4.1 Revenues of the Chapel of Garaison in livres

1782	32,043
1783	34,310
1784	26,931
1788	25,131
1789	37,171

Source: Archives départementales des Hautes-Pyrénées, G 1100 (1756, 1758, 1759), G 1101 (1762, 1763, 1767), G 1108 (1782), G 1102 (1783, 1784, 1788, 1789).

Table 4.2 Breakdown of the Garaison revenues (in livres and %)

Métairies	16,969.20	49.9 %
Dues and charges	6,903.70	20.3 %
Rented land	1,277.75	3.8 %
Mills	4,057.00	11.9 %
Château d' Esclassan	4,797.00	14.1 %

Source: see Table 4.1.

year, cost 12 livres 5 sous the sack. Thus Garaison took in 143 livres. The next year, 1784, 25 sacks were delivered but the price had fallen to 8 livres 2 sous a sack, so the gain was only 153 livres. In 1788, for nine sacks at 10 livres 5 sous the sack, the revenue was 96 livres and in 1789, for 16 sacks at 15 livres 6 sous, 252 livres. The same applies to oats. In 1783 four sacks at 6 livres 16 sous a sack, made 32 livres. In 1784, 8 sacks at 4 livres 16 sous made 28 livres. In 1788, six sacks at 8 livres 19 sous made 44 livres. In 1789, seven sacks at 10 livres 9 sous the sack made 81 livres. A good harvest was no guarantee of a substantial profit.

The accounts for 1783 show the respective size of the different components of the revenues.

Table 4.3 shows how these components were divided between the different *métairies* and gives some idea of the overall structure of the estate.

III.2. Breakdown of the revenues

The *métairies* were the essential element as they brought in half of the total income. They were large compact farms held by *bordiers* who made regular reports on their management to the chapel syndic. Garaison was a special case and operated somewhat differently from the others.

Table 4.3 Structure of the estate in livres

Métairies	Garaison	5,650.00
	Montauban	240.00
	Arné	629.00
	Villemur	804.00
	Betpouy	1,223.20
	Barthe	375.50
	Campusan	811.70
	Anguian	2,166.00
	Mane	998.60
	Esclassan	1,115.30
	Beres	1,818.40
	Bedoura	464.00
	Labastide	673.50
Dues and charges	Garaison	5,165.00
	Arné	145.00
	Bajourdan	168.00
	Villemur	591.00
	Esclassan	98.00
	Monlong	736.70
Rented land	Garaison	977.00
	Tajan	9.75
	Recurt	4.00
	Gassan	8.00
	Villemur	3.00
	Monlong	276.00
Mills	Bajourdan	283.00
	Lassalet	516.00
	Anan	800.00
	Esclassan	1,772.00
	Monlong	686.00
Château	Esclassan	4,797.00

Source: see Table 4.1.

The rented lands (*fermes*) were made up of parcels of land and meadows that had entered the estate in various ways, by bequest or purchase. They were generally too small to make an independent holding for sharecropping. In these circumstances, renting them out to peasants was the simplest and most flexible way to use them but, as they only made up 3% of the total, their economic weight was negligible.

The dues and charges covered feudal and seigneurial revenues as well as charges on the land (*rentes constitutées ou foncières*). These made up 20.3% of the total revenues, showing how persistent and significant were the feudal dues and other charges that burdened the land. This aspect is only mentioned briefly here and needs further study.

The five mills made up 11.9% of the total revenue. They were rented out, but the rent of four of them, which remained fixed, was stated in kind, which affected the amounts received. This explains the variation in revenue already discussed. The following table sets out the statement of accounts for the mills.

The amount of rent in this type of lease makes it possible to see the importance of the mills in the estate as a whole. For example, the mill of Esclassan paid a rent of 125 sacks of wheat, while the *métairie* at Esclassan brought in to Garaison between 27 and 45 sacks of wheat according to the year.

The Château d'Esclassan (14.1% of the total) was like a seigneurial reserve. Its resources included arable fields, meadows, and vines worked 'by our hand', land in fief, *agriers* (the local term for *champart*, a proportionate levy in kind on crops), and various charges.

This portrait of the estate at the end of the period describes the situation that existed for most of the eighteenth century. The sources are too defective to follow the history of how it was built up, but it seems to have been complete by the 1730s at the latest. The two principal means by which the estate reached this stage seem to have been pious bequests and a policy of judicious purchases. These factors, bequests and purchases, explain both the size and the dispersion of the holdings. There were, however, some small changes during this period in response to slight alterations in the management of the estate. The accounts for 1767, for instance, note that the land at Augain was rented out at that time.

Table 4.4 Accounts for the mills

Mill	Rental payment	1782	1783	1784	1788	1789
Esclassan	125 sacks of wheat	1,750 liv.	1,623 liv.	1,184 liv.	1,625 liv.	2,148 liv.
Lassalet	8 sacks of rye	98 liv.	121 liv.	89 liv.	82 liv.	160 liv.
Anan	Cash	800 liv.	800 liv.	800 liv.	800 liv.	800 liv.
Bajourdan	22 sacks of rye	269 liv.	269 liv.	177 liv.	225 liv.	336 liv.
Monlong	56 sacks of rye	686 liv.	686 liv.	451 liv.	574 liv.	856 liv.

Source: see Table 4.1.

IV. The output of the Garaison *métairies*

IV.1. The range of products

The thirteen *métairies* made up the economic heart of the estate but were spread out from two or three kilometres to thirty-odd kilometres around the chapel. They can be put into four groups. The first was close to Garaison, from two to five kilometres from the chapel. It was made up of the *métairies* of Arné and Montauban and the smaller holdings at Trajan, Monlong and Lassalet. A second group lay further to the north east and was made up of the *métairie* at Villemur, that of Mane and lands at Bajoudan. From fifteen to twenty kilometres to the northwest of Garaison, Barthe, Betpouy and Campusan made up the third group. Finally, more than thirty kilometres towards Auch, were Esclassan and Labastide. This brief description of the geography shows that the various groups of estate lands were in regions with different characteristics and different potentials.

There are two characteristics of the estate seen as a whole. The first is the diversity of products. The following table lists them all.

This table, with more than 35 different headings, shows the diversity of the estate's produce. There are concentrations in certain areas. Winter cereals are present with wheat and rye, but also as maslin (*mixture* or *misture*). In spring cereals, barley is predominant and appears in many varieties. The legumes were also numerous and diverse. There were lentils, which were usually used for pigeon feed (although pigeons do not appear in the list). *Pois carrés* (fodder peas), along with barley and oats, were generally kept for animal fodder. Broad beans, haricot beans and vetch were also frequently grown.

Livestock were there for different purposes: for work or for market. The animals noted were oxen, young bulls (30 months), cows with calves, heifers, mares (often in foal), foals, and sometimes a mule. Other horses and bulls were almost never mentioned. Where there was wool, there were ewes, ewe hoggets or sheep. Pigs, male and female, were often noted, in fairly large numbers. Finally the poultry were numerous and diverse. There were also a few additional products, such as flax and wine, which were found in some holdings, but not everywhere.

All the variety of 'words from the past', to borrow Marcel Lachiver's phrase, is seen in this list (Lachiver, 2006). The great range of products of mixed farming reflects the extent of subsistence farming, but the place of stock rearing demonstrates that the market was always important, as does the significant variation in the estate's revenues, which has already been discussed.

IV.2. The differences between the *métairies*

The second characteristic is the difference between the various *métairies*. The table of the income generated by the *métairies* clearly shows that they were not all equally important.

Garaison was the dominant part of the estate. This was both because it was at the centre and because it was managed in a special way. It was not, strictly speaking, a *métairie*, but a varied collection of lands (cultivated fields, meadows, vines, woods) close to the chapel, and benefiting from this proximity in many ways, which was managed on share-cropping contracts.

Table 4.5 Products of the Garaison *métairies*

	Garaison	Montauban	Arné	Villemur	Betpouy	Barthe	Campusan	Anguian	Mane	Esclassan	Beres	Bedoura	Labastide
Wheat			*	*	*	*	*	*	*	*	*	*	*
Rye	*	*	*		*								
Rye and oats			*										
Oats	*	*	*	*	*	*	*	*	*	*	*	*	*
Maize			*	*	*	*	*	*	*	*	*	*	*
Millet		*	*	*	*	*	*		*				
Mil morou (variety of millet)									*				
Millot (variety of millet)													*
Maslin					*	*	*	*		*		*	*
Paumole (variety of spring barley)			*	*	*	*		*		*	*	*	*
Barley			*			*				*	*	*	
Carron (barley and wheat)					*		*	*	*				
Broken grains of wheat				*	*			*	*				
Broken grains of *paumole*								*					
Sarde (variety of barley for poor soil)													
Mousent (unidentified local term)						*							
Pois carrés (variety of fodder peas)			*	*		*		*	*	*	*		
Vetch					*	*		*		*	*		
Broad beans			*		*	*		*		*	*	*	*
Haricot beans			*	*		*		*	*	*	*	*	*
Lentils						*				*	*		

Table 4.5 (Continued)

	Garaison	Montauban	Arné	Villemur	Betpouy	Barthe	Campusan	Anguian	Mane	Esclassan	Beres	Bedoura	Labastide
Chestnuts		*											
Wood	*										*		
Planks	*												
Meadows	*								*				
Hay	*		*	*									
Wine	*			*	*		*	*	*				
Flax		*	*	*	*	*	*	*	*	*	*	*	*
Wool				*	*	*	*	*	*	*	*	*	*
Animals	*	*	*	*	*	*	*	*	*	*	*	*	*
Pigs	*												
Poultry		*	*	*	*	*	*	*	*	*	*	*	*
Geese				*	*	*	*	*	*	*	*	*	*
Turkeys										*	*		*
Eggs		*	*	*	*	*	*	*	*	*	*	*	*

Source: see Table 4.1.

The situation of the other *métairies* varied widely, depending mainly on where they were. Rye-growing country contrasted with wheat-growing country, and the regions of Magnoac and the areas nearer to Auch were more favoured than those close to Garaison. Whatever else was produced, livestock rearing always seems to have been important. It is not suprising that there was a link between the presence of draught oxen and the results of the holding. Anguian, which generated the highest income, was notable for the diversity of its products. In varying quantities, according to the year, the *bordier* produced wheat, oats, maslin, *paumole* (a variety of spring barley), maize, *sarde* (a variety of barley grown on poor soil), broad beans, vetch, *pois carrés*, haricot beans, wine, flax, and wool. The animals were also listed. Fatted geese were mentioned separately from the poultry. All of these items underwent variations in both the volume and value of their production. The question of the profitability and productivity of these *métairies* still remains to be resolved.

V. Production trends

Since the general trend of the eighteenth century was mostly favourable to growth, what was the situation of these *métairies*? Were they entering a period of growth or not? Two points will be discussed with reference to the graphs compiled from data in the accounts.

V.1. Short-term fluctuations

The first point to make is that there were great variations in production. Although all the products were affected only three, animal products, wheat and oats, will be discussed here. The period 1782–1789 has been used because the data for those years is presented in a standard form that allows valid comparisons to be made.

'Animal products' covers a wide variety of activities but these appear in the accounts in terse entries. Only the value, in livres, of 'profits from animals', is noted. There was, however, more information in the earlier years. In 1739 the syndic of the chapel drew up a statement of accounts for the livestock in the *métairie* of Montauban:[5]

> 5 oxen for ploughing (in the margin: 1 sold in 1740); 2 cows of which 1 in calf; 2 heifers; 2 sows; 2 last year's pigs; 3 pigs from this year; 1 mare; 40 ewes; 7 ewe hoggets. 13 December 1739 settled accounts with the bordier of Montauban after deducting all the profits I have received he still owes three livres two sous six deniers. The capital for the oxen bought at 88 l. this year has been reduced to 51 l. by 37 l. from the sale of an ox. The capital of the pigs which was twenty-six livres six sols six deniers has been reduced to 15 l. 6s 6d by means of one male and one female pig taken for the house.

In 1743 the state of livestock for the *métairie* of Betpouy was as follows:[6]

> 4 oxen, 1 cow with this year's calf, 1 mare in foal, 1 female foal aged 30 months; 1 sow, 4 last year's pigs and 6 this year's pigs; 23 ewe lambs or hoggets for which I advanced capital of 43 l. 18s; the capital for the *braux* (young bulls) is 192 l. 5s which belong to us, there are now only 2 *braux* and the *bordier* has the rest of the money to buy more. He paid for the poultry and the eggs and we are now quit of all profits until 21 Dec. 1743.

The *métayers* of Garaison reared oxen, cows, calves, horses, mostly mares and their foals, pigs, male and female, sheep and ewes. Many animals were sold as yearlings. The new animals were rarely kept more than two years. The situations thus varied enormously. This diversity accounts for the variation under this heading. The rhythm of stock rearing does not always fit in the accounting year. The situation is different for the other two products, wheat and oats.

In calculating the values used in these graphs we have used volumes, rather than values. In the Garaison region the measure used for cereals and legumes was the sack of four *mesures*, each *mesure* made up of two *coupeaux*. The sack varied from place to place, from 72.26 litres to 104.10 litres. In order to make the graphs comparable the volumes have been converted into *mesures*.

The variations in agricultural production were much greater than those in stock rearing, both in time and space. They differed slightly according to the product.

In the case of wheat there are eleven *métairies* involved as Garaison and Montauban only produced rye. Production could double from one year to another, and in certain

[5] Archives départementales des Hautes-Pyrénées, G 1098.
[6] Archives départementales des Hautes-Pyrénées, G 1098.

cases rose five-fold. For example the *bordier* of Campusan brought in two sacks, three measures of wheat in 1788 and thirteen sacks one measure the next year. The graph shows that the *métairies* were very different from each other and experienced separate patterns of growth. We can, however, single out five types of development.

Arné, which grew mostly rye, did also produce a little wheat. Since it was a marginal product there are wide variations in the results, but is this significant? There was a relative stability in the results for both the rye and oats. Is there a link between these different figures? At Villemur, Betpouy, Barthe, Anguian and Labastide variations in product, while significant, remained within a range of 20%–30%, although the crisis at the end of the century had a noticeable effect. At Campusan the results were up and down. The year 1784 was a poor one there, even though the situation improved in the other *métairies*. Overall, the results were not good. At Béres the results fell regularly and the one good year, 1789, could not make up for this significant decline. On the other hand, Mane, Esclassan and Bedoura showed unbroken growth, apart from the crisis of 1788, which was compensated for the next year.

The variations were just as great for oats but as the quantities brought in were smaller they were not so obvious. Also, each *métairie* seemed to develop on a different path than its neighbours. It is almost impossible to find common patterns of change.

For both wheat and oats, within a small area the changes were both very large and very different from one holding to another. The logic behind these changes and behind the lack of uniformity is difficult to identify. The influence of climate, in a fairly small area, is difficult to take into account. Probably soil quality and other local factors were more important.

V.2. Medium-term changes

The second point relates to growth of production in the medium term. Two graphs for Barthe and Betpouy show the change in the volume of all the products for which there are figures in the accounts over the whole period. They confirm the extreme variability of production according to the year and the product. At the same time they show certain strong trends, particularly concerning the change in cereal production. Wheat shows the greatest alteration, but *carron* (a mixture of barley and wheat) and oats also changed markedly. There seems to be a decline, or at least a stagnation of production in the middle of the century. On the other hand, the 1780s show a growth in production, though it was irregular at times.

Two tables of the production of wheat and oats at Betpouy and Anguain have been constructed, showing the changes in the quantities produced, the price per sack of grain and the overall income to the chapel.

These tables show once again the great variations in the level of production. But it should be noted that the market was sensitive and that prices fluctuated just as much as production. This confirms what was said earlier: a growth in production was not necessarily accompanied by better economic results and the variations in prices brought about a much more limited gain, both for the *bordier* and the chaplains. The reasons for this weakness remain to be explored.

Table 4.6 Wheat and oats at Bretpouy and Anguain

Betpouy	1782	1783	1784	1785	1786	1787	1788	1789
Wheat								
Quantity in *mésures*	104.00	84.20	136.00				51.00	93.00
Price per sack	16.00	15.00	11.00				14.50	20.00
Value in livres	416.00	320.00	381.00				183.00	465.00
Oats								
Quantity in *mésures*	16.00	30.00	9.00				26.00	23.00
Price per sack	8.00	6.75	4.75				7.00	10.50
Value in livres	32.25	51.00	10.75				46.00	60.00

Anguian	1782	1783	1784	1785	1786	1787	1788	1789
Wheat								
Quantity in *mésures*	204.00	176.00	232.00				101.00	236.00
Price per sack	13.50	12.50	8.25				10.50	17.00
Value in livres	688.50	578.00	498.00				273.00	1,003.00
Oats								
Quantity in *mésures*	44.00	84.00	136.00				56.00	40.00
Price per sack	7.00	5.75	4.50				6.00	9.00
Value in livres	77.00	120.00	153.00				84.00	90.00

Source: see Table 4.1.

VI. The vulnerability of the estate

It is not clear if there was any real growth. Changes in production were not necessarily accompanied by an overall improvement in the results for the holding. The predominant impression is that the results were unimpressive. Two other indications support this impression.

VI.1. The question of productivity

It is difficult to determine productivity, as there is no information on the areas under cultivation. However in certain years there are accounts of seeds supplied and of grains 'for

Table 4.7 Seed, Grain and sheaves in Garaison

Seed	1756	1758	1759	1762	1763	1767
Garaison	36.75	31.00	39.00	45.00	45.00	39.00
Betpouy	11.50	11.50	18.00	18.00	20.00	15.00
Barthe	4.50	3.75	6.50	5.00	6.00	6.00
Esclassan	40.00	36.00	38.00	36.00	30.00	29.00
Beres	63.00	60.00	66.00	48.00	60.00	65.00

Grain	1756	1758	1759	1762	1763	1767
Garaison	150.00	186.50	160.00	195.50	213.25	279.50
Betpouy	11.25	20.25	24.00	25.75	13.50	28.50
Barthe	1.25	6.50	1.50	6.00	7.00	12.75
Esclassan	11.50	22.25	23.00	7.00	11.25	21.50
Beres	32.00	53.00	104.75	49.00	46.00	83.00

Sheaves	1756	1758	1759	1762	1763	1767
Garaison	145.00	185.00	166.00	178.00	228.00	275.00
Betpouy	56.00	60.00	105.00	84.00	80.00	92.00
Barthe	23.00	19.00	13.00	20.00	25.00	37.00
Esclassan	143.00	130.00	147.00	90.00	97.00	111.00
Beres	270.00	290.00	399.00	234.00	258.00	340.00

Source: see Table 4.1.

our share' or sometimes 'grains taken'. Doubling this last figure ought to give the total production. A doubt remains, though, since these figures were often very low. Were they the total portion due to the landlord or only the amount due at the time when the accounts were settled? There are also inventories of sheaves posing similar questions. Were they the whole of the production, or just the share belonging to the chaplains? These sheaves were counted in *beauquiers* (a unit of 11 or 12 sheaves) subdivided into sheaves, which make it difficult to establish the relation to the sack. But still, these raw figures, with all their problems of interpretation, make a preliminary study of productivity possible.

Table 4.7 shows figures for five *métairies*, chosen as representative of the different soil conditions. Garaison produced rye, the others, wheat.

There are several comments to be made on these tables. Generally the seed seems to have been provided in identical amounts, showing that the areas sown were probably

Table 4.8 Productivity (number of sheaves/per unit of seed)

Sheaves/seed	1756	1758	1759	1762	1763	1767
Garaison	3.9	5.9	4.2	3.9	5.1	7.0
Betpouy	4.8	5.2	5.8	4.6	4.0	6.1
Barthe	5.1	5.0	2.0	4.0	4.2	6.2
Esclassan	3.5	3.6	3.8	2.5	3.2	3.8
Beres	4.2	4.8	6.0	4.8	4.3	5.2

Source: see Table 4.1.

constant and that there were no major changes in methods of cultivation. Garaison, which specialised in rye, is different from the other four *métairies*, which grew wheat. The statement of grain production is difficult to interpret because the figures are so small in comparison with those for seed, and it seems likely that they do not represent total production. But again, rye was different from wheat, and the figures show great variations in time and between *métairies*. From 1750 to 1760 the situation was the same as in the 1780s. Similar remarks could be made on the information from the table of sheaves. These figures probably relate to the real production of these *métairies*. They show large variations. It is possible to establish a relation between the amount of seed used and the number of sheaves produced.

The lack of uniformity in these figures makes it impossible to make precise estimates of the yield of these holdings, but some information, though approximate, can be gathered from them. The ratio of seed to production seems to be more favourable for rye than for wheat and there was perhaps some slight progress with rye. In the case of wheat, the ratio seems stable, and not particularly good. These are signs of mediocre and stagnant agricultural production.

VI.2. The indebtedness of the bordiers

The second sign of weakness in the economy was that all the *bordiers* were in debt. The debts continued over several years with some attempt being made to face and liquidate the debt. But even when it shrank it did not disappear altogether.

The case of the *bordier* of the château of Esclassan in 1762 and 1763 may serve as an example.[7] In 1762, according to Jean Deffez, the *procureur* who managed the syndicate (*syndicat*), the *bordier* owed a total of 134 livres 1 sol. He paid 121 livres 8 sous 6 deniers and thus remained in debt for 12 livres 12 sols 6 deniers. In the following year, 1763, he owed 167 livres 1 sol, including the 12 livres 12 sols 6 deniers from the preceding year. He paid 136 livres 9 sols 6 deniers. His debt had more than doubled and had risen to 30 livres 11 sols 6 deniers.

[7] Archives départementales des Hautes-Pyrénées, G 1101.

These two end-of-year statements confirm what has been said about the fluctuations and weakness of agricultural production, but, on the other hand, they emphasise the importance of livestock rearing, which allowed the *bordiers* to make up for the deficiencies of cereals. They also show that although this weakness resulted in an unpromising situation the *bordiers* were able to rise above it, in spite of everything, thanks to the diversity of their activities.

VII. Conclusion

In conclusion, it must be repeated that these accounts are a very useful source. Since there are gaps in them they need to be used carefully. There are many methodological problems involved in collating and using the information in them, but even if the results obtained are approximate, they show the main features of these *métairies* and illustrate the uncertainty and great variability in production, and the large differences between the different holdings. The *métairies* of Garaison were a world that seemed to be on the margins of eighteenth-century growth. The *bordiers* made a very meagre living, but their situation was not desperate, and they still provided the chaplains of Garaison with substantial incomes.

Bibliography

Barifouse, B. (1874) *Études historiques sur le pays des Quatre Vallées*, Saint-Gaudens d'Abadi.

Brumont, F. (2003) 'Le Métayage en Gascogne à l'époque moderne', in G. Béaur, M. Arnoux and A. Varet-Vitu, (eds), *Exploiter la terre: les contrats agraires de l'Antiquité à nos jours.* Actes du colloque international tenu à Caen du 10 au 13 septembre 1997, Rennes: Association d'histoire des sociétés rurales, Bibliothèque d'histoire rurale 7, pp. 133–154.

Brumont, F. (1999) 'Le Métayer et son maître' in A. Antoine (ed.), *Campagnes de l'Ouest: stratigraphie et relations sociales dans l'histoire*, Colloque de Rennes, 24–26 mars 1999, Rennes: Presses universitaires de Rennes, pp. 361–375.

Decroix, X. (1983) *Anglèze de Sagazan et la chapelle de Garaison*, Pau: Imprimerie Marrimpouey.

Desplats, C. (1992) *Pau et le Béarn au XVIIIe siècle*, Biarritz.

Dumoret, J.-J. (1869) *Étude sur le pays des Quatre Vallées*, Bagnères: Père.

Féral, P. (1987) 'Arrentements perpétuels, baux de métayage et à cheptel en Gascogne du XVIe au XVIIIe siècle', in *Les Revenus de la terre: complant, champart, métayage en Europe occidentale (IXe-XVIIIe siècles)*, Actes des Septièmes Journées internationales d'histoire du centre culturel de l'Abbaye de Flaran, 20–22 septembre 1985, Auch, 1987, pp. 145–181.

Frêche, G. (1974) *Toulouse et la région Midi-Pyrénées au siècle des Lumières (vers 1670–1789)*, Paris: Éditions Cujas.

Lachiver, M. (2006) *Dictionnaire du monde rural. Les mots du passé*, Paris: Fayard, 2nd ed.

Labrousse, E. (1933) *Esquisse du mouvement des prix et des revenus en France au* xviii*e siècle*, Paris.

Minovez, J.-M. (1997) *Société des villes, société des champs, en Midi toulousain, sous l'Ancien régime*, Aspet: PyréGraph.

Sarramon, A. (1954) *Les Quatre-Vallées. Aure, Barousse, Neste, Magnoac. Essai historique*, Albi.

Soulet, J.-F. (2006) *La Vie dans les Pyrénées du* xvi*e au* xviii*e siècle*, Pau: Cairn.

Souriac, R. (1978) *Le Comté de Comminges au milieu du* xvi*e siècle*, Paris: CNRS.

Zink, A. (1969) *Azereix: la vie d'une communauté rurale à la fin du* xviii*e siècle*, Paris: SEVPEN.

Zink, A. (1997) *Clochers et troupeaux: les communautés rurales des Landes et du Sud-ouest avant la Révolution*, Bordeaux: Presses universitaires de Bordeaux.

Appendix

In 1762, Jean Deffez wrote:

> The *Bordier* of the Château d'Esclassan owes the previous syndicate sixty-four livres nine sols six deniers. During this year I have lent him forty-four livres five sols in grains for his subsistence plus five livres on account. He also owes eight livres for our share of a sow that he took on his account. Plus eight livres for the second mowing of our meadows plus thirty-two sols for cutting two hedges of which he used the wood plus fifty-four sols six deniers for his share of sainfoin seeds and of remedies for the animals.
> Owes in all 134 livres 1 sol
> In deduction of which he has paid forty-five livres from his share of a foal which we took for the house plus thirty-six livres nine sols six deniers from his share of the sale of a mule which he gave me plus thirty francs paid by three pipots twenty pots of red wine which I have taken & brought here paid also seven livres 10 sols which M Lapeyre gave me at his discharge at the beginning of the year plus forty-nine sols paid by means of some *beauquiers* of straw which he supplied from his store: half of the same and for some other small advances he made to looking after the animals.
> Paid in total 121 livres 8 sous 6 deniers
> Remains owing twelve livres twelve sols six deniers.

The following year, 1763, the statement of account was as follows:

> The *bordier* of the Château owes twelve livres twelve sols six deniers according to the previous syndicate. During the present year I have advanced one hundred and forty-six livres eight sols six deniers to buy grain to live on. He still owes five francs for our share of a sow he kept for himself. Plus three francs for the remainder of the second mowing in front of the Château estimated at twelve livres. Owes in total one hundred and sixty-seven livres one sol. +9Of which he has paid 1. thirty-six

livres nine sols six deniers which he remitted on his share of the sale of a pair of oxen 2. twenty-four francs on his share of the sale of a mule 3. six francs for straw which he supplied for the stables which was his sole property 4. seventy francs by means of seven pipots of wine which he brought here himself at forty livres the cask. All these payments totalling one hundred and thirty-six livres nine sols six deniers he remains in debt for the sum of thirty livres eleven sols six deniers. Thus concluded and agreed with the said *bordier* Jean Ducos at the Château of Esclassan the twelfth December one thousand seven hundred and sixty-three he has paid all the poultry and accounted for all the sales made this year.

5 Dormant agriculture? Some evidence of agricultural change in nineteenth-century Navarre*

José-Miguel Lana Berasain, Public University of Navarre, Iruña/Pamplona

I. Introduction

There has been intensive historiographical debate in Spain about the sluggish economic growth before 1950. The debate has recently been re-examined in convergence studies that have shortened the degree and length of Spanish backwardness. We know now that the years between 1936 and 1952 saw a real break in Spanish economic evolution (Carreras, 1997). However it remains true that the nineteenth century was a period of slow growth, especially for the agricultural sector. The classic treatments of Spanish economic history blamed agriculture for being inefficient and holding back Spanish economic potential. A few years ago, James Simpson renewed this argument in his influential book *Spanish Agriculture*, with the expressive subtitle *The Long Siesta (1760–1960)*, in which he confirms that agricultural growth did take place during the nineteenth and first half of the twentieth century, but says that it was insufficient and uneven, and that consequently Spain was condemned to remain a backward state. Nevertheless, other Spanish historians have acclaimed the accomplishments of Spanish agriculture. L. Prados in his *De imperio a nación* (Prados, 1988) and later Pujol *et al.* in their book *El pozo de todos los males* (Pujol, 2001), found advances in agricultural production and productivity during the nineteenth century and the first third of the twentieth. But the nature of Spanish agricultural growth during the nineteenth century remains an open question.

Moreover, those historians who have tried to measure the advances in agricultural production and productivity in nineteenth-century Spain have generally used indirect methods because the direct sources were few and of doubtful reliability. With imaginative and valuable methods, authors like Garrabou and Sanz, Prados, Simpson and Bringas demonstrated, despite differences over volume and timing, an appreciable improvement in Spanish agricultural efficiency before the 1936–39 Civil War. Regional studies, using a wide range of sources, take the same route and attempt to follow various patterns of

* This article is part of the research projects S3100007H (financed by the Government of Navarre), MEC-HUM2006–01277 and HAR2009–09700 (financed by the Spanish Government). A previous version was presented at the 'Production et productivité agricoles dans le monde occidental (xive-xxe siécles)' conference, INRA, Paris, France, December 18–20, 2003. I am indebted to María-Teresa Pérez Picazo, Gérard Béaur, Joseba de la Torre, Guy Lemeunier, Paul Brassley, Jean-Michel Chevet, Nadine Vivier, Gabriel Jover and the referee, for their comments. Any errors are my sole responsibility.

growth. Indeed James Simpson explicitly called one chapter of his book 'Unlocking the puzzle of stagnation: *Regional variations*'.[1]

It is not possible within the scope of this paper to resolve the enigma of nineteenth-century Spanish 'agricultures'. Here I can only contribute some evidence from a regional perspective, in two ways. First, I have gathered data for a direct estimate of the trends of agricultural production and productivity in the province of Navarre. Second, I have examined some collections of private accounts to verify these items on a micro scale. Both studies are preliminary approaches to the research that I am currently undertaking.

II. An approach to regional agricultural growth: the case of Navarre

Navarre is a small territory (10,421 km^2) in northern Spain with a contrasting and diverse agriculture and climate. Rainfall varies between less than 400 and more than 1800 mm per year. Here we find Mediterranean natural vegetation with holm-oak groves and steppe in the centre and south, alpine vegetation in the northeastern valleys, and humid spaces with beech forest and ferneries in the northwest. The plains of the rivers Ebro, Ega, Arga and Aragon in the southern two-thirds of the territory were historically given over to the production of grains and wines. In the northwest and northeast cattle breeding and forestry were the main activities.

Let us now try to give an impression of agricultural growth in this region throughout the nineteenth century. Several different sources were consulted in order to reconstruct the data and trends of agricultural production. The first are tithe-books (*tazmías*) and derived documents. On various occasions between 1785 and 1807 the authorities of the kingdom of Navarre compiled tithe information for the purpose of deciding whether to permit grain exports.[2] The second are some Government inquiries. A few attempts were made in the mid-nineteenth century to produce agrarian statistics, with dubious results. The main ones were in 1857, 1859 and 1865.[3] The third is a series of reports of agronomists. Since the 1880s the State assumed the responsibility for generating Spanish agricultural statistics and thus created the *Junta Consultiva Agronómica* (JCA) with agronomists in all the provinces sending in annual reports.[4]

---

[1] For a regional approach see Pérez Picazo (2000), Garrabou, Planas & Saguer (2001), Robledo (2010).

[2] The *Diputación del Reino* of Navarre in 1789 and the *Consejo Real* of Navarre between 1801 and 1807 recompiled data, parish by parish, that are very useful in getting to know the agricultural output. In 1803 the Spanish Crown edited a controversial census, *Censo de Frutos y Manufacturas*, with data from 1799. In 1810 the French Government, represented by Jean-Baptiste de Rancy, elaborated other statistics, town by town, enriching it with data from 1800. The Napoleonic Administration also prepared a complete report, dated 15 April 1811, based on 1803–07 tithe information. Learned literature about tithes as a source of information is very abundant. See Goy & Le Roy Ladurie (1972 & 1982), and Coll & Fortea (1995: 95–98).

[3] Pan-Montojo (1993); Coll & Fortea (1995: 98–115). The information gathered in Navarre for the 1857 inquiry was published by F. Sanz Baeza (1858) in a detailed and critical study. Less useful are Ramírez Arcas (1848) and Ripa (1865).

[4] The methodology used by agronomists for calculating production was by estimation. Their reports have a good reputation in general (GEHR, 1991; Simpson, 1996).

Figure 5.1 Map of Navarre

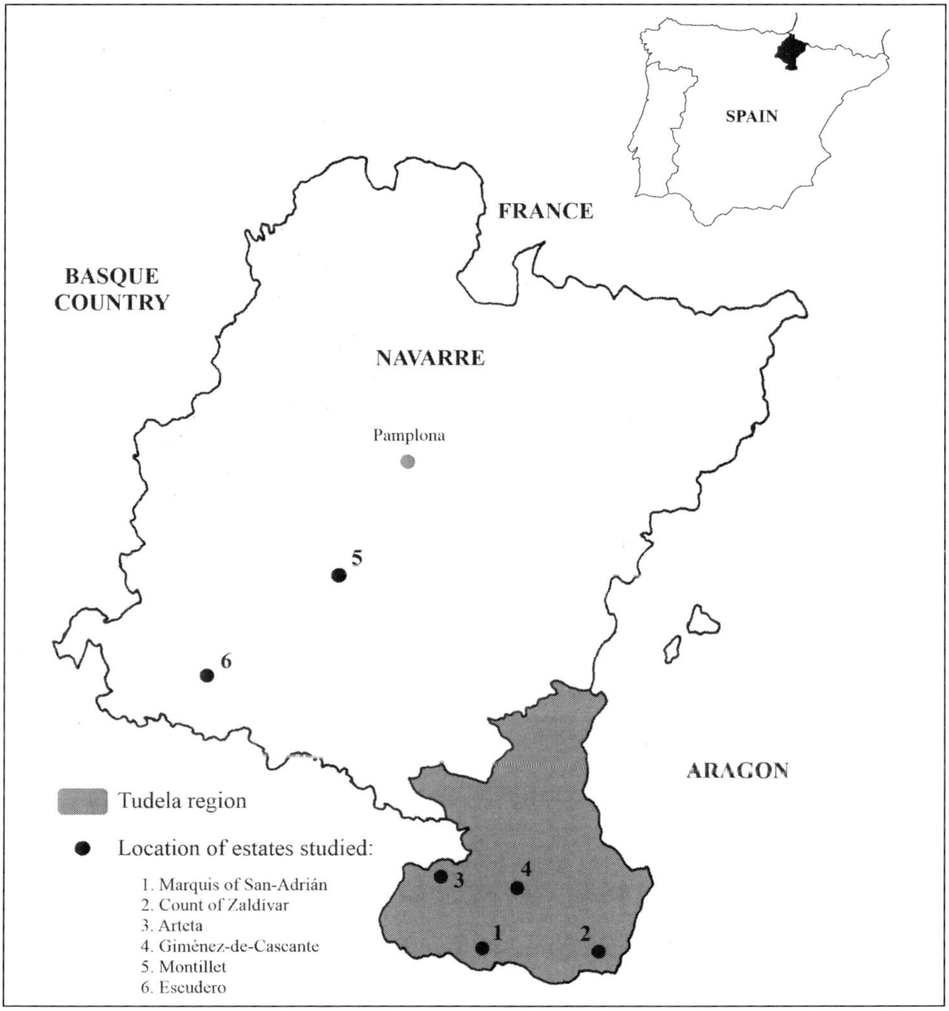

Source. Map by the author.

With these sources we have reasonably complete information about agricultural output, but these data have some problems. We cannot compile annual series of production because the figures for the nineteenth century are discontinuous. We must deal with some chronological breaks. Secondly we do not have good information about farm animal production. Only the report of 15 April 1811 and Sanz-Baeza's book in 1858 specified the annual production of lambs and calfs, wool, hides and cheese. So, for the present, discussion must be limited to crop production. Thirdly, some crops are not fully reflected in these sources. Tithes did not reflect the appearance of new crops like turnips, clover or potatoes. Agronomists, for their part, did not give data about tubers, roots, fodder, or industrial plants until the first years of the twentieth century. The best information is limited to cereals, wine, olive oil and pulses. Finally, we do not know the amount of agricultural products consumed within the sector. The only information we have about seed needs comes from a couple of documents that record figures for the seed yield of cereals and legumes. We have no information on other intermediate consumption of farm products (grain for fodder, wine for farm workers, oil for stable lighting). So, for the moment, we know more about gross production than final production.

This information nevertheless allows us to map the course of agricultural production in Navarre in the nineteenth century.[5] There were considerable advances in the production of the main crops. Wine production, which increased by 178%, was the most successful. Next in line are pulses, with 66%, and olive oil, with 62%. At a considerable distance behind are cereals, with the best results for oats (30%) and wheat (22%), stagnation in barley, and a fall in poorer cereals like rye, emmer, and millet. Finally, GAP (Gross Agricultural Product, calculated using the values of 1857) rose by 59% between 1799–1807 and 1886–1890, at a rate of 0.55% a year in 85 years. If we deduce the amount of seed from the proportionate yields of seed in two reports of 1811 and 1890,[6] agricultural growth in Navarre seems higher in terms of Net Agricultural Product. NAP was definitely multiplied by 1.68 times throughout the century whilst GAP multiplied by only 1.59 times.

Part of this increase was absorbed by population growth. Between 1797 and 1887 the number of inhabitants in Navarre increased from 226,000 to 304,000 a rate of 0.33% a year. So, in per caput terms we found positive rates only for wine, olive oil and pulses. NAP per inhabitant rose only 25% (a rate of 0.27% per annum).

How can we interpret this data? Here are some suggestions. Firstly, there was growth through specialisation. Output of marketable crops such as wine and olive oil grew considerably.[7] Being permanent crops (for which we do not to need to discount seed), they made up a greater proportion of net than of gross production. Secondly, the proportion of fallow appears to have shrunk to some extent, and it was replaced on some land by legumes. This means that the northern European pattern of growth of nitrogenous crops (Chorley, 1981) appeared here too, but to a small extent. Thirdly, the amount of wheat produced per caput fell, despite growth of production in absolute terms, but this did not translate into a significant loss in the quantity of food per person in this country. If we accept Livi Bacci's estimations (1988: 142–145) caloric supply would have been satisfied

---

[5] The Appendix gives a compendium of all statistics for agricultural produce avalaible from 1785 to 1900. For the purposes of this chapter, I take only the averages of 1799–1807 and 1886–1890.

[6] The report of 15–4-1811 gives a yield of 1:4.5 for wheat; 1:8 for barley; 1:6 for oats, beans, haricots, fenugreek, and lentils; 1:5 for rye, peas, chick peas, vetch, and tares; and 1:12 for maize. (AGN, *Reino, Estadística*, box 49) *Avance* of 1891 makes it possible to estimate medium seed yields of 1:5.2 for wheat, 1:9 for barley, 1:5.5 for oats, 1:4.8 for rye, 1:20.5 for maize, 1:6 for peas, fenugreek, tares, and lentils, 1:4 for beans, vetch and chickpeas, and 1:10 for haricots. (JCA, 1891a, II: 474–491).

[7] Olive oil data in 1886/90 is strongly affected by the effects of the frost of 1889. In 1891–95 olive oil annual production was 38,300 hectolitres, and thus the increase was 307%, and in per caput terms the advance was 215%. Van Zanden (1991: 223–226) highlights the importance of specialisation in the growth of productivity prior to 1870.

Table 5.1 A balance sheet of Agricultural Product in Navarre, 1800–1890. Annual averages and growth rate

	Gross Agricultural Product (GAP)			Net Agricultural Product (NAP)			NAP per inhabitant		
	1799–1807	*1886–1890*	%	*1799–1807*	*1886–1890*	%	*1799–1807*	*1886–1890*	%
Wheat	693.60	848.80	+22	539.40	686.20	+27	2.38	2.26	–5
Rye	18.30	11.40	–38	14.60	9.10	–38	0.06	0.03	–54
Maize	115.30	134.30	+16	105.70	127.70	+21	0.47	0.42	–10
Barley	200.80	203.40	+1	175.70	180.90	+3	0.78	0.60	–23
Oats	109.50	142.70	–30	91.20	116.90	+28	0.40	0.38	–5
Total Cereals	1,143.00	1,340.60	+17	931.70	1,120.80	+20	4.11	3.69	–10
Pulses	67.70	112.70	+66	54.90	88.30	+61	0.24	0.29	+20
Wine	380.80	1,060.60	+178	380.80	1,060.60	+178	1.68	3.49	+107
Olive oil	9.40	15.20	+62	9.40	15.20	+62	0.04	0.05	+20
Value at 1857 prices	146.54	233.58	+59	125.17	210.69	+68	0.553	0.693	+25
Population	226.47	304.12	+34						

Note: Production data expressed in thousand hectolitres; population in thousand persons. Value calculated by multiplying the quantities by the 1853–1857 average prices in Navarre. It is expressed in million *reales de vellón* (rvn). Net Agricultural Product (NAP) calculated by deduction of seed.

Source: see Appendix.

at a level of 2.33 hl of wheat per inhabitant per year. So it seems the province still had sufficient supplies in spite of the fall in wheat production. At the end of the eighteenth century Navarre had a surplus of wheat, which José-María Magallón Mencos (Marquis of San Adrián) estimated in 1770 at 42,200 hl. This position would not have changed at the end of the nineteenth century, if we can assume that new crops like potatoes and vegetables counteracted the fall in per caput wheat production.[8] Fourth, a moderate advance in cereals and pulses for cattle fodder (barley, oats, maize, beans, vetch, tares, and fenugreek), 24% between 1803–07 and 1886–90, suggests that there was no substantial increase in livestock at this time. This fits evidence that we have concerning the stocks at the beginning and end of the century, and corroborates the idea of a marked crisis in extensive breeding and a readjustment in the composition of herds (GEHR, 1985; García-Sanz, 1994).[9] Fifth, growth seems to concentrate in the second half of the century (GAP rose 1.06% between 1857 and 1886–90), while the moderate rise in the first half (0.25% from 1799–1807 to 1857) was completely absorbed by demographic growth. These results agree with other studies such as that of Prados (1988: 129), and lead us to think of Navarrese population growth in more modest terms. In fact, Navarrese demographic growth was not very vigorous if we compare it with other regions, and it was concentrated in the first half of the century. After 1860 emigration cancelled out the effect of natural growth, thus producing higher rates of production per inhabitant.[10]

III. Evidence from the 'micro' level: case studies from particular properties

Particular case studies, when available offer another perspective. On the 'micro' level, the analysis has more reliable, rich and complex information. Account books allow us to reconstruct a wide range of data series such as wages, rents, prices, shares, taxes, crops, and yields. If the estate under study was directly managed, we can find out the details of progress in agricultural operations and this allows us to calculate indicators of productivity. Accounts and correspondence books enable us to analyse the concrete behaviour and strategies of historical actors.

However, there are some drawbacks. Often the files come in a fragmentary state and cover only a few years. Moreover, the figures may not be representative of general practice; account books were regularly used on large properties, so that the landowner could audit his managers and agents. But the only accounts existing from middle and small sized properties are those drawn up during the execution of wills. There is also a geographic

[8] Magallón's conjecture, in A.MSA, carton 45, no. 5. The annual production of potatoes in 1896–1900 was 448,000 qm, namely 145 kgs per inhabitant and year.

[9] A drop in natural meadows because of ploughing reduced the amount of food in this period, but was offset by new crops. In 1903–09 cadastral statistics indicated that 128,400 metric quintals (qm) of clover, and 489,700 qm of fodder were harvested in this province. From 1857 to 1903–09 the turnip harvest grew from 299,200 qm to 638,800, while the mangelwurzel harvest rose from 1,500 to 119,500 qm (AAN, cartons 16133–16151).

[10] Between 1787 and 1860 the population of Navarre grew by 0.38%, while that of Spain grew by 0.63%. From 1860 to 1900 the population of Navarre increased only by 0.07% and that of Spain by 0.43%. (Pérez Moreda, 1999).

bias: it is easier to find account books in regions with a property structure characterised by large estates than in regions of peasant property. Another problem is that the books do not always specify which plots were sown on behalf of the landowner, and thus it is very difficult to calculate yields or workforce per hectare. At other times tasks were not paid for on a daily basis: sometimes workers were contracted on a piecework basis or for a yearly salary, with the result that we cannot calculate the real cost of the workforce in this particular task. If we are lucky and we find one or more account books, we have a good, but not a perfect source.[11]

In this case, I was able to consult six sets of private accounts. Two of them cover long periods and are reasonably complete; four are fragments.[12] First, I shall describe the conditions under which these estates were managed in order to understand the logic of the agrarian entrepreneurs and to evaluate the potential of these sources for the study of productivity. After that, I shall present some evidence for increases in productivity of labour and land in vines, olives and cereals.

The income structure (Table 5.2) of a few large and middle-sized properties reveals a management standard that combined direct operation with land leasing. For the most part, direct operation constituted about 50% of income. Proprietors generally managed the cultivation of vineyards and olive groves; sometimes they took on plots for sowing grain; but in general plough-land was leased out to tenants. These tenants, who usually paid their rents in kind, i.e. wheat, and those who leased houses, pastures and gardens, and paid in cash, contributed the other 50% of entries. So, the absentee landowner seems to be the exception rather than the rule.

Moreover, direct management was flexible in character. It varied from one estate to another and was adapted to circumstances, leading in some cases to a gradual (Arteta, 1832/44) or sudden (Montillet, 1865/69) abandonment of direct management and in others to vigorous development by the landlords (Zaldívar, 1862/84). These strategies responded to varied opportunities and to changes in the structure of relative prices.[13]

---

[11] For the possibilities and problems of these sources in other contexts, see Afton (2000), Antoine (2000), Garrabou et al. (2001).

[12] The best set of accounts I used is from the Marquis of San Adrián's estate, with records from 1800 to 1900, missing only 1820. This property occupied, at the end of eighteenth century, about 573 hectares in his manors of Monteagudo (250 ha) and San Adrián (32 ha) and in other villages of southern Navarre. Recently (thanks to J.M.Gastón-Aguas) I was able to consult the private registers of the Count of Zaldívar in Cortes; these records begin in 1862 and run until 1970. The property covers 886 hectares and includes 38 buildings in 1890. The other accounts are fragments and belong to Sebastián Arteta and his widow Manuela Sesma, for his property in Corella (1822–49), Inocencio Escudero's farm in Los-Arcos (1861–67), José María Jiménez-de-Cascante's (and his widow Paz Escribá) estate in Tudela (1820–47), and the inheritance of Eduardo Montillet, which was situated in Mañeru (1858–74).

[13] In these examples, Arteta's property reduced salary expenses and extended the leased land – taking out vines – when demand for wine became feeble and prices remained low. In a similar conjuncture twenty years later, Montillet's vineyard was leased by his executor to sharecroppers. On the other hand, the Count of Zaldívar determined to start large scale cultivation, stimulated by railway building and the boom in French demand for wine.

Table 5.2 Structure of gross income of some estates in Navarre during the nineteenth century

Estates	Years	Direct management	Rents and sales of wheat	Other	Total
Arteta	1822–1832	42.9	51.6	5.5	100
Arteta	1833–1843	38.0	58.0	4.0	100
Arteta	1844–1849	20.7	78.4	0.9	100
Escudero	1861–1867	41.9	58.1	0.0	100
Jiménez-de-Cascante	1820–1831	75.3	24.7	0.0	100
Jiménez-de-Cascante	1841–1847	42.8	53.1	4.1	100
Montillet	1858–1865	91.2	08.3	0.4	100
Montillet	1869–1874	00.0	100.0	0.0	100
Count of Zaldívar	1862–1867	13.5	86.1	0.4	100
Count of Zaldívar	1884–1887	45.1	54.3	0.5	100
Marquis of San Adrián	1801–1820	47.2	52.2	0.6	100
Marquis of San Adrián	1821–1840	54.0	45.7	0.3	100
Marquis of San Adrián	1841–1860	53.5	44.4	2.1	100
Marquis of San Adrián	1861–1880	55.8	41.9	2.4	100
Marquis of San Adrián	1881–1900	49.8	48.4	1.7	100

Sources: Arteta and Escudero, AGN, Fondo Arteta; Jiménez-de-Cascante, AGN, Fondo Jiménez-de-Cascante; Montillet, Archivo familiar Lambea (Mañeru); Count of Zaldívar, Archivo familiar Conde del Real (Traibuenas); Marquis of San Adrián, Archivo del Marqués de San Adrián [A.MSA] (Tudela).

The Navarre social landscape during the nineteenth century thus allows us to construct some indicators for the rhythm of agricultural productivity in this period. Table 5.3 shows the evolution of the productivity of land and labour in the vineyards and olive groves on the estates of the Marquis of San Adrián. I have carefully gone over the cultivation-books where the manager recorded the tasks carried out on the estate and the salaries paid to workers. I have reconstructed the workforce used year by year for each task, and reduced it to a homogeneous 8-hour working day.[14] I identified the plots cultivated in survey books and cadasters, and I constructed numerical records for farm outputs from their accounting books. Thus I have three data series: workforce, surface and output, and from these I have

[14] Bylaws of some villages like Tulebras or Cascante in the 1840s set the work-day at seven hours for diggers, from sunrise to sunset (about twelve hours) for harvesters in summer, and for all others – called *a modo de abina* – at eight hours (Lana, 1995).

Table 5.3 Productivity of labour and land in the Marquis of San Adrián's property. Monteagudo (Navarre), 1798–1920

Years	Vineyard			Olive grove		
	Wf	*Y*	*pL*	*Wf*	*Y*	*pL*
1798/1802	71.43	1203	16.8	–	–	–
1801/1811	–	–	–	37.32	175	4.7
1809/1813	53.77	715	13.3	–	–	–
1843/1847	60.86	1770	29.1	58.50	345	5.9
1867/1871	65.18	1635	25.1	–	291	–
1889/1893	73.52	1848	25.1	52.53	149	2.8
1896/1900	35.81	1786	49.9	56.05	320	5.7
1916/1920	72.20	1781	24.7	–	–	–

Note: Wf = workforce in days/hectare; Y= yields in litres/hectare; pL = productivity of labour in litres per work-day
Source: A.MSA, Accounts and labour books.

obtained three new series: workforce by hectare, yields in litres of output per hectare, and labour productivity expressed in litres per eight-hour working day.

In the vineyard we find considerable growth in land yields, from 7 to 12 hectolitres of wine per hectare at the beginning of the nineteenth century to 17 to 18 hl/ha in the second half of the century. Meanwhile, the workforce used on each hectare fell throughout the first half of the century, when wine markets remained stagnant, and rose again in the export boom of the 1880s. From 1896 to 1900 there is an anomalous result, when the inexorable threat of phylloxera made farmers less careful, as they sought to extract the maximum product from the doomed vine. When normality returned in 1916–20 we again find a cultivation pattern similar to 1889–93. Labour productivity rose from 13 to 16 litres per workday to 25 litres. So, in this property the vineyard productivity grew throughout the nineteenth century by 47% to 49% for land and labour.

Olive groves provide another indicator. Workforce by hectare rose here from 37.3 workdays in 1801–11 (35.7 and 32.3 in Jiménez-de-Cascante's olive groves in 1820–31 and 1841–47, respectively) to 56 to 58 workdays when the trees were at full load. Productivity of labour rose by 21% between 1801–11 and 1896–1900 (the figures for 1889–1893 in Table 5.3 are biased by the effects of the particularly hard frost of 1889). It seems the productivity of land grew by 83% over this period. So, here we have a larger increase in output per hectare, but at a cost of more workforce per hectare, and thus at a smaller growth of productivity per worker.

We can find the explanation for these increases in three factors. Firstly, there was a growing density in planting. In the case of olive groves, the size of plantations at the beginning of the nineteenth century was 95 to 122 trees per hectare; at the end of the century we find 134 to 178 trees per hectare, with 156 in the medium term. In the case of vineyards, in 1800 there were 3,340 vinestocks per hectare while in 1880 the number varies between 5,000 and 7,000 stocks per hectare.[15] Secondly, there was a change in plant varieties. The Grenache (*garnacha*) variety became increasingly dominant in vineyards through the nineteenth century, thanks to its robustness and resistance to oidium, eliminating others like *tempranillo* and *mazuela*. Among olives, *empeltre* (an ingrafted tree) displaced the *acebuche* or *negral*, because of its greater yield (reckoned at a third larger in several reports) and the greater suitability of the fruit for pressing.[16] Thirdly, there was a change in the use of labour. The main change was the replacement of manual digging by mechanical. In Monteagudo there were experiments with new pruning systems in the olive groves between 1838 and 1841. However, new factors like plagues and plant diseases – especially in vines – made it necessary to introduce new tasks.[17]

We cannot do the same exercise for cereals. The sources do not provide information on the seeded plots in the property and so we cannot calculate the workforce used per hectare or the output per workday.[18] Grain production in properties of this size was rarely market-oriented. The aim was mainly to provide fodder for the horses to avoid buying it on the market. There is also another problem with long runs of data. At certain times seeding fell and at other times it rose dramatically: so, in 1846–50, 138 hectolitres were harvested in the Marquis of San Adrián's property, but in 1861–70 the amount was only 34 hectolitres, and in 1891–1900 it rose again to 150 hectolitres. The Count of Zaldívar harvested 3,143 hl of wheat in 1860, but only averaged 420 hl in 1861–68 and 218 hl in 1886–88, while between 1868 and 1886 and after 1888 the crop was abandoned altogether.

The only reliable information on yield ratios is summarised in Table 5.4. Here I have incorporated the data from San Adrián's accounts in Tudela, Monteagudo (his ancestral seigneurial property) and Tulebras (an old church property bought by the State in 1840), and from Zaldívar's estate in Cortes and Buñuel. The most complete series is for barley, while wheat data is concentrated in the middle decades of the century. The high average yields of wheat from 1826–50 are very unusual but despite this, we can confirm an appreciable growth in estimated seed yields in both crops during the nineteenth century: above 30% for wheat and 50% for barley. For barley this increase seems slow and steady. For wheat, the scarcity of observations makes it less sure, but it seems to rise in the central decades of the century.

How can we explain these movements? There is not enough evidence, but we could propose some hypotheses. Firstly, we could consider these results as an illusion, like a simple change of seeding from dry lands to irrigated lands, or from lower quality plots to better fields in the property. In this way the increase in yields at a 'micro' level may be compatible with stagnant yields at a 'macro' level. The unusually high yields of wheat we

[15] AGN, *Protocolos*, Tudela, J.J.Zapata (1800:1); AGN, *Oficio de Hipotecas*, Tudela, books 246–248; JCA (1891b); JCA (1891c).
[16] *Ibid;* Benito López (1879); *La Revista Agrícola* (vol.III, no.13, 5/1/1881); A.MSA, carton 44, no.8.
[17] Lana Berasain (1995).
[18] Overton (1996: 70–88) offers a useful methodological dissection of the concept of productivity, and the different ways of measuring and expressing it.

Table 5.4 Seed-yield ratios of cereals in South Navarre, 1800–1900

Period	*Wheat*					*Barley*				
	n	*av.*	*i.*	*max.*	*min.*	*n*	*av.*	*i.*	*max.*	*min.*
1801–1825	8	5.16	100	6.39	2.35	20	7.37	100	13.75	4.27
1826–1850	22	8.53	165	21.21	4.38	27	9.13	124	16.39	3.12
1851–1875	24	7.25	141	17.14	4.10	46	10.71	145	20.83	1.46
1876–1900	11	6.76	131	9.78	2.90	49	10.98	149	21.85	4.73
1801–1900	65	7.34				142	10.02			

Note: n.- number of observations; av.- average of yield seed/harvest; i.- index base 100 = 1801–25; max.- maximum; min.- minimum
Observations were made on the Marquis of San Adrián's estates in Tudela, Monteagudo and Tulebras, and on the Count of Zaldívar's properties in Cortes and Buñuel.
Source: Archivo Marqués de San Adrián, Accounts and labour books: Archivo Conde de Zaldívar, Libro de frutos.

find in 1826–50 to some extent confirms this: the ploughing of new land, which had previously been pasture, offered good yields at first, but sooner or later the law of diminishing returns set in. However this explanation does not seem very probable in the long run, either for wheat or barley.[19] So we could consider a second hypothesis: a possible increase in fertilisers and soil corrections. This explanation may have some validity on a small scale, but we do not have much evidence. In fact, the amount of manure per cultivated area decreased throughout the nineteenth century, because crop surfaces grew much more than livestock. Guano or chemical fertilisers were very little used in the province at this time. A third hypothesis could be taken into account, suggesting a possible change in wheat or barley varieties. We have limited information about this item. Barquín examines a few testimonies from 1818, 1857 and 1877, and concludes that the map for wheat in Spain does not seem to have changed much during the nineteenth century, nor presumably in the eighteenth. There was however perhaps a larger extension of the *candeal* and *chamorro* varieties, to the detriment of the *redondillo* and others of poorer quality. (Barquín, 2001:26). Local customs offered an opportunity for improving seed quality: farmers believed that seeds degenerated over time and that seed should regularly be brought in from other sources. Failing this, landowners used to lend seed to their tenants with the aim of ensuring the quality of their rents in kind, thus providing them with an opportunity to select and improve strains.[20] Finally, a possible change in cultivation practices could improve yields. Better

[19] Higher yields of wheat in 1826–50 were located in Tulebras, the old monastic property disentailed and bought by the State in 1840. In 1844–45 pasturelands were ploughed and sown with wheat, following a marvellous yield ratio of 21.21 to one. The reverse was possible too. So, low yields in 1886–1888 were obtained in the dry land estate of El Espartal (Buñuel).

[20] López Martínez (1856: 222). Olmstead & Rhode (2002) discovered for nineteenth-century U.S.A., the unsuspected importance of change in wheat varieties, which allowed the extension of arable, increased yields and neutralized plagues.

Figure 5.2 Yields per seed in cereals in South Navarre during the nineteenth century

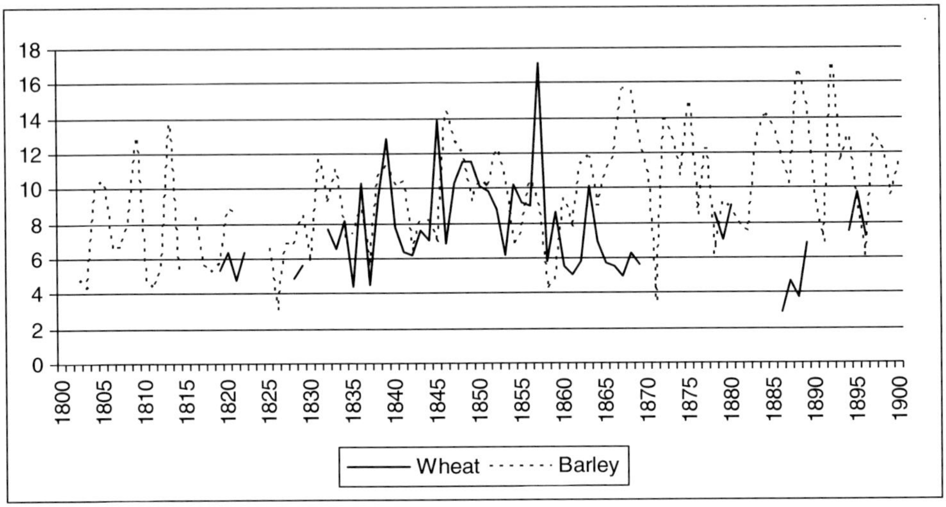

Source: Archivo Marqués de San Adrián, Accounts and labour books; Archivo Conde de Zaldívar, Libro de frutos.

tillage of land, deeper sowing, liming the seed, replacing broadcasting by line sowing, or modifying the seeding frame, were alternatives that reduced expenses. Writers all through the century recommended some of these changes. In 1800 the friar J.M. Larumbe advised in his agricultural catechism: 'Labra junto y hondo y cogerás pan abondo' ('Plough tight and deep and you'll harvest plenty of wheat') (Larumbe, 1800: 65). Sparser seeding had been counselled over and over again by agronomists since 1836, citing the proverb: 'Quien siembra claro, recoge espeso' ('He who sows sparsely, harvests most').[21]

I would like to explore the last hypothesis with some new considerations. Equally as important as the amount of harvest was its regularity, and, as Figure 5.3 shows, this was not guaranteed. Throughout the century deviations from the average yield were very large. Viewed in this context, the vulnerability of peasant farms and of landowners' investments was great.

---

[21] In 1836 *Sociedad Económica Matritense* organised a competition on the theme of the optimum quantity of seed per surface area. Concepción de Arias (daughter of the agronomist Antonio Sandalio de Arias) won the prize with a report that recommended diminishing the amount of seed by around 55% of the average for wheat and barley (Antón Ramírez, 1865: 282). In the mid-nineteenth century this subject was much debated: Casas (1845: 75); Olivan (1849: 54–55); Ramírez Arcas (1855: 192); Del Moral Ruiz, (1979: 35); López Martínez (1856: 224); Blanco Fernández (1857:197–198); Frades (1878); Alvarez Alvistur (1879); Abela (1880: 290). Even by 1880 agronomists still could not agree on the correct formula: 2 hl/ha according to Frades (1878), 1.5 to 2 hl/ha for Tortosa (1887: 203) or 1 to 1.5 hl/ha for Botija, Arce & Rodríguez (1880: 135). See Holliday (1960).

Figure 5.3 Fluctuations in cereal yields in South Navarre, 1801–1900

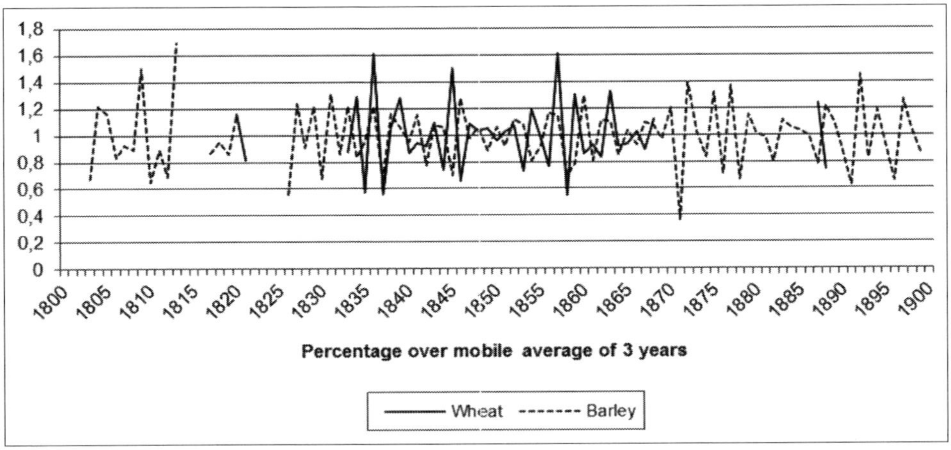

Source: Archivo Marqués de San Adrián, Accounts and labour books; Archivo Conde de Zaldívar, Libro de frutos.

Outlays on seed were closely tied to the availability of working capital, and this was a weak link in nineteenth-century farming. The absence of agrarian insurance companies and the scarcity of capital, together with the high cost of credit and opaque credit markets, all made matters difficult. The purpose of the *positos* (public granaries) in a large number of localities was to alleviate this situation, but they were often badly managed. Could this scarcity of capital be related to the practice that we have verified, namely the direct relation between quantity of seed and quality of land? In Navarre, cadastral evidence from 1881–1890 refers to amounts of about 2.69 hl/ha for seed on irrigated lands and 1.71 hl/ha on dry lands; for 1904–1906 similar sources speak of 2.31 and 1.57 hl/ha respectively. There was an agronomic argument to justify this practice: poor soils could nourish fewer grains than rich soils, but this also implies that less money was spent on lands more vulnerable to crop damage.[22]

This finding does not contradict the fact that on fields of good and medium quality the amount of seed used was excessive. Blanco Fernández (1857: 198) warned of the consequences for the national economy of wasteful seeding, and years later Abela (1880: 290) quantified the amount of seed that could be economised in Spain at nine million hectolitres of wheat! Notwithstanding, this, real savings in seed do seem to have occurred. In the case of Navarre, the figures mentioned in the previous paragraph could be taken

[22] Herrera (1818, I: 56), Oliván (1849:55). Donézar (1984: 214) showed in his study of the Toledan Ensenada Cadaster that in the eighteenth century the quantity of seed normally decreased per acre at the same time as the quality of land deteriorated. See also, Amalric (1985: 45–49). However, agronomists such as Boutelou (Herrera, 1818, I:64), Arias Arimon (1837), Casas (1845:76) and Blanco (1857:197) recommended sowing a quantity of grain in inversely proportionate to soil quality.

as an indicator of this seed reduction on irrigated land, with estimations calculated at between 14% and 26% below the etymological *robo por robada*.[23]

This hypothesis will have to remain unresolved for the moment. If it were true, it would help to explain some clues in nineteenth-century data. A shrinking amount of seed combined with other more efficient practices like deeper tillage or liming the seed could have brought about higher yields. At the same time such practices could have solved one of the farmer's main problems, protection from harvest fluctuations reducing the danger of losing his invested capital. At least, by minimising the risk, even while maximising the output, farmers would have managed to economise the scarcest factor of production in the Spanish context: not land or labour, but working capital.[24]

IV. Conclusion

In this paper I have shown some indications of agricultural change in nineteenth-century northern Spain. Of course this evidence and our interpretations are, for the present, provisional. More evidence will have to be found in order to get a more reliable picture, particularly by increasing the number of private accounts in the sample. However our evidence so far suggests the following conclusions.

There was appreciable agricultural growth in nineteenth-century Navarre. It can be estimated at 0.55% per year in gross terms, and at 0.61% if we leave seed out of our calculations. Gross agricultural output relative to population grew too, but at a lesser extent and despite a decrease during the first half of the century. Private accounts reinforce this picture. On San Adrián's estate we found increases in land and labour productivity in vineyards and olive groves. We also found growth in seed yields for cereals.

Growth stemmed from greater regional specialisation and from closer ties to the market. Landowners profited by this link and enhanced it by their involvement in farming, principally as vine and olive-growers, and in manufacturing wine and oil. In the case of cereals the increase in yields may have reduced the cost of working capital, rather than increased the total quantity of the product, by using a smaller quantity of seed per surface unit.

These results correspond with some general studies such as those of Prados and GEHR, and strengthen the 'optimistic' interpretation of nineteenth-century Spanish agriculture.

23 The figures mentioned were equivalent in traditional Navarre metrology to 13.75, 8.75, 11.8 and 8 *almudes* per *robada*. Sixteen *almudes* make 1 *robo*, and etymologically 1 *robada* (898 m^2) is the space where 1 *robo* (28.13 litres) is seeded. In traditional metrology the dry *robada* was double the size of the irrigated *robada*. There are no studies on this question, but there is some information available. Thus, for inland Catalonia, Garrabou, Pascual, Pujol & Saguer (1995: 109) found that the amount of seed per hectare fell from 3.35 hectolitres in 1716 and 1762 to 1.8 hl in 1886/90. In Málaga top-quality fields received 1.10 hl of wheat seed by hectare in 1752 and only 0.89 hl in 1898 (Sivera, 1988: 143). Blanco (1857:198) ascertained that more than half of the 6.54 millions hectolitres of wheat and 4.31 millions hl of barley used in Spain yearly for seed were misused.

24 One might object that the scarcity of capital does not fit with the considerable extension and improvement in vineyards and olive groves. But these are long-term investments, whereas sowing requires short-term capital. A defective credit market could serve an occasional demand like the former, but would not satisfy a regular demand for working capital.

Bibliography

Abela Sáinz de Andino, E. (1880) 'Reformas convenientes en el sistema de explotación de cereales', *Conferencias agrícolas de la provincia de Madrid*, vol. IV, Madrid, pp. 271–325.

Afton, B. (2000) 'Investigating Agricultural Production and Land Productivity. Methodology and Opportunities Using English Farm Records', *Histoire & Mesure*, vol. XV, no.3/4, pp. 233–245.

Alvarez Alvistur, L. (1879) *Manual de agronomía*, Madrid.

Amalric, J.P. (1985) 'En el siglo XVIII: ¿Una agricultura agarrotada?', in B. Bennassar, (ed.), *Orígenes del atraso económico español*, Barcelona, Critica, pp. 15–79.

Antoine, A. (2000) 'Entre macro et micro. Les comptabilités agricoles du XVIIIe siècle', *Histoire & Mesure*, vol. XV, no.3/4, pp. 247–270.

Antón Ramírez, B. (1865) *Diccionario de bibliografía agronómica y de toda clase de escritos relacionados con la agricultura*, Madrid.

Arias Arimón, C. (1837) *Memoria sobre los perjuicios que causa la excesiva cantidad de trigo y cebada que nuestros labradores arrojan generalmente a la tierra en la sementera, y manifestación de lo que en rigor debieran sembrar para obtener mejores y más abundantes cosechas*, Madrid.

Bairoch, P. (1989) 'Les trois révolutions agricoles du monde développé: Rendements et productivité de 1800 a 1985', *Annales ESC*, pp. 317–353.

Barquín Gil, R. (2001) *Precios de trigo e índices de consumo en España, 1765 1883*, Burgos, Universidad de Burgos.

van Bavel, B.J.P. and Thoen, E. (eds) (1999) *Land Productivity and Agro-Systems in the North Sea Area, Middle Ages-20th Century. Elements for Comparison*, Turnhout: Brepols.

Benito López, G. (1879) 'Estado agrícola de la provincia de Navarra', *Conferencias agrícolas de la provincia de Madrid*, vol. III, Madrid, pp. 239–265.

Blanco Fernández, A. (1857), *Elementos de agricultura*, Madrid.

Botija, A., Arce, J. and Rodríguez Ayuso, M. (1880) *Lecciones elementales de agricultura*, Madrid.

Bringas, M.A. (2000) *La productividad de los factores en la agricultura española (1752–1935)*, Madrid, Banco de España.

Campbell, B.M.S. and Overton, M. (eds) (1991) *Land, Labour and Livestock: Historical Studies in European Agricultural Productivity*, Manchester, Manchester University Press.

Carreras, A. (1997) 'La industrialización: una perspectiva a largo plazo', *Papeles de Economía Española*, 73, pp. 35–60.

Casas, N. (1845) *Tratado de agricultura española teórico-práctica. Parte sexta*, Madrid.

Censo de frutos y manufacturas de España e islas adyacentes (1803), Madrid.

Coll, S. and Fortea, J.I. (1995) *Guía de fuentes cuantitativas para la Historia económica de España. Vol. I. Recursos y sectores productivos*, Madrid, Banco de España.

Chorley, G.P.H. (1981) 'The Agricultural Revolution in Northern Europe, 1750–1880: Nitrogen, Legumes, and Crop Productivity', *Economic History Review*, 2nd Series, XXXIV, 1, pp. 71–93.

Donézar, J. (1984) *Riqueza y propiedad en la Castilla del Antiguo Régimen. La provincia de Toledo en el siglo XVIII*, Madrid, Ministerio de Agricultura.

Moral Ruiz, J. Del (1979) *La agricultura española a mediados del s. XIX, 1850–1870. Resultados de una encuesta agraria de la época*, Madrid, Ministerio de Agricultura.

Frades, L.G. (1878) *Elementos de agricultura*, Valladolid.

Garrabou, R., Pascual, P., Pujol, J. and Saguer, E. (1995) 'Potencialidad productiva y rendimientos cerealícolas en la agricultura catalana contemporánea (1820–1935)', *Historia Agraria*, 10, pp. 89–130.

Garrabou, R., Planas, J. and Saguer, E. (2001) *Un capitalisme impossible? La gestió de la gran propietat agrària a la Catalunya contemporània*, Vic, Eumo.

Gallego Martínez, D. (1986) *La producción agraria de Alava, Navarra y La Rioja desde mediados del siglo XIX a 1935*, Madrid, Universidad Complutense de Madrid (doctoral thesis), 2 vols.

García Sanz, A. (1994) 'La ganadería española entre 1750 y 1865: los efectos de la reforma agraria liberal', *Agricultura y Sociedad*, 72, pp. 81–119.

G.E.H.R. (*Grupo de Estudios de Historia Rural*) (1985) 'Contribución al análisis histórico de la ganadería española. 1865–1929', in R. Garrabou and J. Sanz Fernandez, (eds), *Historia agraria de la España contemporánea, 2*, Barcelona, Critica, pp. 229–278.

G.E.H.R. (*Grupo de Estudios de Historia Rural*) (1991) *Estadísticas históricas de la producción agraria española, 1859–1935*, Madrid, Ministerio de Agricultura.

Goy, J. and Le Roy Ladurie, E. (1972) *Les fluctuations du produit de la dîme. Conjoncture décimale et domaniale de la fin du Moyen Âge au XVIIIe siècle*, Paris and La Haye, Ecole Pratique des Hautes Etudes and Mouton.

Goy, J. and Le Roy Ladurie, E. (1982) *Tithe and Agrarian History from the Fourteenth to the Nineteenth Century. An Essay in Comparative History*, Cambridge, Cambridge University Press.

Herrera, G.A. (1818) *Agricultura General de Gabriel Alonso de Herrera, corregida según el testo original de la primera edición publicada en 1513 por el mismo autor, y adicionada por la Real Sociedad Económica Matritense*, Madrid, 4 vols.

Holliday, R. (1960) 'Plant population and crop yield: part I', *Field Crop Abstracts*, vol. 13: 3, pp. 159–167.

J.C.A., *Junta Consultiva Agronómica* (1891a), *Avance estadístico sobre el cultivo cereal y de leguminosas asociadas en España*, Madrid, 2 vols.

J.C.A., *Junta Consultiva Agronómica* (1891b) *Avance estadístico sobre cultivo y producción de la vid en España*, Madrid.

J.C.A., *Junta Consultiva Agronómica* (1891c) *Avance estadístico sobre cultivo y producción del olivo en España*, Madrid.

J.C.A., *Junta Consultiva Agronómica* (1892) *La ganadería en España. Avance sobre la riqueza pecuaria en 1891*, Madrid, 5 vols.

Lana Berasáin, José Miguel (1995) 'Trabajo, técnica y mercado en la viticultura Navarra: los viñedos del Marqués de San Adrián en Monteagudo durante el siglo XIX', *Historia Agraria*, 10, pp. 135–163.

Larumbe, J. M. (1800) *Epítome cristiano de Agricultura, según las instrucciones del Semanario, y de las puras fuentes de donde se derivan*, Pamplona.

Livi Bacci, M. (1988) *Ensayo sobre la historia demográfica europea*, Barcelona, Ariel.

López Martínez, M. (1856) *Elementos de agronomía, agricultura y economía rural*, Madrid

Nadal, J. (1975) *El fracaso de la revolución industrial en España*, Barcelona, Ariel.

Navarro Faulo, J. (1882) *Geografía militar y económica de la Península Ibérica y colonias de España y Portugal*, Madrid.

Olivan, A. (1849) *Manual de agricultura*, Madrid.

Olmstead, A.L. and Rhode, P.W. (2002), 'The Red Queen and the Hard Reds: Productivity Growth in American Wheat, 1800–1940', *The Journal of Economic History*, Vol. 62: 4, pp. 929–966.

Overton, M. (1996) *Agricultural Revolution in England. The Transformation of the Agrarian Economy, 1500–1850*, Cambridge, Cambridge University Press.

Pan Montojo, J. (1993) 'Fuentes estadísticas', in M. Artola, (ed.), *Enciclopedia de Historia de España. VII. Fuentes. Índice*, Madrid, Alianza, pp. 337–441.

Pérez Moreda, V. (1999) 'Población y economía en la España de los siglos XIX y XX', in G. Anes, (ed.), *Historia económica de España, siglos XIX y XX*, Barcelona, Galaxia Gutenberg.

Pérez Picazo, M.T. (2000) 'Essor de la production et gains de productivité agricole dans une región méditerranéenne au XIXe siècle. Le cas de la province de Murcie', *Histoire & Mesure*, vol. XV, 3/4, pp. 217–232.

Prados de la Escosura, L. (1988) *De imperio a nación. Crecimiento y atraso económico en España (1780–1930)*, Madrid, Alianza.

Pujol, J., González-de-Molina, M., Fernández Prieto, L., Gallego, D. and Garrabou, R. (2001), *El pozo de todos los males. Sobre el atraso en la agricultura española contemporánea*, Barcelona, Critica.

Ramírez Arcas, A. (1848) *Itinerario descriptivo geográfico, estadístico y mapa de Navarra*, Pamplona.

Ramírez Arcas, A. (1855) *Tratados de estadística general y nociones preliminares de su formación*, Madrid, 2 vols.

Ripa, R. (1865) *Observaciones sobre las mejoras que pueden introducirse en agricultura y ganadería de la provincia de Navarra*, Pamplona.

Robledo, R. (ed.) (2010), *Sombras del progreso. Las huellas de la historia agrarian. Homenaje a Ramón Garrabou*, Barcelona, Critica.

Sanz Baeza, F. (1858) *Estadística de la provincia de Navarra*, Pamplona.

Simpson, J. (1996) *Spanish agriculture: The Long Siesta, 1765–1965*, Cambridge, Cambridge University Press.

Sivera Tejerina, M.A. (1988) *Los cambios técnicos de la agricultura en el término rural de Málaga: siglos XVIII-XIX*, Málaga, Diputación de Malaga.

Thompson, F. M. L. (1968) 'The Second Agricultural Revolution, 1815–1880', *Economic History Review*, 2nd Series, XXI, 1, pp. 62–77.Tortosa Picón, M. (1887) *Nociones de agricultura*, Barcelona.

Vicens Vives, J. (1972) *Historia económica de España*, Barcelona, Editorial Vicens-Vives.

Van Zanden, J. L. (1991) 'The First Green Revolution: the Growth of Production and Productivity in European Agriculture, 1870–1914', *Economic History Review*, 2nd Series, XLIV, 2, pp. 215–239.

Appendix

Abbreviations

hl: hectolitre

ha: hectare

qm: metric quintal

rvn: *reales de vellón*

AAN: Archivo Administrativo de Navarra (Pamplona, Spain)

AGN: Archivo General de Navarra (Pamplona, Spain)

AMSA.: Archivo del Marqués de San Adrián (Tudela de Navarra, Spain)

GEHR: Grupo de Estudios de Historia Rural

JCA: Junta Consultiva Agronómica

Table 5.5 **Gross Agricultural Product in Navarre between the eighteenth and nineteenth centuries. Information based on tithe-books, governmental inquiries and engineers' reports***

Product	Unit	1785/89*	1799	1800	1801/02*	1803/07	1846	1857	1859	1886/90	1891/95	1896/00	1903/09
Wheat	Hl (10^3)	740.9	755.8	824.9	615.2	686.2	796.2	715.0	752.4	848.8	918.2	946.1	1361.4
Rye	Hl (10^3)	20.1	25.9	23.7	13.2	17.7	20.5	14.0	10.6	11.4	11.5	10.0	3.6
Emmer	Hl (10^3)	5.9	7.0	5.0	6.0	5.2	6.2	3.1	w.d.	w.d.	w.d.	w.d	1.9
Maize	Hl (10^3)	126.4	111.0	100.6	118.5	117.9	138.8	172.6	144.4	134.3	146.3	151.2	193.8
Barley	Hl (10^3)	194.5	242.4	222.5	188.5	193.0	220.3	159.1	178.5	203.4	233.1	265.1	621.4
Oats	Hl (10^3)	123.5	112.0	102.1	123.9	104.6	125.0	177.7	136.1	142.7	171.3	175.8	250.3
Cereals	*Hl (10^3)*	*1.211.5*	*1.254.2*	*1.278.8*	*1.065.3*	*1.124.7*	*1307.0*	*1241.5*	*1221.9*	*1340.6*	*1480.4*	*1548.1*	*2432.4*
Pulses	Hl (10^3)	68.1	69.0	77.3	w.d.	65.5	85.4	123.2	61.5	112.7	129.8	179.0	174.8
Wine	Hl (10^3)	410.5	421.8	376.2	310.0	401.3	470.6	428.3	176.3	1060.6	878.7	600.2	w.d.
Olive oil	Hl (10^3)	4.5	6.4	13.9	8.8	9.3	10.5	22.5	9.5	15.2	38.3	34.8	51.5
Flax	q (10^3)	1.6	1.1	1.2	w.d.	1.3	2.1	2.6	1.4	w.d.	w.d.	w.d.	5.2
Hemp	q (10^3)	4.2	3.2	8.5	w.d.	5.0	5.7	4.7	5.0	w.d.	w.d.	w.d.	0.6
Chestnut	q (10^3)	4.3	7.3	8.0	w.d.	9.9	w.d.	23.1	w.d.	w.d.	w.d.	w.d.	w.d.
Potatoes	q (10^3)	w.d.	w.d.	w.d.	w.d.	w.d.	w.d.	163.2	152.0	w.d.	w.d.	448.0	496.9
Turnips	q (10^3)	w.d.	w.d.	w.d.	w.d.	w.d.	w.d.	299.2	w.d.	w.d.	w.d.	420.9	638.8
Beet	q (10^3)	w.d.	w.d.	w.d.	w.d.	w.d.	w.d.	1.5	w.d.	w.d.	w.d.	446.0	708.1

(Continued)

Table 5.5 (Continued)

Product	Unit	1785/89*	1799	1800	1801/02*	1803/07	1846	1857	1859	1886/90	1891/95	1896/00	1903/09
a) GAP (1811 prices)	Rvn (10^6)	*71.25*	*73.47*	*76.37*	*60.23*	*71.38*	*84.10*	*84.71*	*65.76*	*113.28*	*120.59*	*112.47*	*129.41*
b) GAP (1857 prices)	Rvn (10^6)	*153.70*	*158.88*	*163.52*	*124.61*	*146.91*	*172.52*	*167.88*	*135.21*	*233.58*	*238.43*	*221.50*	*226.13*
c) GAP (1910 prices)	Rvn (10^6)	*139.54*	*144.11*	*147.27*	*112.18*	*134.17*	*158.50*	*155.45*	*118.75*	*222.86*	*225.23*	*205.24*	*213.97*

Notes: Data in thousand hectolitres (hl) and in thousand metric quintals (q).
The estimate of Gross Agricultural Product (GAP) includes only cereals, pulses, wine and olive oil. It is expressed in million reales de vellón (rvn). I established three series using different prices:
a) 1811 prices from 'Estado general de los productos territoriales, comerciales e industriales', 15 April 1811 (Archivo General de Navarra, AGN, Reino, Estadística, lg.49);
b) 1857 prices (average for 1853–1857) from Sanz Baeza, 1858;
c) 1910 prices from Gallego Martínez (1986).
* Data are unavailable for some municipalities during the years 1785–89 and 1801–02. I estimated the overall figure from their percentage shares of the 1800 total. Data for legumes are incomplete for 1891–1895: peas, lentils, tares, blue vetch and fenugreek are lacking. In 1896–1900 they represented 20% of legume production; I have thererfore increased the 1891–95 figures by that percentage.
Sources: 1785–89 and 1800: A.G.N., Reino, Estadística (lg.32, 41, 43 y 44); 1799: Censo de frutos y manufacturas (1802); 1801–02: AGN, Archivo secreto del Real Consejo, tit.32, f.1; 1803–07: A.G.N., Reino, Estadística, leg.49. Ramírez Arcas (1848) for 1846. Sanz Baeza (1858) for 1857. Navarro Faulo (1882: 215) for 1859. Data for 1886/90, 1891/95 and 1896/1900 are from estimates made by the agricultural experts of the Junta Consultiva Agronómica, transcribed and assigned values by Gallego Martinez (1986). Data for 1903–09 are from cadastral records (Archivo Administrativo de Navarra, AAN, DFN, cj.16133–16151). Wine production was reduced by phylloxera during these years.

6 Reducing production costs and improving productivity in the agrarian systems of the south-east Iberian peninsula during the nineteenth century: a micro-economic approach*

María Teresa Pérez Picazo (†), University of Murcia

I. Introduction

This article focuses on an aspect of my research into the economic operations of large estates and small agricultural holdings in the river valleys of a particular region of southeast Mediterranean Spain in the nineteenth and twentieth centuries. This study was started many years ago (Pérez Picazo, 1991 and 2000), applying the methodology of micro-history and the *longue durée*. The work was prompted by a belief that agrarian accounting records could be of great use in overcoming the limitations of nineteenth-century statistical sources and the macroeconomic indicators derived from them.[1] This is especially true as regards the production function and land and labour productivity.

The search for new heuristic and methodological approaches seems just as necessary as the old debate over the 'backwardness' of agriculture and its negative influence on economic growth, which continues to preoccupy Spanish researchers. Certain recent contributions from scholars in various parts of Europe have helped to change the terms of the debate. For example, it has been shown that the agricultural revolution was not the fundamental factor in early British industrialisation, but rather just one among many, of various kinds (O'Brien, 1986; Mokyr, 1993). Moreover we now know more about the pace and stages of the phenomenon and of its protagonists (Allen, 1992, 1999, 2000; Overton and Campbell, 1996), and this knowledge decisively established a new basis for comparing French and English agriculture (Chevet, 1996 and 2002). But, above all, environmental restrictions are now taken into consideration, and they make it clear that agrarian technologies are not interchangeable, but tied to their own specific energy and ecology cycles. This explains why the successes of the Atlantic agronomy could not easily be shifted to Mediterranean agrarian systems, where the environmental conditions were so different (González de Molina and Martínez Alier, 2001).[2]

---

* Revision of the translation by Judith Le Goff.

1 The first publication of statistical sources for the nineteenth century did not take place until 1991 (Grupo de Estudios de Historia Rural, GHER [*GHER Rural History Studies Group*]), but the starting point of the series does not usually go back farther than 1860, and in many cases no further than 1890. Longer series with a greater extent of economic detail can be found in *La productividad de los factores en la agricultura española (1752–1935)*, (Bringas, 2000).

2 The development of agroecology in recent decades has raised the question of the need to analyse agrarian production, not just as an economic or social phenomenon, but also as a physical and biological process (Altieri, 1989; Gliessman, 1998 and Sieferle, 2001). These authors have

These debates have renewed the controversy on the progress achieved by Spanish agriculture in the second half of the nineteenth century and the first decades of the twentieth. Historians who emphasise the scant progress achieved in productivity per person and hectare (Simpson, 2003: 29–30) confront those who prefer to highlight changes in land use, which made it possible to introduce new products that improved the price/quality ratio (Pujol et al., 2001). According to this latter hypothesis, agrarian activity gained in efficiency, but technological change took place very slowly. The problem can be posed in the following terms: were the levels of land and labour productivity achieved in Mediterranean agrarian systems during this period inferior to those potentially possible using the available technology, or were they, despite the comparative advantages of the new productions, low because of the slow pace of technological change? Recent attempts to answer this question came out in 1996 and 2001. The titles of the books summarising the arguments for and against are very suggestive: *The Long Siesta* (Simpson, 1996) and *El pozo de todos los males* [*The Pit of all Evil*] (Pujol et al., 2001). It should be pointed out that both works extend the range of variables considered to include in particular the characteristics of the labour supply and the institutional context (the agrarian structures) affecting product demand.

II. The context of the study

This work proposes to use a set of agricultural accounting records to test the previous statements. These records come from Murcia, a typical Mediterranean region of 11,317 km^2 in the southeast corner of the Iberian peninsula (Map 1). The region has an arid climate with high average temperatures (17°C), an elevated and irregular pattern of precipitation, (360 mm), and high levels of evapotranspiration. Under these conditions, with the rainfall varying from 200 mm in the mountainous area of the northeast to 700 mm on the coast, water shortage was structural. There is no doubt that the 'technological package' that came out of the nineteenth-century English agricultural revolution did not offer real solutions to the problem.

The documentation comes from the private papers of two of the highest-taxed landlords of the region at the end of the nineteenth century. The Count del Valle de San Juan, who was first on the tax roll, and the Count de San Julián, who was seventh, were owners of, respectively, 10,353 and 5,973 ha covering several municipalities, and containing land worked under all the main agrarian systems (dry farming, irrigated land and middle mountain).[3] The estates had existed for a long time – three generations of owners

highlighted the fact that the technological progress linked to the Agricultural Revolution was designed for warm and wet climates, very different from that of the Mediterranean.

[3] The lands of the Count del Valle were distributed among dry-farming land (3,117 hectares), mountain land (4,967) and irrigated land adjacent to the Segura river (1,053), and they belonged to nine different municipalities. The estate of the Count de San Julián, was also divided among these systems (3,204, 1,011 and 1,758, respectively), although the horticultural lands were not irrigated by the Segura river, but by the Guadalentín, which had far lower flow rates), was somewhat more concentrated from a municipal point of view: the various farms were distributed among four regional municipalities and two extra-regional municipalities. The documentation is preserved in the Municipal Archives of Calasparra (Counts Del Valle) and Lorca (Counts De San Julián).

Figure 6.1 Map of Murcia

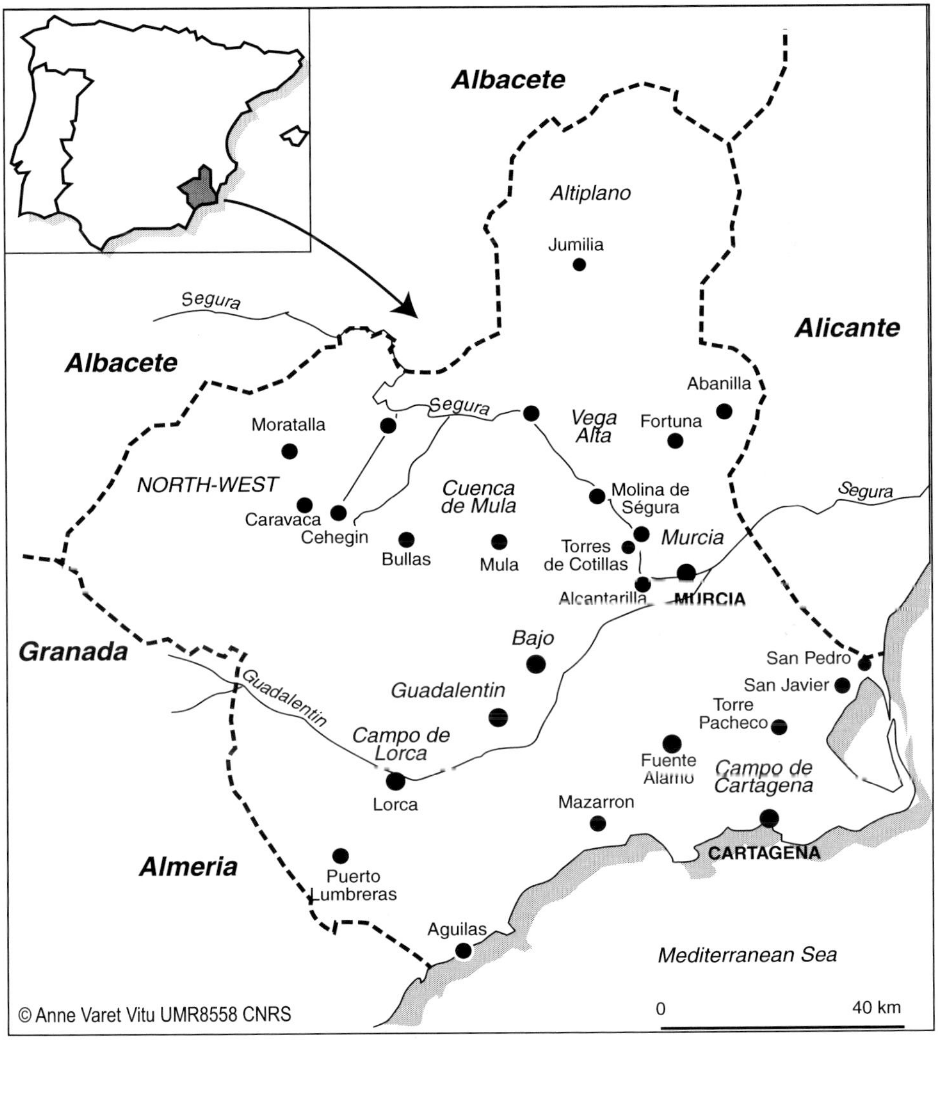

succeeded each other at their head during the nineteenth century – and it so happens that the last two of them were the most entrepreneurial ones. Thus, the information from these sources helps provide answers to a wide range of questions: the organisation of labour; the details of the production cycle; the limitations set on technology by the natural environment, to say nothing of the dynamics of growth, the attitude of owners of large estates to the challenges of the market economy; and it allows us to put forward some ideas on such controversial subjects as labour productivity. C. Sarasúa (2000: 88–89) has recently indicated how specialists are dissatisfied with the way the productivity variable is constructed in the primary sector. In her view, the variable can only be calculated rigorously for agrarian operations if we can be certain about the number of workers employed, the cultivated surface areas and the techniques applied.[4]

These advantages do not come without inconvenience. In this particular case, the accounts cover more than a century – from 1800 to 1902 – and their state of conservation is excellent, but it is hard to know if they are representative. These documents come from large estate administrations, the only ones that kept books; small and medium operations have barely left a mark. And it must be remembered that, until well into the nineteenth century, agricultural accounting records cannot be considered as accounting documents in the current meaning of the term, but rather as balance sheets drawn up by the property manager for the owner's information. This sometimes means that the data necessary for a deeper investigation of various agrarian topics are absent.[5]

Finally, the management of these extensive estates must be explained. They shared two fundamental traits: dispersion, especially in the dry farming areas,[6] and the predominance of indirect management, which usually took the shape of small or medium farm units subject to lease agreements for cash, in the case of irrigated land, or sharecropping on dry farmland. The most conspicuous trait of these agrarian structures consists precisely of this coexistence between large land owners and small operations, very different from the situation on the landed estates predominant in certain regions of southern Spain, such as in western Andalusia or Extremadura. But this situation was not an exception. We find similar systems in regions as diverse as Cataluña (Garrabou *et al.*, 2001), Valencia (Calatayud, Millán and Romero, 2000) or Castilla la Vieja (Carmona, 2001). For example, the 657 hectares that the Count del Valle owned outside the capital were split up between 176 lessees in 1836 (an average of 3.8 hectares), and among 360 in 1900 (1.7 hectares).[7]

[4] The study of private accounting has progressed in Spain since the 1990s. Aside from confirming the statistics the objective of researchers has been to find new ways of approaching the issues raised by agrarist historiography. The following research teams stand out: Catalonia (Garrabou and al., 1995, 2001); Aragon (Sabio, 1998), Navarra, (Lana Berasain, 1996); Galicia (Baz, 1997); Murcia, (Pérez Picazo, 1991) and Castilla, (Carmona Pidal, 2001). Recently an international symposium was held in Spain, which facilitated the debate about this type of source (Universidad de Salamanca. 15–16th November 2004).

[5] The accounting systems of the nineteenth century do not include certain categories that are common in double-entry accounting, nor do they distinguish sometimes between operational costs and consumption. Balance sheets or summaries of the main entries are often absent.

[6] The reason is that these groups of farms had existed for centuries, protected from the market, and from division by inheritance, by the institution of Mayorazgos (primogeniture), which disappeared in 1836–1842 as a result of liberal reforms. For Murcia, Pérez Picazo, 1990.

[7] These systems were considered to be inefficient by the founding fathers of classical economics, since A. Smith (1979: 484–495 and A. Young, 1929), in whose opinion agrarian development requires the landowners or major tenants to have initiative and an enterprising spirit, in a context of considerably sizaeable operations and an abundance of capital and labour. The modest success achieved in the nineteenth century by small operations in Mediterranean agriculture detract from the validity of these affirmations.

As for the management of the large dry farming farms, their more complicated organisation associated the indirect system with the direct system, thereby giving rise to a kind of pyramid with the following organisation:

A. At the top was the manager or administrator who resided on the hacienda. He received the fruits of the sharecroppers and directed the cultivation of the part of the estate managed directly by the owner, an area rarely more than 40 to 60 hectares of top quality land.[8] He was paid partly in cash and partly in kind.

B. Next came the sharecroppers, whose operations rarely covered more than 20 hectares. The owner received one-sixth of their harvest, but he was not bound to help cover the costs of cultivation, although he had to provide the seed. This is the reverse of what happened in the case of grapes and olives, where the owner's share was greater (including day-wages, fertilisers, and sometimes planting) and where the money earned from the sale of the product was distributed equally between the owner and the sharecroppers. Moreover, the sharecroppers usually had the right to a house on the estate, at a token rent. On the other hand, the agreement also included fairly onerous duties such as helping to work the lands managed directly by the owner, at a wage set by him, and providing work animals for the owner when he needed them. The system had many similarities to the feudal organisation of Eastern Europe, which was maintained until relatively recently.

C. Landless peasants formed the last tier. They were day labourers who received unbroken ground and whose function was to bring it into cultivation at their own cost until the first crops were obtained, when they would become sharecroppers.

III. Towards more competitive farming

Throughout the period studied, there were two main strategies for dry farming crops. The first was to expand the area under cereal crops, since the increases in the size of harvests, which approximately doubled on the haciendas studied, had much more to do with breaking new land than with technological improvements.[9] This increase in soil under cultivation, a response to demographic pressure, was widespread in southern Spain (Llopis, 2002: 34–87) and in a large part of the Mediterranean basin in the first half of the nineteenth century, where a wide range of medium-quality land was still available. In Spain we also have to take into account the progress of internal market formation, as evidenced by the increasing convergence of price movements (Barquín, R.; 1997: 199 and Martínez Vara, 1999:61–62).

---

[8] In certain situations the landowners, without changing the predominant regime of sharecropping, undertook the direct operation of some lands. At times this was to introduce certain improvements in the wheat cultivation (such as new species or chemical fertilizer) and at others the aim was to spread crops such as vines, olives and almonds. In Murcia (Pérez Picazo (1991, 1998) and in Catalonia (Pujol, 1998) this was very common practice.

[9] There was little possibility of increasing the performance of grain farming on the dry lands in the southeast of the peninsula because of the scarcity of water and fertilizers, so attempts were made to implement new extensive farming techniques such as foothill farming and conversion to grazing.

More significant for our purpose are the changes in the composition of cereal crops in the interior, which were driven by the environment and the change in demand. First, wheat declined in relation to barley, which is better adapted to the climatic and soil conditions of the region; the yields per hectare were relatively higher than those for wheat, and the cultivation costs lower. Second, rye was grown much less, even in the mountainous areas. The makeup of the total grain harvest in both groups of haciendas leaves no room for doubt: on the lands of Count del Valle, wheat represented 29.5% of the total in 1800 while barley made up 46.5% and rye, 24%; in 1855, the respective proportions had become, 27.2%, 58.5% and 14.5%; and in 1900, they had changed to 18.9%, 79.3% and 1.8% (Table 6.1). This is a trend found across the country throughout the nineteenth century – an advance in feed grain cereals at the expense of cereals for human consumption, and a decline in poorer cereals such as rye. This latter phenomenon is linked to urbanisation and modest improvements in the standard of living.

However the most important change in land use concerns the expansion of bush crops (grapevines) and tree crops (olives, almonds, carob trees, figs) in the second half of the nineteenth century. This contributed to agricultural specialisation as well as to intensification, since both kinds of crops made more intensive use of labour and capital than cereal crops. The change was driven by the increase in the relative prices of wine and oil, although the prices corresponding to the latter had lost pace by 1870. Among the remaining tree crops, there was a veritable frenzy of almond-planting in the years before 1860. In that year, the second of the two Counts, the Count de San Julián, put 62 varieties on display at the Agricultural and Industrial Exhibition of Lorca. Foreign demand, especially from England, was responsible for the strong increase in the production and cultivation of these and other nut crops.[10]

The data on the percentage of surface area occupied by the various crops under study show that the surface area occupied by cereals dropped, but that cereals continued to lead, in spite of increased planting. This evolution is quite contrary to changes in the pattern of profits made in marketing the respective crops. From the moment when grapevines and tree crops began to bear fruit (the decade from 1840 to 1849), income from wine and oil sales increased much faster than that from sales of grain. On the estates of the Count del Valle, the cereals mage up 85.9% of the total from 1800 to 1809 was and wine/oil only 14.1%; while from 1890 to 1899 the proportions had become 53.6% and 46.4%, respectively. On those of the Count de San Julián, the results were rather less brilliant because the phylloxera epidemic was particularly virulent and intense in the Lorca countryside. Thus, from 1840 to 1849 the percentages reported, 86.9% and 13.3% of the total, were very similar to those of the Count del Valle, but from 1890 to 1899 they had changed only to 69.3% and 30.7% (Table 6.1).[11]

---

[10] Even more than the progress on the surface of the cultivated land, the changes in the composition of the cereal harvest are signs of the advance of physiocratic principles, an essencial component of economic liberalism. The idea is that both agrarian production and rent should not only be maintained, but should also increase substantially, as much as possible (Naredo, 1979). In the correspondence of the Count Del Valle V we find frequent references to these principles (Archives of Murcia, File L).

[11] The expansion of vines and olives was perfectly compatible with the environmental context of the southeast and, from an economic perspective, with the price of factors in Mediterranean

Table 6.1 Grain production in the land of the Counts of Valley and Saint-Julien (*quintales métricos*)

Quinquenium	Calasparra		Campo Carthagène				Caravaca				Lorca			
	Rice	I	Wheat	I	Barley	I	Wheat	I	Bar.	I	Wheat	I	Bar.	I
1800–1804	1,286	*100.0*	479	*100.0*	1,883	*100.0*	173	100	214	100	652	100	2,197	100
1805–1809	110	*8.0*	446	*93.0*	999	*53.0*	150	86	124	58	324	49	1945	88
1810–1814	119	*9.2*	563	*117.0*	1,406	*79.0*	112	64	159	74	345	52	2,004	91
1815–1819	890	*69.0*	368	*760.0*	1,996	*106.0*	73	42	102	47	436	66	2,261	102
1820–1824	910	*70.0*	709	*148.0*	1,890	*100.3*	189	109	249	108	711	109	2,389	108
1825–1829	873	*67.8*	799	*166.0*	2,285	*121.0*	198	114	267	124	756	115	2,566	116
1830–1834	948	*73.0*	772	*161.0*	2,274	*120.0*	237	135	301	140	793	121	2,789	126
1835–1839	1,349	*104.0*	780	*162.0*	2,650	*140.0*	296	171	328	153	845	129	2,854	129
1840–1844	1,456	*113.0*	678	*141.0*	2,796	*148.0*	309	178	367	171	901	138	3,096	140
1845–1849	934	*72.0*	529	*110.0*	1,945	*103.0*	123	71	218	101	347	53	1,568	71
1850–1854	1,399	*108.0*	538	*112.0*	3,890	*206.0*	301	173	398	185	1,078	165	3,997	181
1855–1859	1,580	*122.0*	402	*83.0*	2,897	*153.0*	283	163	525	245	689	105	4,156	189
1860–1864	1,782	*138.0*	310	*64.0*	3,768	*200.0*	569	328	766	358	1,123	172	3,871	176
1865–1069	3,211	*249.0*	316	*65.0*	3,390	*180.0*	321	185	662	309	996	159	4,894	222
1870–1874	3,341	*252.0*	298	*71.0*	5,343	*203.0*	547	316	685	320	1,257	192	4,996	227
1875–1879			294	*61.0*	5,564	*295.0*	608	351	761	355	1,342	205	5,461	248
1880–1884	2,362	*183.0*	238	*49.0*	5,127	*272.0*	561	324	765	357	1,286	197	5,320	242
1885–1889	4,105	*319.0*	218	*45.0*	6,101	*324.0*	505	291	807	377	1,459	223	5,897	268
1890–1894	6,287	*488.0*	220	*45.9*	6,190	*328.0*	481	278	954	445	1,504	230	5,991	272
1895–1899	4,428	*352.0*	218	*45.5*	6,699	*355.0*	583	336	961	449	1,580	242	6,045	275

Source: Harvest Accounts Books. Family Archives of the Comte del Valle, Calasparra, Annual balance-sheets, File III – XXIII; Family Archives of the Comte San Julián, Lorca, Annual balance sheets, File II – XIV.

In the irrigated farming systems intensification and specialisation advanced at a quicker pace. The increase in the number of leases alerts us to the changes being introduced, and the chronology was similar to the sequence found in dry farming. The substitution of more for less profitable crops and of commercial products for subsistence products accelerated. In the plains, horticultural plants and tubers became an essential component of complicated crop rotations while wheat began to disappear from them. Fruit trees were planted on the mountain slopes above river valleys, on terraces, constructed at great cost, designed to facilitate drainage. These plantations were accelerated by the decline of sericulture, due not only to various epidemics affecting silkworms (nosema), but also to increased competition on the world market from Oriental silks. The new political and economic situation stimulated large landowners, such as those studied here, to adopt a strategy aimed at uprooting the old mulberry orchards and replacing them with fruit trees – citrus trees in some cases and stone-fruit trees in others. The second generation of the two landlord families faced a problem: their tenants resisted taking out the mulberry trees, since the sale of silk cocoons gave them the necessary cash to pay their rents. In the case of Count del Valle, agreements were renewed on condition that the trees would be cut down at the count's own expense. In other words, in spite of the predominance of indirect management, the owner had found a means to intervene in the production process. Under these conditions, both the productivity of the land and the profits that it generated increased enormously: for the horticultural crops, because there were three or four harvests a year; and for the fruit trees, because the net income per surface unit increased, owing to the high prices.[12]

Special attention should be given to the effort made to consolidate and expand irrigated lands, a *sine qua non* for improving crop yields. During the last two generations, both families invested along these lines. The networks of irrigated land improved, and, in some cases, were extended. Waterwheels and motors were installed (steam, producer gas and electric engines) to facilitate raising river water to the terraces. Artesian wells and subterranean water prospecting were encouraged. It all required progressively more powerful motors and, obviously, a clear advance in water technology, although real progress in this sense would not be achieved until the early decades of the twentieth century.[13] Modest improvements were even carried out in the dry farming system, though still pertaining to small and medium water works. For example, underground water was found by

regions (Simpson and Carmona, 2003: 27; Herr, 1989: 584–596); hence their success in the area. Adaptations of this kind can also be seen in other regions of Spain with other types of commercial products, for example cattle farming in Galicia and the coast of Cantabria, (Carmona and Puente, 1988).

[12] The advance of the new agricultural cycle accelerated in the last two decades of the XIX century, as an alternative to the decrease in the price of cereals resulting from the Great Depression at the turn of the century. The chronological progress went from north to south: first Catalonia (Pujol, 1988), then Valencia (Calatayud, 1989) and finally Murcia (Pérez Picazo, 2000) and Almeria (Sánchez Picón, 1997). The results of the process can be appreciated on a national scale as an increase of the final agricultural production generated by vines, olives, fruit and vegetables of 21–40% of the total (Gallego, 2001:178–179).

[13] The list of hydraulic techniques used highlights the fact that these were still the days of small and medium hydraulic power. The only true advances recorded are those made in the improvement of the pumping motors of underground water (Calatayud and Martínez Carrión, 1999).

excavation or tunnel building, the existing *boqueras* on dry riverbeds were repaired and new ones were constructed, and spring water was distributed by pipe.[14] The objective was to ensure some annual irrigation for the new plantations. It should be pointed out that similar projects are to be found in southern France and the Mezzogiorno at about the same time (Bevilacqua, 1992).

Changes in land use were likewise reflected in the amount of investment, which was mostly concentrated in the period between 1845/50 and 1875. The detailed statements preserved from the various operations carried out during these years allow us to know how much was paid, and on what. The Count del Valle spent 415,212 reales, and the Count de San Julián, 294,765. The amounts went, in order of importance, on irrigation, on building terraces on the slopes, on digging the holes needed to plant vine stocks and young trees, on purchasing and caring for the new plants and, to a much lesser extent, on renovating agricultural equipment. Finally, the material used to prepare juices was modernised, an area in which the second Count de San Julián, who had already installed a hydraulic press for producing oil in 1854, was prominent.

IV. What about productivity?

Given that cereal cultivation dominated the operations under examination here, the study of yields can be an indicator of the advance of agricultural modernisation. However, the figures calculated from the data in the accounting records show that yields from the entire seeded area were very low and remained that way throughout the nineteenth century. And what is even more significant is that they showed the strong fluctuations characteristic of Mediterranean cereal farming. The wheat yield per seed unit oscillated between 4.6 and 5.5 between 1830 and 1900, while barley varied between 6.3 and 8.7, as yet more data demonstrated the rationality of substituting the second crop for the first.[15] Moreover, the yield variation coefficient calculated by ten-year periods shows a deviation with respect to the ten-year means with very high values oscillating between 39.5 in Caravaca (farms belonging to the Count del Valle) up to 50.4 in Lorca (farms belonging to the Count de San Julián). The coherence of these results can be appreciated by comparing them with the yields per unit of surface area. This is easy to calculate because the accounts of the large farms record the surface area seeded and the seed provided to the sharecroppers by the owner. Making the usual allowances for the procedure followed, it can be said that the yields of cereal group in the dry-farming areas varied between 8 and 10 hectolitres per hectare in the second half of the nineteenth century.[16]

---

[14] A *boquera* is a kind of sluice for rain-water retained along the course of dry-river beds by the construction of small reservoirs.

[15] These yields have been obtained by multiplying the owner's share by six, and dividing the result by the seed sown. This information is usually included in the accounts of the various operations, because most of the time the economic agent in question advanced the seed to the sharecroppers. See the accounts of Count Del Valle, Archives of Murcia, File XLIII.

[16] Accounts of Count Del Valle, Archives of Caravaca, File IX and accounts of Count De San Julián, File XVII.

These values, which are clearly low, were similar to those recorded in other Spanish areas with similar climates, such as the interior of Cataluña (Lérida), where they have been calculated very rigorously (Garrabou *et al.*, 1995: 107–111), while in the districts of Cataluña where natural conditions were more favourable, the figures are higher, varying between 15 and 23 in the years from 1838 to 1900 (Garrabou *et al.*, 1995: 112). A comparison with the evolution of wheat yields in Western Europe, both between countries and between the most productive areas, provides clear evidence that the yields obtained at the farms in Murcia stayed far below the European average.[17] In my opinion, the reasons for the low land productivity were the same in Lérida as in Murcia, and probably in most of the arid regions of Spain. Leaving aside the scant availability of water, which has been frequently mentioned, there was a second factor limiting agricultural production, the insufficiency of nutrients, especially nitrogen. The techniques put into practice by the agricultural revolution (crop rotation and the inclusion of leguminous and pasture species) could not be applied in arid environments where, moreover, the thin plant layer made it difficult to use the biomass. The only alternative was natural fertiliser, the production of which increased both on the estates studied and in the whole of the region due to the larger number of work animals. Although we do not yet know the exact figures, the increase was not big enough to resolve the problem. This only happened with the introduction of artificial fertilisers, which did not take place in dry-farming systems until 1910–1920. This does not mean that Count del Valle or Count de San Julián did not know about them, but, that, like almost all large land holders of the region, they kept them for the most profitable crops: rice in Calasparra (which tripled its yields between 1850–1860 and 1900 as had similarly happened in Valencia [Calatayud, 2002: 70–71]), and for horticulture and vineyards on some lands owned by the Count del Valle in the Cartagena countryside. They had the same attitude to mechanisation, which advanced very slowly. Although the mouldboard plough (the Jaén, Dombâle and Hallie models) was very common, tractors and combine harvesters were notably absent.

When the data are analysed they confirm the hypotheses put forward by most researchers who have studied the agriculture of other areas of the peninsula: given the difficulty of increasing cereal grain yields, other, locally diverse, alternatives were sought. With respect to the Mediterranean regions, it was decided to develop crops better adapted to the natural environment and/or those that responded to market demand: wine, oil, nuts and horticultural crops. As we know, this was the direction that the Counts del Valle and de San Julián took in their management. The changes in land use helped them to develop a type of growth that was intensive in labour and not in capital, and which was particularly well-adapted to the context of the Southeast corner of the Iberian peninsula, where the relevant production factors were abundant and cheap labour and a lack of fertile soil and capital.

Did all of the changes described have decisive effects on the growth of total factor productivity? Economists usually affirm that the impact of technological change on the growth of productivity can only be appreciated in the medium and long term,

[17] Garrabou has compiled a collection of data on the evolution of the wheat yield in western Europe from Bairoch, 1989. These data enable us to appreciate the modest position occupied in this respect by the properties that we are studying (Garrabou *et al.*, 1995: 112–114).

and the case that we are studying offers evidence in this regard.[18] Without denying the dynamics and business spirit of the two generations of owners considered in this work, the weight of the traditional dry-farming crop was so strong that the effect of the changes on the modernisation of their estates was only moderate. It was not really felt until the final years of the nineteenth century and, above all, in the first decades of the twentieth.

The most useful indicator for confirming these conclusions is labour productivity, given that the data in hand, though difficult to measure, allow us to say with a certain confidence that its growth was scarce. This problem is present in all the Spanish 'agricultures' during the nineteenth century, to such an extent that the national mean was one-third lower than that of neighbouring countries, except for Portugal.[19] In the case of Murcia, we must likewise take into account certain characteristics of the supply and demand of the production factor in question. First of all, agricultural activities were carried on essentially within the framework of small farm units, and this meant that the male family members who worked as day labourers at peak times of the agricultural year did not have any real specialisation since machinery was scarce. In addition, the population was predominantly rural and dispersed, which, added to the small investment in primary education by the local governments during the second half of the nineteenth century, made field hands significantly less literate than the general population; in 1900, their literacy rate was much lower than the national average (29% as opposed to 43%).

However, there was some real, though modest advance, even though it is difficult to quantify. Some indirect evidence points in this direction. For example, there were fewer salaried workers hired for ploughing, reaping and grape harvesting, and yet there was no corresponding decrease in the surface area occupied by cereals and grape vines. This was the result of small improvements in agricultural tools (ploughs), an increase in the number of beasts of burden and, for vineyards, the advances in winemaking through changes in the species and selection of grapes. On the large farms of Count del Valle, the number of day workers employed each year declined by 10% between 1820–1830 and 1890–1900 for cereals and by 12% for wine and oil crops; the equivalent reduction on the farms of Count de San Julián was 8.5% in the first case and 15% in the latter. The greater meticulousness of some of the administrators of the Count del Valle has been highly useful to us, because they tended to calculate the labour costs by unit of product obtained. As a result we have clear evidence of moderate progress, concentrated in the final decades of the nineteenth century (Table 6.2).

[18] On the subject of the Industrial Revolution in Great Britain Mokyr wrote the following: 'Clearly it is not justified to hope that the great technological breakthroughs entailed a more or less simultaneous increase in productivity. The majority of the benefits of these breakthroughs occur in the far-off future and extend over a long period of time' (Mokyr, 1999: 25).

[19] Data from O´Brien and Prados de la Escosura, 1992, Table 6. With wheat production levels similar to those in Spain, labour productivity in cereal growing in the United States increased fourfold between 1840 and 1910 (Simpson, 1995: 228).

Table 6.2 Evolution of the wages in farming grains in Roda, 1800–1900

Periods	Ploughing		Seeding		Weeding		Harvesting		Threshing	
	Number of hired hands	Days	Number of hired hands	Days	Number of hired hands	Days	Number of hired hands	Days	Number of hired hands	R/Hl
1800–1825	35	14	28	10	144	15	205	20	199	2.00
1826–1850	35	14	26	11	123	17	208	21	187	1.99
1851–1875	34	13	29	10	135	16	196	20	171	1.90
1876–1900	28	10	22	9	105	12	145	18	118	1.60

Source: Harvest Accounts Books, Family Archives of the Comte del Valle, Calasparra, Annual summaries of managers' expenditure, Files V – XXIII; Family Archives of the Comte San Julián, Lorca, Annual summaries of managers' expenditure, Files IV – XIV. R/Hl. Réaux per hectolitre of grain.

V. Income and investment

The system that we have described seems to contradict some of the views of Adam Smith and Arthur Young, especially their claim that sharecropping and modest leases are a sign that owners lacked initiative and entrepreneurial attitudes. According to this widespread belief, agrarian development required the presence of landowners with a spirit of initiative and an eye for business, or, failing that, large agricultural entrepreneurs with a strong contribution of capital and labour.[20]

The information set out in the preceding pages makes it difficult to apply this explanatory scheme. The alternative position that favours indirect management cannot be attributed to the weight of tradition, but rather to a well-considered option, inspired by the environmental and social realities of the various districts (Pérez Picazo *et al.*, 1998: 50–51), taking into account costs and profits. This explains, for example, the generalised use of sharecroppers in dry-land farming, where the harshness of the climatic conditions made the cereal harvest a gamble. In this event, then, the physical limits were decisive, while in other cases it was the institutional context or the economic conditions that determined the path to follow. As far as institutions were concerned, the new liberal legislation, highly favourable to owners, helped make it possible for leases to be maintained on irrigated lands. As for economic conditions, the movement of prices inspired a certain see-sawing between the kinds of agreements. In the case of rice cultivation, for example, the money lease predominated when prices oscillated or tended to drop, as occurred during the Great Depression at end of the century. Both the Count del Valle and the Count de San Julián ended up leasing large dry farming operations to a single person in Caravaca and Lorca during these crises. Conversely, the payment of

[20] The modest success achieved by the small operations of the colonies of the Counts Del Valle and De San Julián disproves the theories on the inefficiency of leasing and sharecropping on a small scale. This is especially so in the case of sharecropping, which has had a poor reputation amongst historians (Cheung, 1969) and has received criticism from opposing political positions, by Marshall, Marx and Kautsky (Hayami and Otosuka, 1993: 4).

rent in kind gained ground in the improving political and economic situation between 1850 and 1870 (Pérez Picazo *et al.*, 1998: 67). Other considerations cannot be ignored, such as the dispersion of the estates, which made it extraordinarily difficult to control the workers. But, above all, there is the fact that, given the state of existing technology, there were no fundamental differences between the technology that the owner could use and that used by indirect operators. In my opinion, the two generations of owners studied followed a rational strategy in their indirect management. Similar behaviour was seen in like circumstances in Murcia and in the Mediterranean regions previously mentioned. This is all the more evident in the fact that at no time did they wash their hands of the management of their farms; rather, they took part in the production process, selecting the personnel hired and, above all, investing a percentage of the moderately high income on improvements (between 14.9% from 1840 to 1849 and 17.8% from 1860 to 1869). It is clear that their objective was to increase the income that they received, but they could have obtained it through other mechanisms that did not require investments on their part and which, of course, were also present: breaking new ground, splitting up operations whenever the progress of intensification and specialisation allowed (as in the mean reduction of the size of the cultivation units on irrigated lands around the capital of Murcia), the systematic increase of rent, thereby taking advantage of the pressure on the land from a growing field-hand population, etc. In such economies where there are few economies of scale, high labour supervision costs and not much risk, small holdings could be efficient.The positive evolution of landed income (Figures 6.1 and 6.2) shows how effective this strategy was for the owners' purposes. Obviously, a rising trend of this magnitude was more pronounced on irrigated lands than on cereal operations, which made up for their drop in income by marketing esparto grass and wood.[21] Furthermore, reassigning resources from a low- performing product such as wheat to high value crops such as fruit, allowed the landowners to increase their income during a period of falling cereal prices.

The continuity of growth and the limited impact of the Great Depression at the century's end are evident. Simpson has recently pointed out that income increased in Spain more than wages (Simpson y Carmona, 2003: 38), unlike other western countries. This evolution, visible in various Spanish regions such as Castille (Robledo, 1984) and Cataluña (Garrabou, Planas and Saguer, 2000: 162–170) can be attributed both to general factors (protectionist tariff policies) and local factors (the boom of horticultural products not affected by falling prices, and the strong control exercised by the oligarchies of property owners from Murcia in local government).[22] This facilitated accumulation by large landowners, especially during the boom period of the central decades of the nineteenth century, which encouraged a high level of investment. But the profits from that investment were not realised until the final decades of the nineteenth and the early decades of the twentieth centuries, when fruit plantations were in full production.

[21] The increase in demand of esparto and cheap wood from the paper factories in Great Britain benefited those properties which had areas of scrubland. For example, in Caravaca (Archives of Caravaca, File XI) the Count Del Valle V managed to increase his income by 35% between 1860 and 1875 thanks to the exportation of the aforementioned prime materials. A similar improvement occurred in Lorca where the Count De San Julián (File IX), increased his income by 36.2% over the same period.

[22] The tendency to increase income contrasts with the well-known 'defeat of the rentier', present in all western countries from the end of the XIX century (Prados de la Escosura, 2003; Simpson and Carmona, 2003; O´Rourke and Williamson, 1997).

Table 6.3 Income account (%), 1805–1902 (*reales de vellón*)

	Comte del Valle de San Juan			Comte of San Julián		
Decades	Incomes	Sales	Total. Index	Income	Sales	Total Index
1805–1814	64.6	35.4	429,224 100			
1815–1824	70.8	29.2	437,311 100			
1825–1834	71.3	28.7	473,121 110			
1835–1844	73.4	28.7	546,088 121			
1845–1854	78.6	21.4	655,167 152	57.6	42.4	396,534 100
1855–1864	75.2	24.8	699,546 162	49.9	50.1	445,675 112
1865–1874	70.7	69.3	756,475 176	46.7	53.3	509,956 128
1875–1884	68.5	31.5	823,422 193	43.8	56.2	428,673 108
1885–1894	70.8	29.2	805,403 187	52.8	47.2	416,870 105
1895–1902	66.3	33.7	836,802 206	51.6	48.4	488,390 123

Table 6.4 Expenditures Account (%), 1805–1902 (*reales de vellón*)

	Comte del Valle de San Juan					Comte de San Julián				
Decades	Wages	Invest.[1]	Taxes	Send. M	Total	Wages	Invest.	Taxes.	Send. M[2]	Total
1805–14	14.9	15.5	13.8	39.3	370,511					
1815–24	14.8	15.7	11.5	37.4	325,229					
1825–34	14.7	15.9	11.5	40.9	395,211					
1835–44	16.3	34.9	11.5	38.6	467,987					
1845–54	17.9	37.2	12.7	35.9	590,675	19.9	31.8	12.7	29.8	391,765 100
1855–64	17.8	29.3	12.7	26.8	680,436	18.5	29.6	12.7	28.3	446,239 114
1865–74	14.4	21.8	12.7	38.5	741,895	13.8	15.7	12.7	37.9	498,650 127
1875–84	12.3	16.7	13.9	39.1	799,056	12.7	14.8	13.9	36.5	399,123 101
1885–94	12.2	16.9	13.9	39.9	785,456	12.6	14.9	13.9	38.3	493,345 125
1895–02	12.5	15.8	13.9	38.2	791,853	12.1	15.4	13.9	40.4	476,147 121

(1) Investments ; (2) : Sending money to owner.

References. Income and expenditure account, Books 1–10, Family Archives of comtes del Valle and San-Julian, Calasparra and Caravaca.

VI. Conclusions

The example of the two estates analysed contributes new evidence to the debate about the degree of progress or backwardness in Spanish agriculture during the nineteenth century. First of all, the results achieved through strategies that skilfully combined continuity and change are undeniable. Agrarian structures were maintained, but new clauses were introduced into agreements, which made it easier for owners to intervene in managing the operation. Cereal cultivation maintained its hegemony, but at its core, the cereals destined for human consumption became less important than those destined for livestock. Dry farming retained its imposing presence, but the expansion of vineyards and of tree plantations diversified the production structure. Above all, there was a rapid increase in irrigated small units, responding to the growing demand for fresh products favoured by the rise in the standard of living and the presence of the railway.

In summary, output grew, and in turn, specialisation and intensification advanced. The result was that regional agriculture was oriented more towards a range of products where it had comparative advantages: the relative costs decreased. The data presented here leave no room for doubt. There were also improvements in land productivity, although due more to crop substitution than to the introduction of new inputs (such as machinery or chemical fertilisers). Conversely, and similarly to what occurred at a national level, labour productivity advanced only modestly, so much so that the weakness of migratory movement and the scarce labour demand from industry in southeastern Spain kept the number of agricultural workers static through the nineteenth century. This evidence demonstrates conclusively that these landowners did not behave like rentiers or absentees, investing little or nothing on their lands and avoiding the risks of investment while taking little interest in its management. The numerous clichés abounding in Spanish agrarian literature on this subject should now be considered disproved.

Bibliography

Allen, R.C. (1992) *Enclosure and the Yeomen. The Agricultural Development of the South Midlands, 1450–1850*, Oxford: Clarendon Press.

Allen, R.C. (1999) 'Tracking the Agricultural Revolution', *Economic History Review*, 52, pp. 209–235.

Allen, R.C. (2000) 'Economic Structure and Agricultural Productivity in Europe, 1300–1800', *European Review of Economic History*, 83, pp. 852–876.

Altieri, M.A. (1989) *Agroecology: The Science of Sustainable Agriculture*, Boulder: Westview Press.

Barquin, R. (1999) 'El precio del trigo en España (1814–1883)', *Historia Agraria*, 17, pp. 127–217.

Bairoch, P. (1989) 'Les Trois révolutions agricoles du monde developpé: rendements et productivité de 1800 à 1985', *Annales E.S.C.*, (mars-avril), 2, pp. 317–353.

Baz, M.J. (1996) *Señorío y propiedad foral en de la alta nobleza en Galicia (siglos XVI-XX)*, La Casa de Alba, Madrid : MAPA.

Bevilacqua, P. (1992) *Storia del'agricoltura italiana in etá contemporanea. I. Spazi e paesaggi*, Venezia: Marsilio.

Bringas, M.A. (2000) *La productividad de los factores en la agricultura española (1752–1935)*, Madrid: Banco de España.

Calatayud, S. (1989) *Capitalismo agrario y propiedad campesina. La Ribera del Xúquer, 1860–1930*, Valencia: Instituto Alfonso el Magnánimo.

Calatayud, S. (2002) 'Tierras inundadas. El cultivo del arroz en la España contemporánea (1800–1936)', *Revista de Historia Económica*, XX, 1, pp. 39–80.

Calatayud, S. and Martínez Carrión, J.M. (1999) 'El cambio técnico en los sistemas de captación e impulsión de aguas subterráneas para riego en la España mediterránea', in R. Garrabou and J.M. Naredo, (eds), *El agua en los sistemas agrarios. Una perspectiva histórica*, Madrid: Argentaria-Visor, pp. 15–39.

Calatayud, S., Millán, J. and Romero, M.C. (2000) 'El rentismo nobiliario en la agricultura valenciana del siglo XIX', *Revista de Historia Económica*, XVIII,1, pp. 79–107.

Carmona Badía, J. and Puente, L. (1988) 'Crisis agraria y vías de evolución ganadera en Galicia y Cantabria', in R. Garrabou, (ed.), *La crisis agraria a fines del siglo XIX*, Barcelona: Crítica.

Carmona Pidal, J. (2001) *La aristocracia terrateniente y el cambio agrario en España en el siglo XIX: La Casa de Alcñices, 1790–1910*, Valladolid: Junta de Castilla y León.

Cheung, N.S. (1969) *The Theory of Share Tenency*, Chicago: University of Chicago Press.

Chevet, J.M. (1996) 'Quelle "révolution agricole" en Angleterre? À propos de deux livres récents sur l'agriculture anglaise du Moyen Âge au milieu du XIXe siècle', *Histoire & Mesure*, XI, 3–4, pp. 389–419.

Chevet, J.M. (1998–99) *La Terre et les paysans en France et Grande Bretagne. Du début du XVIIe siècle à la fin du XVIIIe siècle*, Paris: Editions Messene.

Gallego, D. (2001) 'Historia de un desarrollo pausado: integración mercantil y transformaciones productivas en la agricultura española (1800–1936)', in J. Pujol et al. (eds), *El pozo de todos los males*, Madrid: Crítica, pp. 147–215.

Garrabou, R., Pascual, O., Pujol, J. and Saguer, E. (1995) 'Potencialidad productiva y rendimientos cerealícolas en la agricultura catalana contemporánea (1820–1935)', *Historia Agraria*, 10, pp. 89–130.

Garrabou, R., Planas, J. and Saguer, E. (2001) *Un capitalismo imposible? la gestió de la gran propietat agrària a la Catalunya contemporánea*, Vic: Eumo editorial.

G.H.E.R. (Grupo de Estudios de Historia Rural) (1991) *Estadísticas históricas de la producción agraria española, 1859–1935*, Madrid: Ministerio de Agricultura.

González de Molina, M. (2001) 'El modelo de crecimiento agrario del siglo XIX y sus límites ambientales. Un estudios de caso', in M. González de Molina and J. Martínez Alier, (eds), *Naturaleza transformada. Estudios de Historia Ambiental*, Barcelona: Icaria.

Gliessman, R.P. (1998) *Agroecology. Ecological Process in Sustainable Agricultura*, Chelsea: Ann Arbor Press.

Hayami, Y. and Otosua, K. (1993) *The Economics of Contract Choice. An Agrarian Perspective*, Oxford: Clarendon Press.

Herr, R. (1989) *Rural Change and Royal Finances in Spain at the End of the Old Regime*, Berkeley and Los Angeles: University of California Press.

Llopis, E. (2002) *La crisis del Antiguo Régimen y la revolución liberal (1790–1840)*, in F. Comín, M. Hernández and E. Llopis, (eds), *Historia Económica de España, siglos x-xx*, Barcelona: Crítica.

Lana Berasain, M. (1996) 'Trabajo, técnica y mercado en la viticultura Navarra: los viñedos del marqués de San Adrián en Monteagudo durante el siglo xix', *Noticiario de Historia Agraria*, 10, pp. 135–163.

Martínez Vara, T. (1999) 'La integración del mercado del trigo en el Norte y la Castilla del Duero, 1800–1860', *Historia agraria*, 19, pp. 43–73.

Mokyr, J. (ed.) (1993) *The British Industrialisation. An economic perspective*, Boulder: Westview Press.

Naredo, J.M. (1987) *La economía en evolución. Historia y perspectivas de las categorías básicas del pensamiento económico*, Madrid: Siglo XXI.

O´Brien, P.K. (1985) 'Agriculture and the Home Market for English Industry, 1660–1820', *English Historical Review*, C, pp. 771–799.

O´Brien, P.K. and Prados de la Escosura, L. (1992) 'Agricultural Productivity and European Industrialization, 1890–1980', *Economic History Review*, XIV, 3, pp. 514–536.

O´Rourke, K. and Williamson, J.G. (1997) 'Around the European periphery 1870–1913. Globalization, Schooling and Growth', *European Review of Economic History*, 1, pp. 153–190.

Pérez Picazo, M.T. (1991) 'Riqueza territorial y cambio agrícola en la Murcia del siglo xix. Aproximación al estudio de una contabilidad privada, 1800–1902', *Agricultura y sociedad*, 61, pp. 39–94.

Pérez Picazo, M.T. (2000) 'Essor de la production et gains de productivité agricole dans une región meditérranéenne au xixe siècle. Le cas de Murcie', *Histoire & Mesure*, xi, 3/4, pp. 217–312.

Pérez Picazo, M.T., Pérez de Perceval, M.A. and Martínez Carrión, J.M. (1998) 'Ceux qui peinent et ceux qui prennent. Conjoncture et faire-valoir dans les systèmes agraires du Sud-Est Espagnol (1830–1960)', *Histoire et Sociétés Rurales*, 10, pp. 47–81.

Prados de la Escosura, L. (2003) *El progreso económico de España (1850–2000)*, Madrid: Fundación BBVA.

Pujol, J. (1998) 'Las innovaciones biológicas en la agricultura española antes de 1936: el caso del trigo', *Agricultura y Sociedad*, 86, pp. 163–178.

Pujol, J., González de Molina, R., Fernández Prieto, L., Gallego, D. and Garrabou, R. (2001) *El pozo de todos los males. Sobre el atraso de la agricultura española contemporánea*, Barcelona: Crítica.

Sabio, A. (1998) 'El capitalismo agrari a través de la renda en una agricultura orgànica. Les estrategias d´un ministre a finals del segle XIX a l´Aragó', *Recerques*, 37, pp 57–80.

Sánchez Picón, A. (1997) 'Los regadíos de la Andalucía árida (siglos XIX and XX). Expansión, bloqueo y transformación', *Areas. Revista de Ciencias Sociales*, 17, pp. 109–129.

Sarasúa., C. (2002) 'El análisis histórico del trabajo agrario: cuestiones recientes', *Historia Agraria*, 22, pp. 79–97.

Sieferle, R.P. (2001) '¿Qué es la historia del Medio Ambiente?', *Encuentro Estatal de Historia y Medio Ambiente*, Andujar, mimeo (en prensa).

Simpson, J. (1995) *Spanish agriculture. The Long Siesta, 1765–1965*, Cambridge University Press.

Simpson, J. and Carmona, J. (2003) *El laberinto de la agricultura española (1850–1936)*, Zaragoza: Prensas Universitarias.

Smith, A. (1979) *The Wealth of Nations*, London: Penguin.

Young, A. (1783 [1929]) *Travels in France during the years 1787, 1788 and 1789*, Cambridge University Press.

7 Agricultural production and productivity in eighteenth- and nineteenth-century France: new evidence from the Hospices de Dijon*

Tim J. A. Le Goff, York University, Toronto / IRCOM, Paris

I. Introduction

The Dijon Hôpital Général received a large but varying proportion of income from its rural properties.[1] As Christine Lamarre has shown, most of its land was obtained in the half-century before 1750; these acquisitions seem to have been motivated by distrust of *rentes* (fixed non-property investments), particularly state securities after the manipulation of securities and currency during the Mississippi Bubble and subsequent write-down of state debt in the period from 1718 to 1724. The hospital administrators also augmented their landed endowment by annexing the properties of a few smaller charitable institutions in the region. Then, in 1778, they acquired the property of a religious order, the Hospitallers of the Holy Spirit, after its suppression and the death of its last Commander. Other rural properties were added by way of legacies, exchanges and purchases. At the beginning of the eighteenth century, the Hôpital Général had ten or so rural holdings producing an annual income of barely 3500 livres (Lamarre, 2004: 7–13, 30–33, 67–94). By the end of the Old Regime, in 1787, it had fifty-three rural properties producing 31,843 livres in annual rents.[2] After 1789 its property was further augmented by the gradual integration of lands belonging to the Hospice Sainte-Anne, a charitable establishment dedicated to the training of poor girls (Callerand-Combémorel, 1984). The process by which the Hospice Sainte-Anne acquired its property before 1789 is less well known than that employed

---

* This is a substantially revised and developed version of an article which originally appeared in French (Le Goff, 2010). I wish to express thanks to my colleagues Marc Perrichet, Donald Sutherland and Jeanette Neeson and to Christian Choron, former archivist of the Hôpital Général de Dijon, for their help.

[1] This article draws principally on the Archives des Hospices civils de Dijon [AHCD]. For the Hôpital général, series B1 (baux); E1 (registres des délibérations); E11 (comptes administratifs); E12 (comptes moraux) and E16 & 19 (comptes de détail) have been used. For Sainte-Anne, the relevant séries were B3 (domaines ruraux) and E5 (comptes de détail); sources and methods used for the calculation of TFP are listed in the Appendix. The archives of the Hospices civils have recently been transferred to the Archives départementales de la Côte d'Or [ADCO] where the have been classified under the heading H. dép. 239/1/E.

[2] AHCD, E16 270. In fact, during the 1787 accounting year, the Hôpital Général received only 26,962 livres in rural rents, the remainder being in arrears; for more on the potential impact of arrears, see below. The figures in Lamarre (2004: 93) and Le Goff (2010: 191) overlook a change in the Hôpital's accounting procedure which artificially inflated the size of the hospital's landed and investment income after 1767, but these revised sums are still substantial.

by the Hôpital Général but, by 1787, Sainte-Anne owned 21 farms and other properties producing an annual income of nearly 18,000 livres.[3]

During the Revolution there were plans to sell off the property of the Hôpital Général and the Hospice Sainte-Anne, along with that of all similar institutions in France, as 'national property'. But inflation induced by the introduction and multiplication of paper money, the notorious *assignats*, wrecked hospital income from *rentes*, and the new French state was unable to find enough resources to subsidise these charitable institutions. Inevitably, French hospitals could not be stripped of their landed estates and income. The property holdings of the Dijon Hospices, at the end of the Revolution, as in many parts of France, remained mostly intact. In 1812, the Hôpital Général owned some 38 farms and other rural properties covering a total of 1832 hectares with rents stipulating income of 55,000 francs a year, while the Hospice Sainte-Anne had 20 farms with a total surface of 350 hectares and leases worth around 30,900 francs. At that point then, the resources of the combined 'Hospices de Dijon' were 58 farms and other holdings, with a total surface of 2182 hectares, producing an annual landed income of about 86,000 francs, or around about half of their total income.[4] During the nineteenth century, the Hospices de Dijon continued to receive legacies, and buy and exchange lands, so their endowment changed continuously, but the total surface went on increasing until the long agricultural depression that begin at the end of the 1870s. Even as late as 1886, the Hospices de Dijon still owned 86 farms, producing a total annual landed income of 172,160 francs, about 46% of their annual income.

Thus a large number of properties acquired in the first half of the eighteenth century, or even earlier, stayed in what amounted to the same hands until the 1920s, immune to the dispersion through inheritance that was the bane of private holdings, and to the confiscations and sales that Church lands underwent during the Revolution. And, as is often the case with hospital archives, those of the Hospices de Dijon were carefully kept, not only during the last century of the Old Regime and through the nineteenth century, but even during the Revolution. This extraordinary continuity gives French hospital archives in general an almost unique value for research on economic history, making it possible to construct very long statistical series for key elements of agricultural history such as rent, income and investment. Frequently, they can also be counted on to yield a wealth of evidence on property management in a given region. This essay attempts to present some of these elements as they emerge from the archives of the

[3] AHCD, E5 146. As with the Hôpital Général, Sainte-Anne's rents actually received in that accounting year were only 6,696 livres, a good deal less than what was due.

[4] AHCD E16 300 (Hôpital Général) and E5 183 (Sainte-Anne): Tableau général des revenus & ressources pour l'exercice an 1812. The Hôpital earned 3524 francs that year from the sale of 464 hl of wine from Chambolle; the remaining 353 hl was used for its own consumption. It also took in 453 hectolitres of grain or rents in kind (worth about 9100 francs at average market prices) for its own consumption and 7421 livres from woodcutting. In all the calculations of the overall revenues of the two institutions in parts I to III of this article, only cash income from rented agricultural property has been taken into consideration. The total cash income of the institutions in 1812 (including urban rents, income from loans and bonds, pensions etc.) came to 117,558 fr. for the Hôpital and 54,232 fr for Sainte-Anne.

Figure 7.1 Hospices de Dijon – Agricultural rent (excluding viticulture) in the Dijon region by municipality, 1812

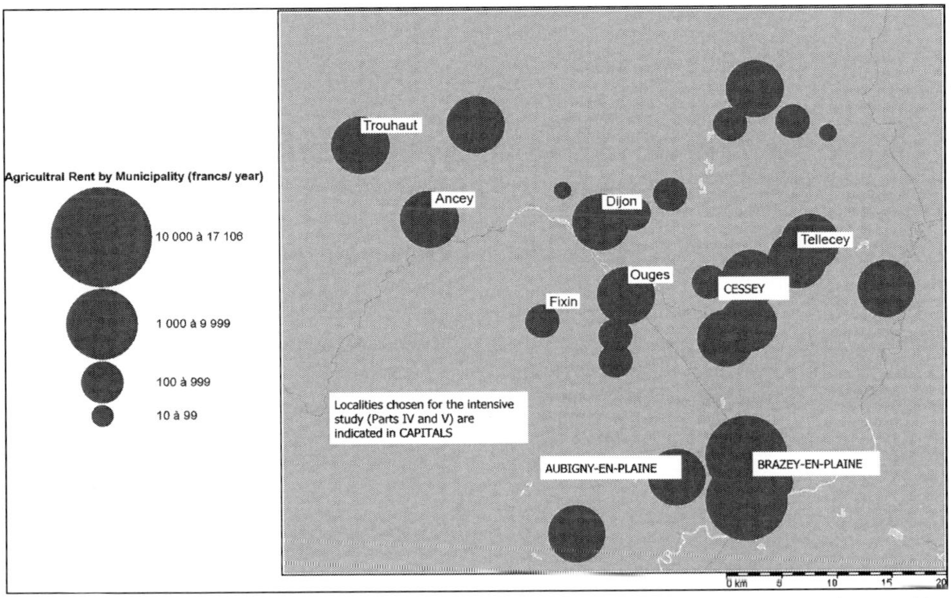

Source: AHCD E16 300; map base: © 1988–2010 Microsoft Corporation and/or providers. All rights reserved. © 1984–2010 Tele Atlas N.V. All rights reserved. http://www.microsoft.com/france/mappoint . Sources © 2010 Tele Atlas N.V. This product contains material licensed by Ordnance Service, authorised by the Controller of Her Majesty's Stationery Office. © Crown copyright, license number 100025324. © NACTEQ. All rights reserved.

Hospices de Dijon, and to draw some general conclusions from them and similar data elsewhere in France.

To this end two approaches have been adopted. The first was to use the total mass of data on the rural agricultural properties of the Hospices de Dijon, while taking into account variations in the composition and dimensions of their endowment. This is the documentation used primarily in sections I to III of this article. The other was to examine in greater detail a smaller set of properties from a micro-region around Saint-Jean-de-Losne, where there were abundant data on long-term evolution. These were the data employed in the final two sections (IV and V).

In the second set of documents, for the Saint-Jean-de-Losne area study, properties where part of the pre-1789 revenue came from seigneurial income have been excluded from analysis, because when seigneurial dues were abolished during the Revolution, the rental on these properties was reduced by an amount which is difficult to determine. It has also been necessary to select properties whose surface did not change over the period considered. In the end, five farms fulfilling all these criteria were selected for study. Two originated in the endowment of the Hôpital Général and three from that of the Hospice Sainte-Anne:

> Properties belonging to the Hôpital général:
> farm at Brazey-en-Plaine (57 hectares)
> farm at Cessey (59 hectares)
> Properties belonging to the Hospice Sainte-Anne:
> farm at Aubigny (27 hectares)
> Jeannelle farm at Brazey-en-Plaine (10 hectares)
> Girod farm at Brazey-en-Plaine (5 hectares)

These farms were in what can be broadly termed the Saône valley, and situated, like most of the lands of the Hôpital Général and the Hospice Sainte-Anne, to the south and east of Dijon. This region had good communication by roads and waterways, notably by the rivers Saône, Ouche, Tille and their confluents. It was crossed by the Burgundy Canal, whose construction began in 1775 and which reached the region around 1788.

All these features helped integrate these farms into regional and inter-regional market systems: Burgundy wheat travelled down the Saône and Rhone to Lyon and even Marseille and beyond. The hospices' lands in the region were well adapted to this purpose; they were situated in a region of alluvial land and 'herbues' (sedimentary, clay and silica soils). These fields were 'fertile, the best soil around Dijon' (Lamarre, 2004: 85). They were capable of bearing good yields, but needed adequate ploughing and fertilising; consequently they required a reasonable number of cattle to provide manure and horses for the heavy ploughing.

The rather modest dimensions of these farms were fairly typical of the other properties owned by the Hospices de Dijon. A farmer from the Île-de-France would have found them small, but in Burgundy, even at the end of the nineteenth century, these were considered a respectable size. According to one study dating from 1911, in the Dijonnais and the Saône plain, a holding of more than forty hectares was considered to be *grande culture*, and an average-sized holding between ten and forty hectares (Guicherd, 1911: 203). So in this case we have two instances of *grande culture* (on a Burgundian scale), two of average size, and one smallholding.

Almost all the property of the Hospices de Dijon was farmed out. The purpose of these farms was not to provide food for the two institutions, which got their victuals for the most part in the Dijon markets or from local suppliers on contract; rather, they were leased out for rents in cash, except for a few instances of small payments in kind. Most holdings were let on leases of the sort typical in the region, usually for nine-year periods, occasionally for six or twelve years. From 1740 onwards, the Hospital appears to have tried to elicit competitive bidding (Lamarre, 2004: 67), a practice followed more or less consistently over the following century and only abandoned in the mid-nineteenth century when bidders became less numerous and more recalcitrant.[5] The administrators of both institutions always managed to have the leases subscribed in advance, usually two

[5] AHCD E1 57 Registre des délibérations de la Commission administrative de l'Hôpital général de Dijon, 26–07–1857.

years before the date of entry. The farmer took possession of the farm on Saint George's Day (23 April) to use the meadows and fallow (*sombres*) and after harvest time for the other lands and crops. The first payment was usually made on the Christmas (sometimes at Martinmas, 11 November) following the date of the farmer's entry into possession. Later, in the nineteenth century, it became common to take payment in two terms, on New Year's Day and on 1 July.

What was the role of these proprietors in agricultural production? In answering this question, most histories of French farming, for lack of documentation, are forced back on the formulaic and rigid texts of the leases to be found in notarial archives, and their conclusions suggest that the landlords' role was minimal. But in reality farm leases often obscure rather than illuminate the role of the landed proprietor in agricultural development and management, and are slow to reflect actual developments on the land. One of the great advantages of documentation from hospitals is the existence, in Dijon as well as several other centres, not only of series of leases, but also of well-kept accounts and records of administrators' meetings, which allow us to reconstruct a great deal of the effective forms of property administration and gain an appreciation of its multiple dimensions.

II. Payments and arrears: a system of short-term credit

In traditional French rural historiography, rents were always due immediately after the harvest – therefore when the prices were at their lowest, and the farmer stood least chance of making an honest profit on his labour. And it is true that, for the Hospices de Dijon in the eighteenth century, rents fell due either on Christmas Day or, more rarely, at Martinmas (11 November). Moreover, in his first year, a new farmer would have practically nothing to sell when he had to make his first payment, since he entered possession just after the harvest. And finally, under the Old Regime, the accountants of the two institutions closed their books on 31 December, imposing a seemingly draconian deadline for payment, and gave extensions of only a couple of months at best before they inscribed overdue payments into a special section of their account books bearing the ominous title 'arrears' (*reprises*).

At first glance, the proportion of arrears appears astonishingly high in the eighteenth century, but when we look more closely into the account books from the two institutions, we see that the administrators were very flexible in demanding payment. This appears most clearly at the start of the Revolution, when, perhaps short of liquid cash, the administrators of the Hôpital Général decided to issue farmers legal summonses for payment of these arrears: at that point they defined 'arrears' to mean two years' worth of rent.[6] This two-year rule appears to have been standard practice in the eighteenth century and continued well into the nineteenth century. In 1818, it was loosened again; thenceforth the administrators decided that payments due in November or December were to be counted as due in the following year. A contemporary accountant noted the following:

> This sort of inversion [...] has the advantage of ridding the accounts of a great number of arrears, since it is well known that this income is almost never paid on the dates

[6] AHCD E1 41, 08–11–1789.

> fixed by the leases, and scarcely paid during the course of the following year, no matter how hard we try.[7]

A logical development of this view was to extend, at this time, the accounting year to cover two whole calendar years. In 1836, the administrators experimented with a shorter accounting year of eighteen months; at the end of it, farmers were considered to be in debt to the hospital and their arrears listed under a separate accounting entry. Finally, in 1842 the accounting year was reduced further, to fifteen months. During the same period, the customary winter due date was shifted to 1 January. If we adopt the administrators' own practice to eighteenth-century bookkeeping and define 'arrears' as two years' rent, the percentage of laggards before 1789 becomes more reasonable.

In moments of crisis, the administrators showed even more flexibility. This seems to have been the case during the last years of the Old Regime, a time when the hospital administrators, like most French landlords, managed to rack up leases considerably. Perhaps to make the rise more palatable, we find often dramatic examples of delayed payments at this time. The total picture for the Hôpital Général is shown in Figure 7.2, while two particular examples are shown in Figure 7.4. At the start of the Revolution, the administrators seem to have tried to exact more prompt payments, but the years from 1793 to 1797 saw a further rash of deferred payments. In the first part of the nineteenth century, late payments became rarer, except for a few years surrounding the Revolution of 1848; but in the last decades of that century, during the 'agricultural depression' which began around 1878, serious arrears once again became common (Figure 7.3). On 31 March 1887, in the depths of that crisis, 66% of the 1886 rents were due, plus 17% of the 1885 and 5% of the 1884 payments (Figure 7.3),[8] a situation comparable to that of the late eighteenth century.

This practice of generous deadlines for rent payments in normal times and more than generous extensions in hard times meant that the two institutions were in effect suppliers of free short-term credit to their farmers. This made sense for the hospices: finding good tenants was not easy. Indeed, at critical moments, the administrators had not only to keep on old tenants for fear of finding worse, but also to grant them more favourable leases. Thus, after the hard times of the 1840s, the Hospices de Dijon gave up the practice of leasing their lands to the highest bidder in open auction, and granted substantial rent reductions, a policy that the administrators somewhat shamefacedly explained in 1855 in describing how

> [...] auctions almost always [provoke] coalitions of farmers and moreover [cause] necessarily high costs which the farmers, who are good cultivators and eager to make a success of their business are quite adept at manipulating to justify lower bids. So whenever the administration sees that it has capable farmers who work well and pay well, it tries to make the hospice lands attractive for them, without neglecting however to get whatever increases from them it thinks practicable. Thus the hospital lands are generally rented out nowadays just as advantageously as those of others like them, considering the layout and quality of the land of which they are composed.[9]

---

[7] AHCD E16 306 (1818), note by the accountant inserted before Article 41, Title 2 ('fermages').

[8] AHCD E19 61 Livre de détail des recettes et dépenses, exercice 1887.

[9] AHCD E12 3 Compte moral, 1855.

Figure 7.2 Arrears as a proportion of annual rents, 1750–1789

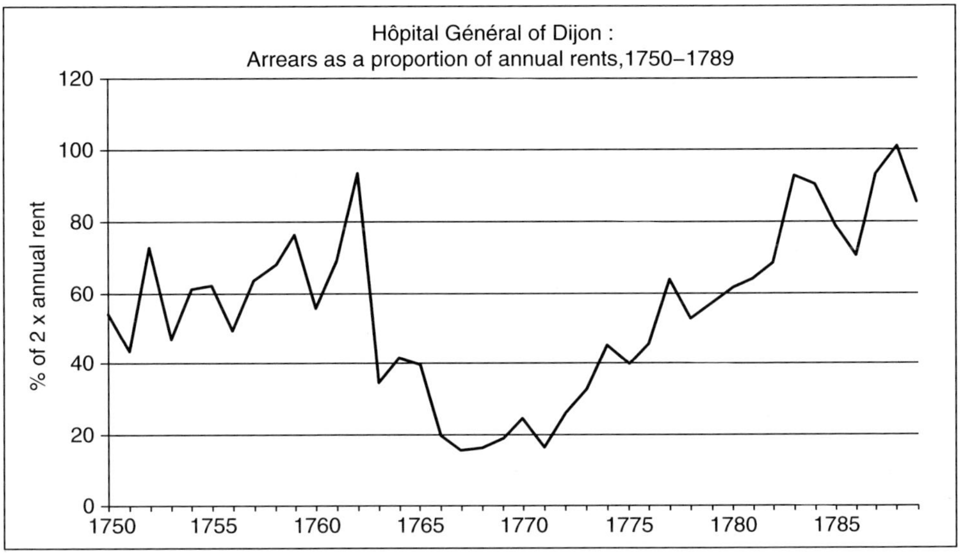

Source: AHCD E16 233–294: comptes de détail 1750 – Year XIII.

Figure 7.3 Proportion of annual rents in arrears, 1827–1901

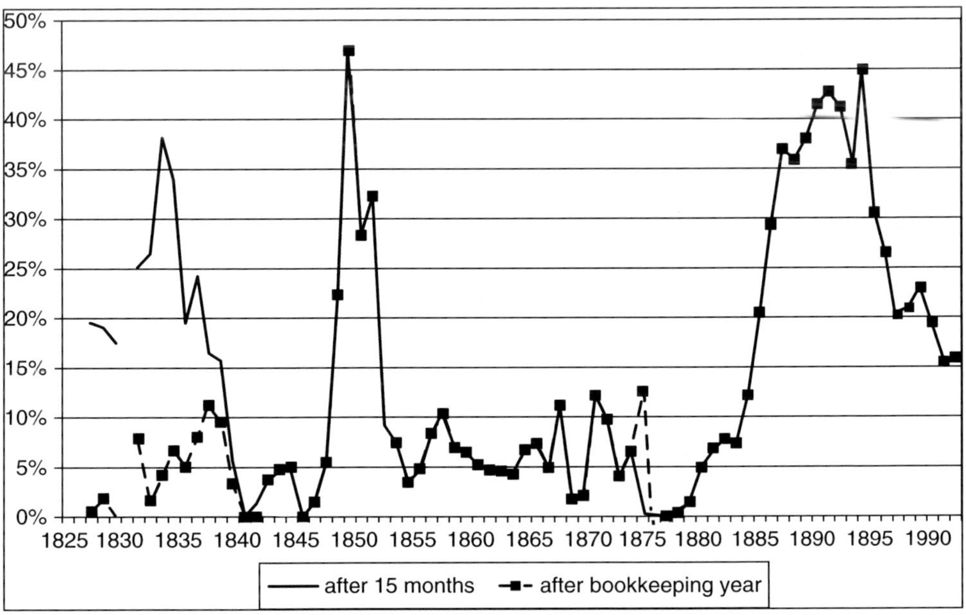

Source: AHCD E11 1–2: comptes administratifs 1851–1901; E12 3–5: comptes moraux 1866-1895; E19 1–63: comptes de détail 1827–1889.

Figure 7.4 Delays in payment on two farms (late eighteenth century)

A. *Farm of Cessey*

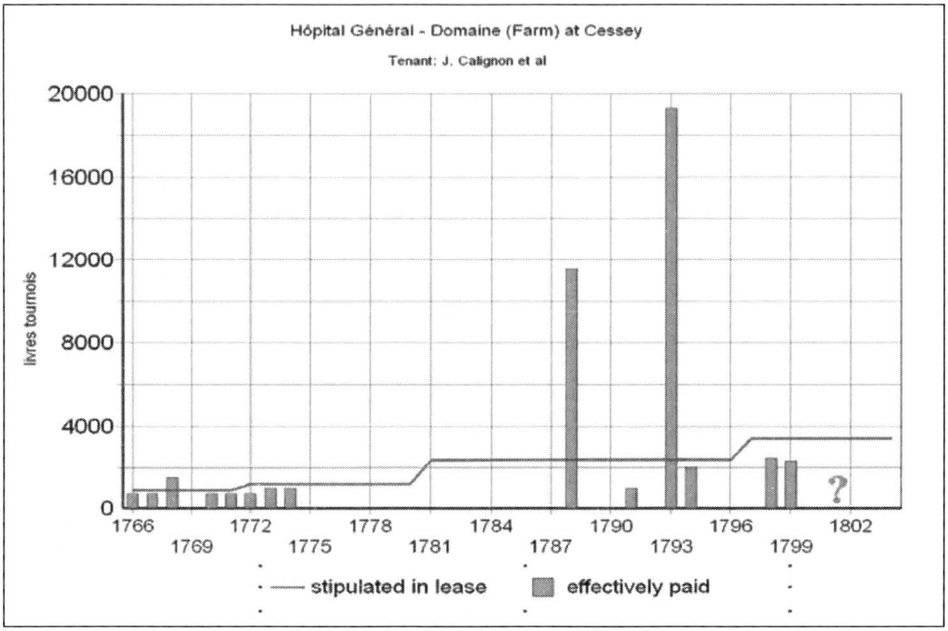

B. *Farm of Brazey*

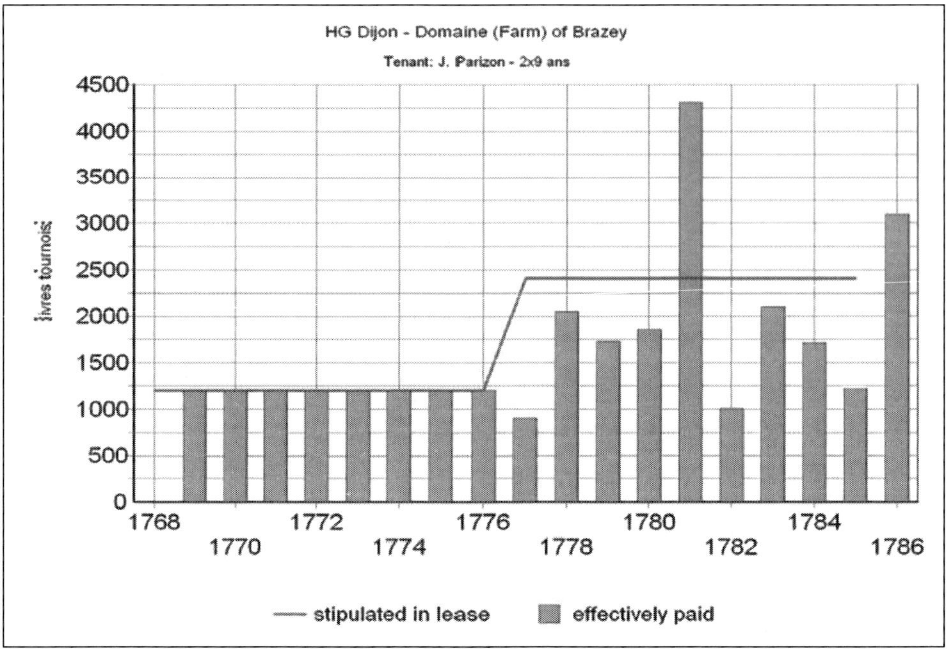

III. Investment in repairs and construction: the role of the hospices

Most works on agricultural history in France have little to say about the role of the landlord in rural investment, tending to assume that it was minimal or non-existent, especially given the nation-wide habit of leasing on short terms of nine years or so. This presumed repugnance for investment was not characteristic of our two institutions, to judge from data covering the last forty years of the old regime and most of the nineteenth century (see Table 7.1 and Figures 7.5 to 7.6).[10] They show that the Hospices de Dijon did make considerable efforts to maintain and improve their rural holdings.

What sort of investment was involved? Nineteenth-century accounts distinguished between 'maintenance and repairs' (*entretien et réparations*) and 'constructions and major repairs' (*constructions et grosses réparations*). But the distinction is arbitrary. To repair a two-hundred year old house could easily become a job of total reconstruction, as the proud administrators announced in 1856, after restoring a dozen or so farm buildings: 'All these buildings are now in a fit state, considering their age, which for half of them is more than two centuries'.[11] This, plus the evident coincidence with periods of heavy construction when we can measure it, in the nineteenth century (Figure 7.7), makes it reasonable to think of the two types of spending as landlord investment and reinvestment. In theory, such investment was distinct from 'tenant improvements' (*réparations locatives*) and investment in stock and equipment, which were usually matters for the tenant farmer. But landlord investment could have a spinoff effect, by increasing tenant output and, in turn, tenant investment.

Where was this institutional landlord investment applied? Except for some drainage works during the nineteenth century, crucial in these damp regions, little went directly into fields and meadows. Most spending was for what we would call 'infrastructure', particularly barns, milk-sheds and houses. While restoring a farmhouse does not appear at first glance to have the same potential economic impact on production as a constructing a barn, if the health of the farmer, his family and his hired hands was improved by the new dwelling, or if these changes put them in a position to use their own means to improve their livestock or buy agricultural equipment, particularly during the phase of farm mechanisation, the effect could be just as positive as if the landlord had made the latter investment himself.

A look at annual patterns of construction and repairs makes it possible to say more about the relation between these investments and what is known of the state of agriculture (Table 7.1 and Figures 7.5 to 7.6). Investment was at record levels in the 1750s and probably in the preceding couple of decades too; these were periods in which the Hôpital was in the

---

[10] AHCD E16 217–227, compte de la recette et dépense, 1749–1789; E19 1–3, 5–25 comptes de détail, 1827–29, 1831–51; E11 1–2 comptes administratifs 1851–1901; E12 2–5 Comptes moraux, 1836–1975. The figures from the hospices' summary accounts on which these graphs are based may, in the period 1852–1878, include repairs to one or two houses which the hospices still possessed in town. Conversely, those drawn from the detailed accounts before 1852 are minimum figures: only expenses specifically designated as being made on rural property have been counted. Gaps in figures for 1830 and 1852 have been filled by linear interpolation.

[11] AHCD E12 3, compte moral, 1862.

Table 7.1 Construction and repairs as a proportion of farm rents, 1750–1789, 1830–1899

Years	% of rents
1750–59	41.3
1759–59	15.9
1760–69	10.5
1770–79	7.6
1780–89	14.0
1830–39	3.1
1840–49	4.8
1850–59	8.8
1860–69	7.7
1870–79	8.1
1880–89	10.2
1890–99	5.4

process of acquiring new properties, and they had to be put into shape.[12] It remained at impressive levels, peaking again in the years just before the Revolution. Investments during the Revolution and Empire (1789–1815) still have to be studied, but it is hard to imagine that the Hôpital had much cash to spare at that point. There appears to have been a surge of activity in the 1820s, a decline in the 1830s, and more or less steadily rising investment thereafter. Particularly noteworthy is the effort made in the 1850s, first of all in an initially gloomy agricultural economy, and then in a progressively improving situation. In the early 1870s, a good level of rent income made another investment surge possible. Towards the end of that decade, the 'agricultural depression' set in, but, far from discouraging further investment, the rise in tenant arrears seems to have convinced the hospices that they were condemned to continue putting money into their farms in order to preserve whatever income they could; the subsequent drop-off in investment after 1890 may be a sign that landlords felt that they had now done what was necessary – or perhaps all that was possible.

Thus it appears that with the almost certain exception of the period of the Revolution and Empire, the hospices never completely failed to do their duty to maintain and, on occasion, improve, their rural property. The nineteenth-century levels were of the same order as investments on the farms of the hospices of Bourg-en-Bresse, on the southern fringes of Burgundy, which reached 8.9% of gross rents in the 1860s.[13] In an English

[12] AHCD E16 217–227, compte de la recette et dépense, 1736–1746 suggest investment levels equal to 26% of annual rents due. On land acquisitions see Lamarre, 2009, pp. 82–88.

[13] Archives départementales de l'Ain, Hospices de Bourg (fonds non classé), Administration des hospices de la ville de Bourg. Rapport de l'Économe externe sur le revenu comparé des propriétés rurales depuis l'année 1866 jusqu'à 1870, 22–07–1871, based on accounts for 57 farms.

Figure 7.5 Construction and repairs in the eighteenth century

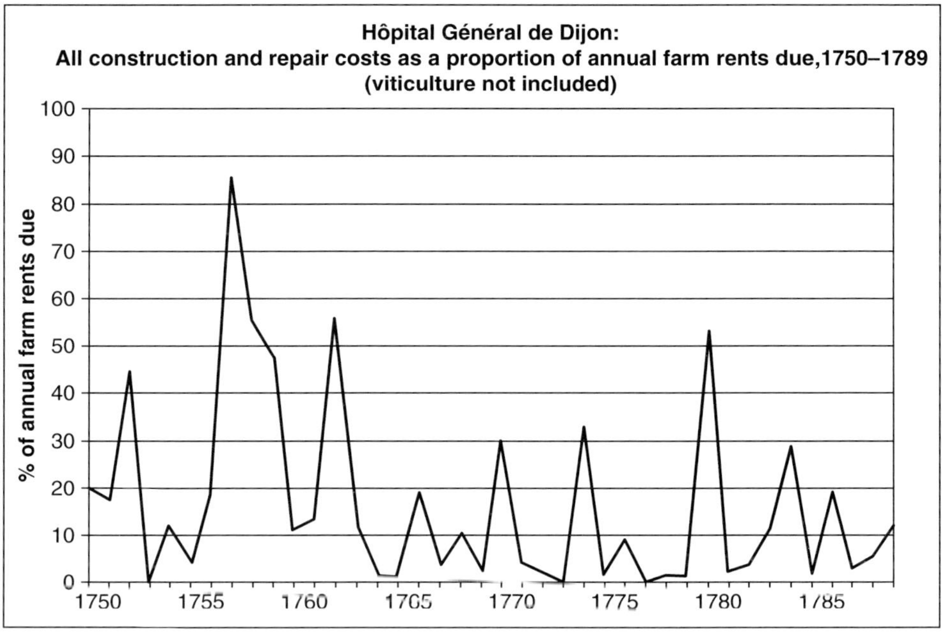

Figure 7.6 Construction and repairs in the nineteenth century

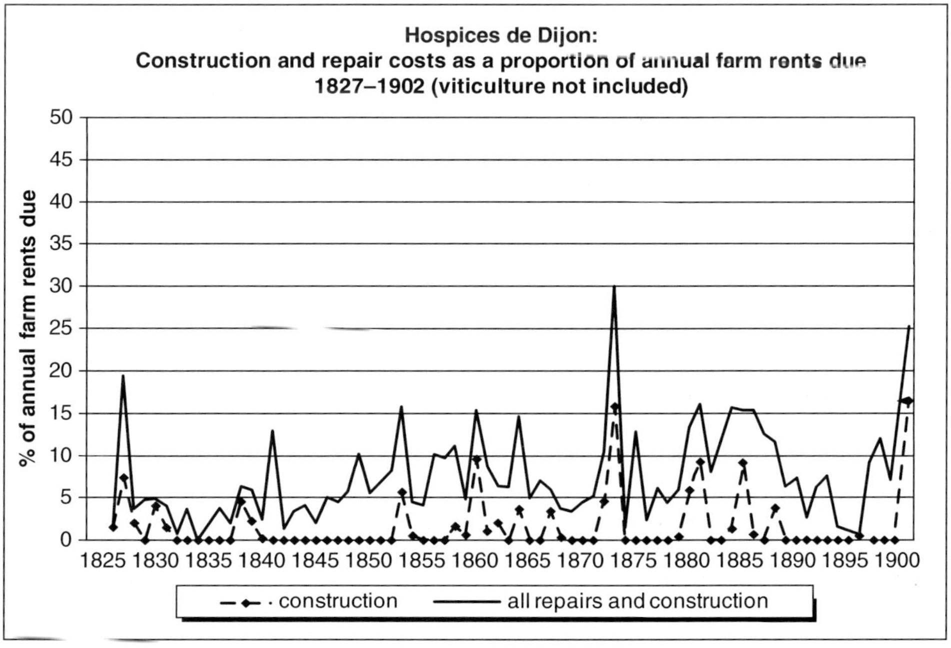

study, concerning Guy's Hospital in London, we find a comparable 9.5% of rent income going into investments between 1762 and 1815 (Trueman, 1980: 41). Research on English landlords (but not institutional landlords) for the middle decades of the nineteenth century suggests that they were spending around 12–14% of gross rents in repairs and improvements (Thompson, 1963: 250; Holderness, 1989: 187–189; Holderness, 2000: 863–929). This was somewhat more than the Dijon and Bourg-en-Bresse hospices, but not grossly disproportionate.[14] In both the Burgundian, and the London institutions, a common constraint on expenditure may have kept the institutions from higher levels of investment: spending priority went to giving adequate care and assistance to the poor and sick people in their charge. This, however, was not the only limitation on the potential impact of investment by the Dijon hospices, and doubtless other landlords in the region as well.

IV. Land management, social and agrarian structures

What sort of property did the hospices rent out, who were the tenants of these holdings and what aims did they pursue? A closer look at the situation, through an examination of the hospices' property around Saint-Jean-de-Losne, provides some answers.

One fundamental trait stands out: the hospital's farms in the Dijon region all bear the mark of fragmentation that is a characteristic of Burgundy. The farms that made up their endowment were scattered, rather than united in single contiguous units. They were assemblages of small parcels which the hospices acquired by legacy, purchase or exchange, and they were integrated in the great three-field systems that were still characteristic of the local villages. The hospices of Dijon made no serious effort to consolidate these parcels. A general survey of the lands of the Hôpital Général in the commune of Brazey in 1869 showed that the institution's land there was split up into 162 parcels, with an average size of 34 ares per parcel. At the end of the nineteenth century, the accepted belief in this region was that agricultural mechanisation could work only on parcels of at least 40 ares (Guicherd, 1911: 206), but of these 162 parcels, 129 were less than this minimum size.

Who were the tenants? The Hôpital Général and the Hospice Sainte-Anne seem to have looked for tenants of a certain substance. During the first three quarters of the eighteenth century, on its farm in Brazey, a large unit (57 hectares) by local standards, the Hôpital Général preferred to lease out its land to bourgeois from the closest urban centre, the little town of Saint-Jean-de-Losne: Jacques Convert, receiver of the *châtellenie* of Brazey, followed by another man with the same name, who was clerk of the same *châtellenie*. After the death of this second Jacques Convert in 1739, François Chenevoy, merchant and bourgeois of Saint-Jean-de-Losne, took up the lease, and when he and his wife got into difficulty in 1748, they found a guarantor in the person of their son, sieur Estienne Chenevoy, a merchant living in the town of Auxonne. some twelve kilometres distant. When this younger Chenevoy himself died in the course of his lease, his children and

[14] More recent studies of farm investment in nineteenth-century England give higher rates, but they use a different method and what they consider as investment appears to include a wider range of expenditures. Turner, Beckett and Afton (1997: 23; 2000: 2020–2026) propose a range from 26–31% of annual rents.

heirs sublet the farm to sieur Thomas of Saint-Jean-de-Losne, a former sub-tenant of their father's, in 1763, and jointly guaranteed payment with him. On the other sizeable farm in our selection of leases, the one belonging to the Hôpital Général in Cessey (59 hectares), the tenants were mainly millers and merchants from Cessey. As in the case of the Brazey farm, these were people who might at some point in their lives have ploughed a field, but were mainly identified with the rural bourgeoisie.

The participation of these bourgeois tenants in the first three quarters of the eighteenth century depended on the existence of a subordinate stratum of peasants who took on all or part of these holdings as sub-tenants, and in fact we do find many traces of such people in the documents in these years. During the last generation of the Old Regime, however, a change can be noticed. Thenceforward, the tenants almost always call themselves *laboureurs* or *manouvriers*; then, during the Revolution and afterwards they are termed *cultivateurs* in leases and official documents. The tenants also became more numerous on each holding, taking on leases in joint tenancy, with a collective responsibility for paying the rent and carrying out the terms of the lease. The record-holders were found on the Hospitals' farm at Brazey, leased out in 1794 to no less than sixteen people (seven *cultivateurs* and nine *manouvriers*). There was also a marked tendency for these farmers to chose their co-tenants among their relatives or in-laws. In 1785, four *laboureurs* from Brazey put their resources together to take on the lease of the Hospital's farm there. One was Jean Tissot, married to Marguerite Fichot; Marguerite was herself probably related to two of the other associates, François and Claude Fichot. The fourth tenant, Philibert Personnier, was married to yet another Fichot, Françoise. These characteristics of multiple tenancies among kin and in-laws carried on through the nineteenth century. This was the sign that the Hospices de Dijon had decided that they no longer needed to lease their land through bourgeois intermediaries – or perhaps that they no longer could find such middlemen – and that they would deal henceforth with the people who actually worked the land, people who had previously been subtenants, or who were children of former subtenants.[15] The joint tenancy agreement was required in order to guarantee the landlord the reliable income so necessary to the smooth functioning of charitable institutions.

What was the social position of these peasant farmers, and what sort of resources could they call on? Sources that give us a general idea of all the possessions of residents in a village community – and not just what they had on a particular farm or holding – are not very abundant, and, paradoxically, they become harder rather than easier to find in the nineteenth century. There is, however, one excellent source, the *nouveaux pieds de taille*, drawn up in Burgundy mainly towards the end of the Old Regime, with a view to a general reformation of tax assessments. Using one such document, the *pied de taille* for Brazey-en-Plaine in 1783, we can group the taxpayers in order of increasing wealth, into four categories, defined by the proportion of the tax paid by each group: the most taxed inhabitants (group 4 in Figure 7.2 above) paid one-quarter of the total tax; group 3 was less taxed but more numerous, accounting for the next-lowest quarter, and so on in descending order. At the end of the Old Regime, when the Hôpital Général and the Hospice Sainte-Anne chose their farmers, they took them from categories 3 and 4, among the solid peasants, but not those at the very pinnacle of rural wealth.

[15] AHCD B1 58–69 (Brazey-en-Plaine); B1 72–84 (Cessey-sur-Tille).

Table 7.2 Taille assessments and taxpayers in Brazey, 1783

Tax paid in individual assessments	Number of taxpayers	Cumulated proportion of tax paid
1. 0.5 to 22.5 l.	164	24.8%
2. 23.3 to 47.5 l.	42	49.9%
3. 47.8 to 83.5 l.	22	74.6%
4. 88.4 to 195.5 l.	12	100.0%

Source: Archives départementales de la Côte-d'Or [ADCO] C5989: Brazey, pied de taille, 1783.

These people were country-dwellers, who owned a few fields and meadows, but who leased, or even sub-leased, most of the land that they worked. In this situation, managing the farms of the Hôpital Général and the Hospice Sainte-Anne was not necessarily their main preoccupation in life. Take for example Claude Fichot, one of the four farmers of the Hôpital Général's farm at Brazey in 1785. He had a house, and owned outright 4.3 hectares of arable both 'good and bad', and 0.17 hectares of good quality meadow. He rented another farm for 350 livres a year from the nuns who ran the Hospice Sainte-Anne, and he sub-let 1.5 hectares of meadow for 22 livres 10 sous. He had eight cows and had undertaken to raise 36 sheep under a separate livestock lease. In addition he paid 577 livres a year to lease the right to collect part of the tithe belonging to the Sainte-Chapelle of Dijon and to the abbey of Cîteaux; half of his share he collected in his own name and half of it as a sub-tenant of another tenant. Claude Fichot paid 79 livres 16 sols in taille, which placed him among the highest taxed people in Brazey, ahead of his farming partners Jean Tissot (51 livres 13 sols) and Philibert Personnier (68 livres), also in the third group. The exception to the rule was the fourth co-farmer, François Fichot, *laboureur*, who paid 157 livres 16 sols. This François Fichot was not the highest-taxed member of the village community, but he was one of the wealthiest: he owned 3.4 hectares of land in the neighbouring community of Saint-Usage, which he leased out to another peasant; and in addition possessed 1.4 hectares of land at Brazey and Montot. He rented 2.1 hectares from his brothers-in-law and was also a tenant on several farms belonging to the Hospice Sainte-Anne, including the splendid farm of Champ-Corbeau (François sublet out a half of this farm to another tenant). He rented the right to take part of the local tithe; he had a house in the little town of Saint-Jean-de-Losne which he rented out, as he also rented out part of another house. On his own farm he had a dozen cows, and leased out two cows and twenty sheep. François was clearly a man of many resources. But farther down in the scale of wealth, as measured by the taille in Brazey, in groups 3 or even group 2, one finds the same multiple activities. Most of these people were farmers or sub-tenants, but less frequently landowners than in the higher groups. These were all, to be sure, entrepreneurial people – they certainly had to be, in order to manage all these different activities – and solid tenants, but in competing for resources, they were caught in an extremely complicated system of property, of farming and sub-farming, and in complex arrangements of land division and networks of parentage made even more confusing by their coexistence with a large number of very small peasant landowners.

There was little or no question here of any physical consolidation of farms, or even of joining together parcels of land. This was a long way from the situation of the *grands fermiers* described in monographs on the Île-de-France (Moriceau, 1992; Moriceau, 1994: 628–645). This fragmentation and division of property among multiple tenants, themselves subtenants and sub-renters are the sign of old and tenacious social structures over which the landlords had little mastery. Just like their peasant tenants, landlords like the Hôpital Général and the Hospice Sainte-Anne were subject to the weight of history and their margin of manoeuvre was small. All this meant that a guaranteed good return on investment for landlords and tenants themselves was not a forgone conclusion, and particularly not when the nature of agriculture changed in the last third of the nineteenth century.

V. The results: landed income and productivity

How well did these two institutions and their farmers perform in these circumstances? A first indication can be gained from the gross income they expected to gain from the farms, as indicated in the leases.[16] Figure 7.8 shows the evolution of the leases on the five farms in the Saint-Jean-de-Losne region. It is similar to that found in the shorter series for eighteenth and nineteenth-century Burgundy, (Saint Jacob, 1960: 618; Germain Martin and Martenot, 1909: 105–107).

It is interesting to compare the evolution of these farm leases with those for some other regions more or less distant from the Dijon area (Figure 7.8), in this instance leases from hospital archives for Upper Normandy (Rouen), Picardy (Compiègne) and Maine (Le Mans). For the purposes of comparison, all leases were converted to comparable units by 'deflating' them with regional grain prices. As is well known, the eighteenth century saw a general rise in rural rents, and this is faithfully reflected in all these regions. However, the data for Normandy show, after a remarkable rise, a decline in mid-century not witnessed elsewhere – an eloquent testimony to the unusual circumstances of Upper Normandy (Le Goff and Sutherland, 2000). But this is an exception; the Burgundy leases behaved much as did those of Le Mans and Compiègne.

When we examine the patterns in the nineteenth century, it is impossible not to notice the relative stagnation in Burgundy from around 1820 onwards; like the other regions, Burgundy enjoyed an agricultural boom in the 1850s and 1860s, but here leases barely returned to the levels reached in the 1820s, during the Bourbon Restoration. Finally the fall in lease income after 1878 is very decisive, much more so than in the other regions – a sign that landlords in the other regions may have been better able to surmount the difficulties of the 'agricultural depression'.

The growth in landlord income in nineteenth-century Burgundy thus pales by comparison with its remarkable increase in the eighteenth century, and the urge to invest in the 1850s should probably be seen as a defensive measure aimed at maintaining whatever could be saved of landed income in the region. This should be seen in the context of falling

[16] See the Appendix for sources and methods used to calculate rents and TFP in this section.

Figure 7.7 Saint-Jean-de-Losne region: money value of rents on five farms

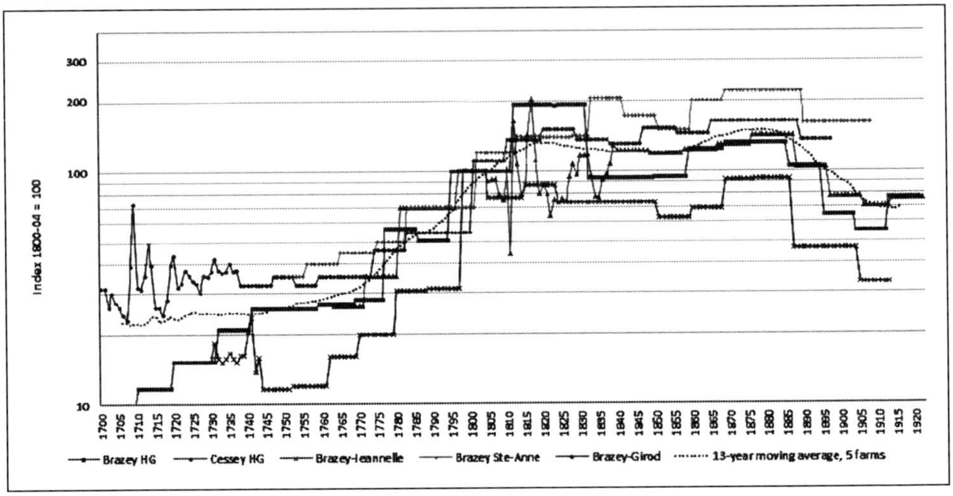

Figure 7.8 Rents in wheat equivalents: regional comparisons

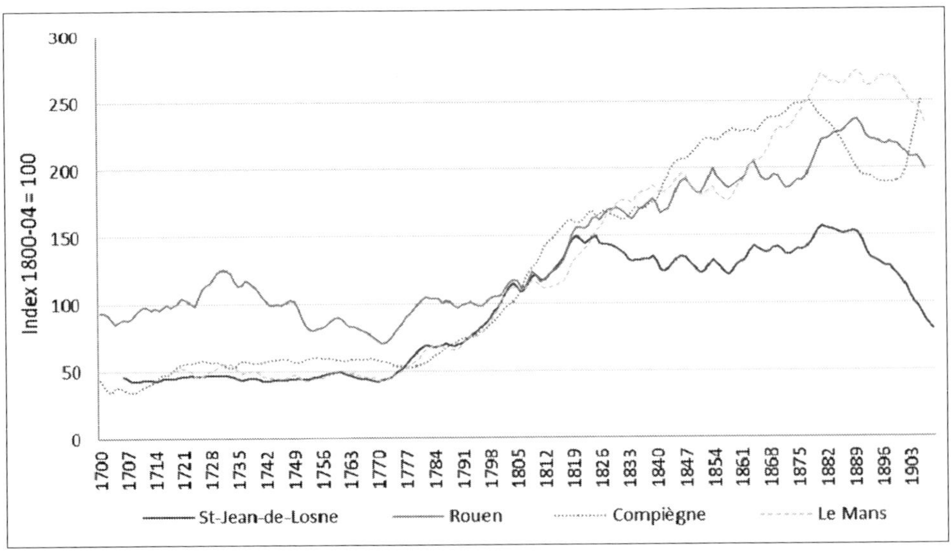

land rents, rising agricultural salaries, and a rural proletariat no longer ready to put up with the meagre salaries of former times – the typical picture of Burgundian agriculture often met with in the official enquirics, treatises and monographs of the second half of the nineteenth century.

Figure 7.9 TFP – regional comparisons

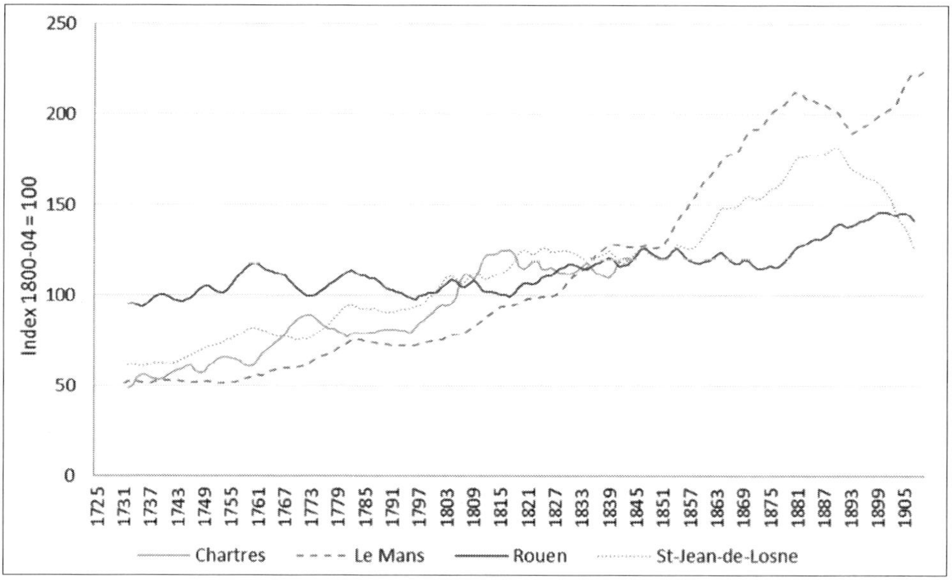

However, it is important to remember that the movement of lease income does not represent the total picture of agriculture in Burgundy or anywhere else. Rent paid to landlords was only one of the elements of production and of agricultural revenue, along with taxes, salaries, equipment, livestock and other components. In order to get a view of the overall evolution of rural production, economic historians sometimes have recourse to calculating *total factor productivity* (TFP). This is a measure which, at least in theory, makes it possible to evaluate the productive capacity of all resources used on a farm and all the revenues they generate, or, to put it another way, the ability of the land to bear the burden of all expenses weighing on it (Hoffman, 1996; Le Goff and Sutherland, 2000).

When we compute this measure and compare it with similar calculations for other regions – in this instance, Chartres, Rouen and Le Mans – two conclusions emerge. First, the quite respectable performance of Burgundian farms down to the first third of the nineteenth century. In this regard, it would seem that the grim picture of the eighteenth-century agricultural economy in Burgundy painted by Pierre de Saint Jacob requires some revision (Saint Jacob, 1960: 397–525). The lease income we have presented, the TFP index, and the comparison of our data with other regions all suggest that the eighteenth century saw strong growth and increased productivity. Burgundy was no exception to what seems to be emerging as a general pattern for eighteenth-century France (Figure 7.9).

Secondly, the usual description of nineteenth-century growth and crisis seems to require some revision. For one thing, the first half of the nineteenth century seems to have seen a prolongation of eighteenth-century growth. In the conclusions to his 1931 thesis for the *Diplôme d'études supérieures*, René Laurent evoked a 'quasi-stagnation of agriculture during the first half of the nineteenth century', leading to a sort of 'impasse' (Laurent, 1931: 216). But although growth slowed down between the Napoleonic Consulate and the end of the July Monarchy (1805–1848), it was never totally interrupted. Moreover the figures for yields given by René Laurent himself demonstrate definite and continual progress throughout that period. Perhaps what occurred in the 1820s and 1830s was a sort of catching-up on reality; as Pierre de Saint Jacob implied when he described the rise in rent income at the very end of the old regime as 'speculative' (Saint Jacob, 1960: 384–393, 466–475, 499–500). The landlords of the late eighteenth century, anticipating rising food prices, managed to raise rents by squeezing their farmers' margins or even (as in the case of the Hôpital Général) by accepting greater arrears from them. Effective increases in landlord income may have taken a little longer to accomplish.

VI. Conclusion

If the traditional historiography paints the eighteenth century against a foreboding landscape, it reserves perhaps even grimmer colours for the second half of the nineteenth century, best summarised by a lapidary description of the region dating from 1909, from the pen of Henry Germain Martin and Paul Martenot: 'The Côte d'Or, as an agricultural centre [was] smitten with all the ills that have weighed so heavily on French agriculture for the last fifty years' (1909: 41). This point of view was echoed, at the other end of the twentieth century, by Jean-Baptiste Viallon, who, speaking of the long period running from the 1850s to the 1970s, wondered, whether Burgundian agriculture had not simply 'failed to modernise' (1977a: 135–142; 1977b).

It would be foolish to deny the difficulties of rural people in Burgundy during the 'great depression' at the end of the nineteenth century. Not only peasants, but also the landlords, including the Hospices de Dijon, suffered from it, as we have seen. Nevertheless, the TFP index seems to contradict this verdict for the first three quarters of the century, down to the 1880s, and because of the methods of calculation used, it may well give an excessively pessimistic picture of the situation even at the very end of the century. The material used to weight the factors employed in the analysis came from the beginning of the nineteenth century and thus ignores the effect of the introduction of new crops, such as the sugar-beet, in the 1860s, and the beginnings of mechanisation; the result is that the TPF curve is probably more depressed than it should be at the end of the period.[17] The qualitative evidence in the monographs and official and semi-official enquiries from the end of the nineteenth and the start of the twentieth century too, has to be read with caution. Despite their overall gloom, these texts are full of empirical observations that suggest a dynamic demand for the agricultural products of the region and a strong sensitivity to the market on the part of agricultural producers and landlords. Studies by local historians seem to confirm this more cheerful impression (François, 1973: 224–226).

This apparent contradiction has two possible causes. First of all, demand seems to have become more unreliable in the course of the nineteenth century. The situation of

[17] This is also a defect common to the other series (Rouen, Le Mans and Chartres) used for comparison here.

Dijon and its region in relation to its traditional markets certainly changed in this period. In the eighteenth century, local demand for agricultural products was reinforced by the general population increase, and accentuated by social diversification driven by the rise of Burgundy vineyards and rural industry. The Saône and the Rhône opened the way to exports towards Lyon and the Midi. In response, tenants, without asking permission from their landlords, converted their meadows into fields and brought in new crops.[18] But in the nineteenth century, bit by bit, these windows of opportunity shrank or closed. Consumer demand from workers in the crisis-ridden metal industries in northern Burgundy declined as did that from winegrowers hit by phlylloxera, and from a demographically stagnant rural population. As for demand from more distant horizons, waterways no longer gave the Burgundy region the same advantages as in the past, now that railways put other regions into direct competition with it. In the meantime, labour supply shrank as rural people moved to towns or fell back on cultivating their own smallholdings.

But the market and demand were not everything; there was also the weight of social and agrarian structures into which, as we have seen, institutional landlords were just as caught up as were the peasants. Until the 1880s, the fragmentation of parcels, compulsory crop-rotations and the recourse to expedients such as the temporary swapping of fields and complex sub-tenancy arrangements did not get greatly in the way of agricultural modernisation. It was only after that difficult transition that they became, not insurmountable, but a perpetual challenge. This is what lay behind the ambient unease and ambiguity that marks the agronomic literature at the end of the nineteenth century. It can even be read in the figures of the account books of the Hospices de Dijon, arid in appearance, but full of answers and ideas for those who take the trouble to ask the right questions.

Bibliography

[Anon.] (1895) 'Prix du blé, et de l'avoine et d'autres denrées depuis 1549 jusqu'en 1870, d'après le registre du greffe du tribunal civil de Langres, concernant les gros fruits', *Bul letin du comité des travaux historiques et scientifiques. Section des sciences économiques et sociales Année 1894*, Paris, pp. 342–350.

Biollay, L. (1886) *Études économiques sur le XVIIIe siècle. Les prix en 1790*, Paris: Guillaumin.

Callerand-Combémorel, J. (1984) 'L'Hospice Sainte-Anne à Dijon de 1633 à 1789', *Annales de Bourgogne*, LVI, pp. 177–181.

Encely, R. (1955) 'Les Prix des céréales sur le marché de Montauban de 1691 à 1789', D.E.S. Lettres, Toulouse, printed in G. Frèche, (ed.), *Les prix des grains, des vins et des légumes à Toulouse (1486–1868)* (Paris, 1967), pp. 101–103.

François, R.J. (1973) 'Agriculture d'hier et d'aujourd'hui. Quelques aspects de son évolution dans un village du Val-de-Saône (1864–1968)', *Annales de Bourgogne*, XLV, pp. 217–237.

George, J. (1920) 'Les Mercuriales d'Angoulême, de Cognac et de Jarnac (1593–1797)', *Bulletin et mémoires de la Société archéologique et historique de la Charente*, pp. 86–93.

[18] AHCD E16 280 (1794) lease of 30 germinal an 2 / 19–04–1795; ACHD E1 42 30 30 floréal and 20 prairial an 2 / 19–05–1794 08–06–1794; B1 64 lease of 20–08–1820; see also François (1973: 218) and Ligeron (1968, 1972, 1975).

Girod, P.-E. (1906) 'Les Subsistances en Bourgogne et particulièrement à Dijon à la fin du XVIIIe siècle, 1774–1789', *Revue bourguignonne*, XVI, pp. 122–128.

Guichard, J. (1911) 'L'Agriculture en Côte-d'Or', in *Dijon et la Côte d'Or en 1911*, Dijon: E. Jacquot.

Germain Martin, H. and Martenot, P. (1909) *Contribution à l'histoire des classes rurales en France au XIXe siècle: La Côte-d'Or, étude d'économie rurale*, Dijon: Damidot frères.

Holderness, B.A. (1989) 'Prices, Productivity and Output', in J. Thirsk, (ed.), *The Agrarian History of England and Wales, VI 1730–1850*, Cambridge: Cambridge University Press, pp. 187–189.

Holderness, B.A. (2000) 'Investment, accumulation and agricultural credit', in J. Thirsk, (ed.), *The Agrarian History of England and Wales*, VII, 1850–1914, Cambridge: Cambridge University Press, vol. 1, pp. 863–929.

Hoffman, Ph.T. (1996) *Growth in a Traditional Society: The French Countryside 1450–1815*, Princeton University Press.

Labrousse, E. (1933) *Esquisse du mouvement des prix et des revenus en France au XVIIIe siècle*, 2 t., Paris: Dalloz.

Labrousse, E., Romano, R. and Dreyvus, F.-G. (1970) *Le Prix du froment en France au temps de la monnaie stable (1726–1913)*, Paris: S.E.V.P.E.N.

Lamarre, C. (2004) *L'Hôpital de Dijon au XVIIIe siècle*, Langres: D. Gueniot.

Laurent, R. (1931) *L'Agriculture en Côte-d'Or pendant la première moitié du XIXe siècle. La Révolution en Côte-d'Or*, Nouvelle série fasc. 7, Dijon: Rebourseau.

Le Goff, T.J.A. (2010) 'Essai sur les biens ruraux de l'Hôpital général de Dijon (XVIIIe-XIXe siècles)' in C. Lamarre, (ed.), *L'Hôpital et la Ville: 800 ans d'histoire hospitalière à Dijon*, Fontaine-les-Dijon: Virgile, pp. 191–209.

Le Goff, T.J.A. and Sutherland, D.M.G. (2000) 'What Can We Learn from Leases? A Preliminary View', *Histoire & Mesure*, XV, 3/4, pp. 289–320.

Ligeron, L. (1968) 'Notes sur la culture du maïs dans la vallée moyenne de la Saône', *Annales de Bourgogne, XL*, pp. 197–204.

Ligeron, L. (1972) 'L'Assolement dans la vallée moyenne de la Saône', *Annales de Bourgogne*, XLIV, pp. 5–47.

Ligeron, L. (1975) 'Le Maïs dans la plaine dijonnaise', *Annales de Bourgogne*, XLVII, pp. 35–38.

Moriceau, J.-M. (1992) *Ferme, entreprise, famille: grande exploitation et changements agricoles: les Chartier: XVIIIe–XXe siècles*, Paris: Éditions de l'EHESS.

Moriceau, J.-M. (1994) *Les Fermiers de l'Ile de France: l'ascension d'un patronat agricole, XVe-XVIIIe siècle*, Paris: Fayard.

Muteau, H. (1906) *L'Évolution économique, au point de vue agricole d'un département français dans le cours du dernier demi-siècle*, Paris: Librairie générale de droit et de jurisprudence.

Saint Jacob, P. de (1960) *Les Paysans de la Bourgogne du Nord au dernier siècle de l'Ancien Régime*, Paris: Les Belles Lettres.

Trueman, B.E.S. (1980) 'Corporate Estate Management: Guy's Hospital Agricultural Estates, 1726–1815', *Agricultural History Review*, XXVIII, pp. 31–44.

Thompson, F.M.L. (1963) *English Landed Society in the Nineteenth Century*, London: Routledge and Kegan Paul.

Turner, M.E., Beckett, J.V. and Afton, B. (1997) *Agricultural Rent in England, 1690–1914*, Cambridge University Press.

Turner, M.E., Beckett, J.V. and Afton, B. (2000) 'Capital' in J. Thirsk, (ed.), *The Agrarian History of England and Wales, VII, 1850–1914*, Cambridge University Press, pp. 2020–2026.

Viallon, J.-B. (1977a) 'L'Agriculture bourguignonne a-t-elle manqué sa modernisation?', *Annales de Bourgogne*, XLIV, pp. 135–142.

Viallon, J.-B. (1977b) *La Croissance agricole en France et en Bourgogne de 1850 à nos jours*, New York: Arno Press.

Appendix: Sources and calculations of TFP index

1. Leases

Saint-Jean-de-Losne region: AHCD B1 63–64 (Hôpital – Général, Brazey, 1573–1921); B1 75–76 (Hôpital Général, Cessey 1738–1912; B3 30–32 (Sainte-Anne – domaine Girod à Brazey, 1699–1899); B3 5 (Sainte-Anne, Aubigny 1747–1887); B3 35 (Sainte-Anne, domaine Jeannelle, 1639–1902).

2. Prices

General
Biollay (1886).
Labrousse (1933).
Labrousse, Romano and Dreyfus (1970).
Archives statistiques du ministère des travaux publics, de l'agriculture et du commerce, publiées par le ministre d'État de ce département (Paris, 1837).
Statistique de la France. Agriculture. Résultats généraux de l'Enquête décennale de 1862. [*2e série, T. XVI. Agriculture*] (Strasbourg, 1870).
Statistique agricole de la France (Algérie et colonies) publiée par le ministre de l'Agriculture. Résultats généraux de l'Enquête décennale de 1882. (Nancy, 1887).
Statistique agricole de la France publiée par le ministre de l'Agriculture. Direction de l'Agriculture. Résultats généraux de l'enquête décennale de 1892 (Paris, 1897).

Regional
Cereals, vegetables etc.:
Encely (1955)
George (1920)
Girod (1906)
[Anon] (1895)

3. Farm animals (mares, donkeys, cows, bulls, sheep, pigs)

1727–1797: ADCO B2 705/1, 705/3, 807/1, 919/3, L 3922 , L 3923 Post-mortem sales of property.
1808–1811: ADCO 1F 38 Statistique du département de la Côte-d'Or (Statistique Vaillant)
1837: *Archives statistiques du ministère des travaux publics…* (Paris, 1837), pp. 186–187 tableau XIV
1843: Reverchon, 'Rapport de M. le Médecin vétérinaire du département de la Côte-d'Or sur la situation des animaux domestiques au 1er septembre 1842', *Journal d'agriculture et d'horticulture. Rédigé et publié par le Comité Central d'Agriculture de la Côte-d'Or*, 7e année (1843), pp. 161–178.
1841, 1845, 1850: Reverchon, 'Statistique animale du département de la Côte-d'Or', *Journal d'agriculture et d'horticulture. Rédigé et publié par le Comité Central d'Agriculture de la Côte-d'Or*, 14e année (1851), pp. 10–23, 31–43.
1862: *Statistique de la France. Agriculture. Résultats généraux de l'Enquête décennale de 1862.*
1882: *Statistique agricole de la France… Résultats généraux de l'Enquête décennale de 1882.*
1892: *Statistique agricole de la France…Résultats généraux de l'enquête décennale de 1892.*
Interpolation for gaps by linear regression.

4. Labour Costs

1726–1789: Wages for 1790 from Biollay for Dijon, used as base for values derived for earlier years by regression using national figures from Labrousse (1933: 493).
1808–1812: ADCO 1F 38 Statistique du department de la Côte-d'Or (Statistique Vaillant).
1852: Laurent (1931: 49) (arrondissement de Dijon).
1868, 1909: Germain Martin & Martenot (1909: 526) (journalier à Viévigne, belle saison).
1882, 1892: Muteau (1906: 141–142) (journalier en été).
1912: *Enquête sur les salaires agricoles* (Paris: Imprimerie nationale, 1912).

5. Taxes

Taken from real figures from eight communities in the Saint-Jean-de-Losne region (Aisery, Aubigny, Bessey, Brazey-en-Plaine, Echigey, Esbarres, Montot and Trouhans).
Taille: ADCO C4885–5111 (1695–1786).
Dixième: ADCO C5319 (1744–1756).
Vingtième: ADCO C5849–51 (1750–90).
Contribution foncière: ADCO L2055 (1792); 2P4 B4 (1803); 1F 38 (1807–09); 2P6 (1820–1823), 2P12 (1839–1840); 2P17 (1855–1856); 2P20 (1861–1862); 2P27 (1875–1876); 2P 40 (1893).
These were all related to the surfaces for the communes as reported in *Journal d'agriculture et d'horticulture. Rédigé et publié par le Comité Central d'Agriculture de la Côte-d'Or* (1820).

6. Factor shares

The basis for calculation was ADCO 1F 38 Statistique du département de la Côte-d'Or (Statistique Vaillant).

Average output and input (physical product multiplied by prices) were calculated for years 1808–1812. Total input was assumed as follows: operating costs 30%; land: 40%; labour 30%.

Costs for land were calculated as the sum of tithes/hectare, rent/hectare and tax/hectare. Tithes were estimated as 25% of rent/hectare; rents and taxes were calculated from real figures as in the notes on sources above.

8 Productivity and farm management. The hospitals of Le Mans, 1661–1913

Donald M.G. Sutherland, University of Maryland

I. Introduction

The agricultural surveys of the nineteenth century are a wonderful source of information about production and productivity. Jean-Claude Toutain, for example, has used these records to examine the problem of growth in enormous detail (Toutain, 1992–93). The problem with the enquiries, however, is they date well after the 'agricultural revolution' in France had begun. Attempts to reconstruct the history of productivity before the enquiry of 1840 requires the use of scattered sources. Until very recently, there was a consensus that breakthroughs in productivity did not occur in the Old Regime. Productivity in France fluctuated within fixed limits, limits that did not change from the Middle Ages until after the Revolution (Morineau, 1971; B. H. Slicher van Bath, 1964: 280–1; Leroy Ladurie, 1973: 271–80; Goy and Le Roy Ladurie, 1982: 174–5; Béaur, 2000: 64–6).[1] The question merits another look. One of the goals of this paper is to show that at least in one region, the agricultural revolution began much sooner.

For all their enormous detail, the nineteenth-century surveys also do not explain how this productivity increase occurred. It is possible to outline the changes and even establish a chronology, but how the general surveys do not explore very deeply the question of how the 'agricultural revolution' occurred, who financed it, and the successive stages through which it passed (See for example, Désert, 1975, 3, 221–34).[2]

One source that would address this question would be the archives of hospitals. No private landlord could match a hospital's record keeping. Estate papers like these also provide a glimpse into management techniques, investment decisions, and financial strategies. Like many hospitals, the archives of the two hospitals of Le Mans contain leases and other papers that go back to the beginning of the seventeenth century and which finally disappear with the sale of the last farm in 1957! The Hôtel Dieu and the Hôpital général of Le Mans owned about thirty farms or *métairies*, and in the carefully preserved dossiers of each one, there are innumerable leases, correspondence, invoices, receipts, and so on.[3] Although several other hospitals could be chosen to illustrate the point, the archives of these two hospitals do record the beginnings of the 'agricultural revolution,' something that would be more difficult to do for some other regions. Secondly, the province of

[1] Long term stability in grain yields was the norm in western Europe as a whole (see B. H. Slicher van Bath). E. Le Roy Ladurie has argued for a very long stability until about 1750 with a true growth began. See also Gérard Béaur who concludes that the 'révolution agricole reste un mystère.'

[2] Gabriel Désert attributes expansion to rural out-migration which stimulated mechanisation of agriculture. This is only part of the story.

[3] For methods and sources see Sutherland, 2002 and appendix.

Upper Maine had a destiny as a cattle raising region and so offers a useful counterpoint to the more standard vision of the wheat growing plains of Picardy and the Ile de France.

II. Total factor productivity

Examining grain yields and analyzing the curve of tithe records have been the standard methods of estimating productivity before the nineteenth century. A more recent technique is to calculate the Total Factor Productivity (TFP). The justification for inferring productivity through the manipulation of prices has been done elsewhere, notably by Philip Hoffman and George Grantham (Hoffman, 1996; Grantham, 1996). One of the problems in the method is to know what weight to attach to the factors of production. Attaching too great a weight, for example, to animal production risks distorting the results and especially the chronology of change. In the case of the hospitals of Le Mans, pure luck led to the discovery of a document that avoids this danger and so to a reasonable calculation of the proper weights of the factors of production. While making its calculations of the land tax in the early nineteenth century, the *administration des contributions directes* used the farm of La Grève in the village of Etival to verify its estimates of net taxable revenue.4 In the event, La Grève belonged to the hospital of Le Mans and its file in the hospital archives contains a continuous series of leases that date from the reign of Louis XIV and which continue until the end of the Fourth Republic.[5] We also have the *inventaire apres décès* of one of the farmers taken ten years before the fiscal verification.[6] As everyone knows, this document lists the personal possessions of the farmer, especially the financial papers which give a brief summary of the marriage contract, debts, and so on, his tools, his animals, his stocks of grain, etc. This inventory as well as the fiscal verification can be used to calculate an approximate budget for the farmer and thus the weights to use in calculating the TFP.

The first conclusion from our calculations is the long period of stability between 1661 and the Seven Years War. This confirms Philip Hoffman's conclusion who also argued for stability outside the Paris basin in the same period. It is possible to see the effects of individual bad years or their aftermath like 1694, 1710, or 1741, but on the whole, the curve is fairly flat until well into the eighteenth century. Since the line does not appear to be responsive to obvious major events like wars, one suspects other factors might be at work. It seems reasonable to suppose that this might have something to do with taxation, local and regional markets, and population stability, but information of this sort is very scattered and unsystematic for this region. Still, the curve is surprising for what is not there. Whatever the case, from the 1760s until the Revolution, the curve began an unmistakable upswing. It never fell below the series mean again and from the beginning until 1790, TFP grew by 40%.

This climb continued until the eve of the First World War, once again oblivious to the major events of national history. The long climb of the TFP curve from the 1760s to 1914 was almost continuous with the clear exception of the Great Depression after the mid-1870s. In spite of these setbacks, this was a remarkable take-off. From 1800 until

---

4 AD, Sarthe, 3P 1903, expertise communale.

5 *Ibid.*, HG 1207.

6 *Ibid.*, 4E XVII, 73–4, inventory of 27 prairial An VII.

Figure 8.1 Hospital of Le Mans (Sarthe) – Approximate location of the farms

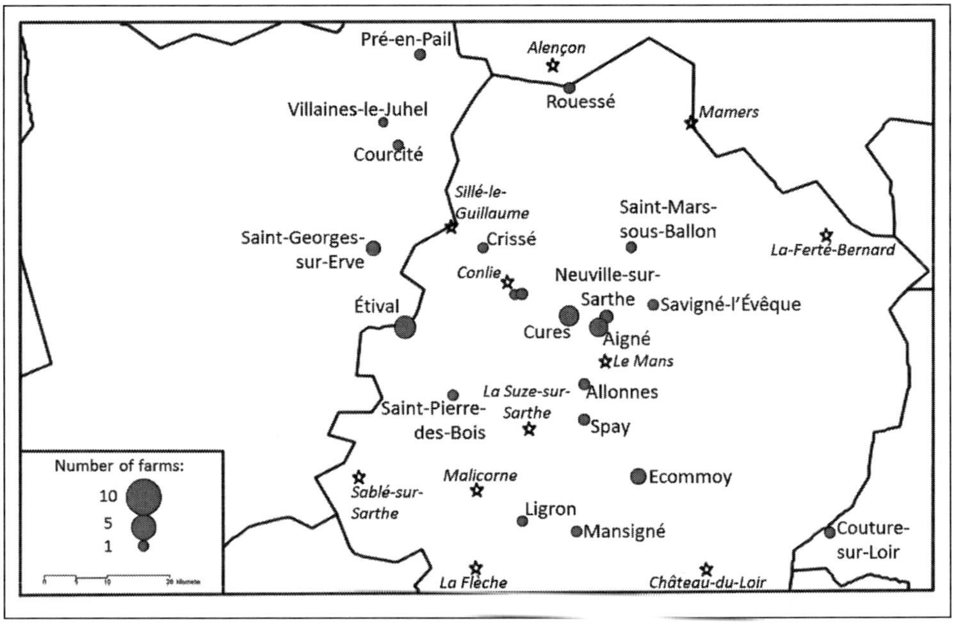

Figure 8.2 Total Factor Productivity, Hospitals of Le Mans, 1661–1789

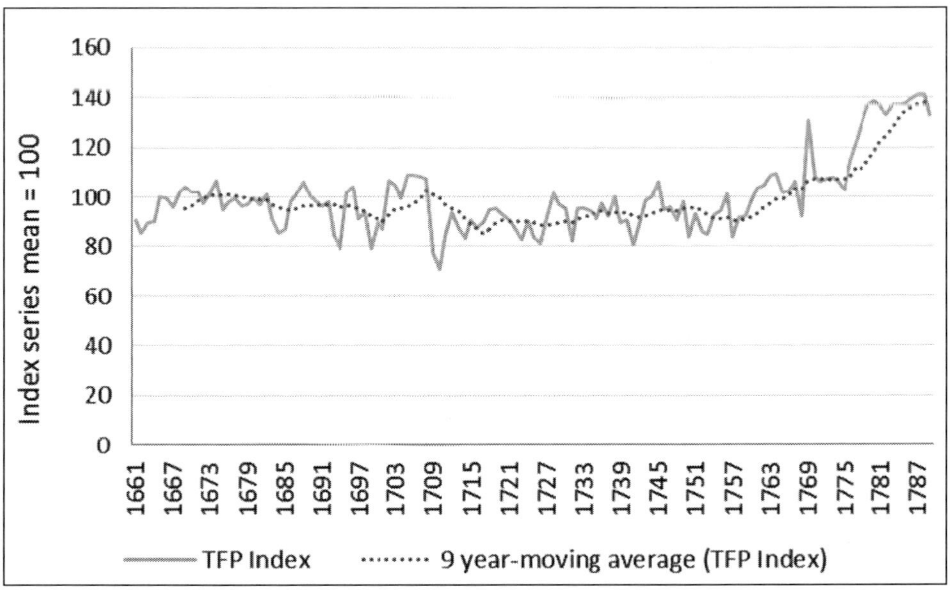

Sources: 'Peasants, Lords, and Leviathan: Winners and Losers from the Abolition of French Feudalism, 1780–1820,' *Journal of Economic History*, LXII, no. 2, (March 2002), 1–24.

Figure 8.3 Total factor productivity, hospitals of Le Mans, 1661–1913

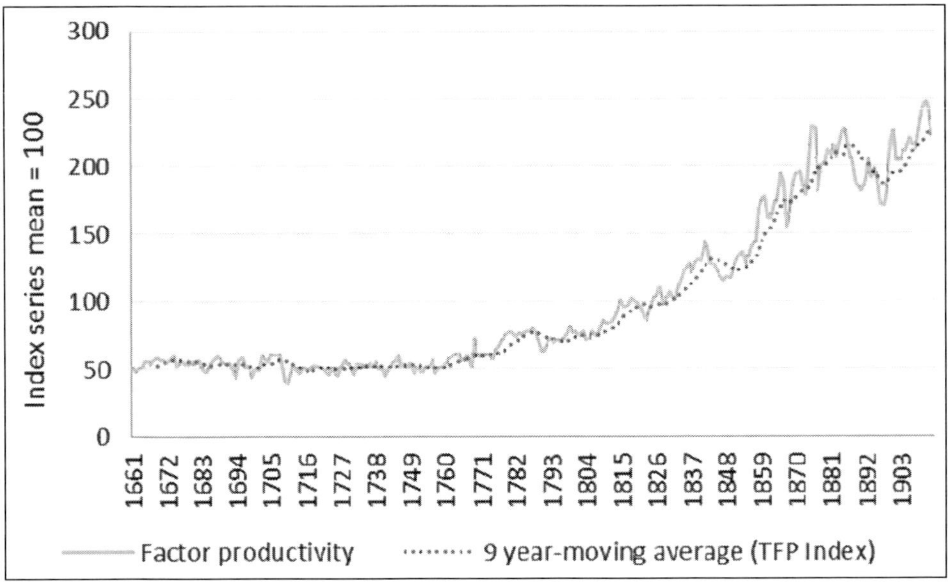

Sources: 'Peasants, Lords, and Leviathan: Winners and Losers from the Abolition of French Feudalism, 1780–1820,' *Journal of Economic History*, lxii, no. 2, (March 2002), 1–24.
Note: Index Series mean = 100.

the dawn of the Great War, total factor productivity tripled. That is, annual growth was a little less than 1%, and sometimes more.

It remains to explain this growth. We must leave aside the question of local and long distance markets because the sources we have used do not contain this information. It is an important question, however, because in a society where sources of credit were so limited, profits that were generated from markets must have been an important source of investment. For the sake of argument, let us assume a closed world of proprietor and farmer. Where did the sources that financed the growth of the Old Regime and the post-revolutionary period come from?

III. Landowners' investments

In the Anglo-Saxon world there is a myth that goes back at least to the Anglomania of the eighteenth century that French landowners did not invest in their properties. This hypothesis presupposes that it was their historic responsibility to lead the agricultural revolution but in most cases, their ability to so was quite limited. Even so, they did invest. The administrators of the Hospitals of Le Mans demanded specific types of work from their farmers that usually involved maintenance of the fences and buildings. Thus, they demanded so many days repairing hedges and fences, maintaining roofs, repairing barns, trimming and planting fruit trees, and so on. Possibly because the verification of these kinds of requirements was time consuming, other proprietors took the responsibility of repairs themselves. In these cases, it is possible to estimate how much the cost of maintenance and repairs were. It was impressive. For example, the Hôtel Dieu of Paris spent 20% of its annual revenues in 1789 in repairs, and 12% in 1818. These were high rates especially given the impression the literature gives that proprietors were simple parasites (Fosseyeux, 1912: 172–73; anon., 1823: 167–170).

Investment beyond maintenance seems to have been rare in the earlier period. But for the hospitals of Le Mans, an investment in the fixed capital of the farms began in the 1830s with the construction of new granges, stables, cider presses, dwellings and so on. In four farms for which there is specific information, the administrators spent 13,000 francs, or about 3000 francs per farm. The pace of new construction fell off until the early twentieth century. Then, improvements and new construction on three farms cost a little more than 30,000 francs, or about 10,000 francs per farm.

These are, of course, large sums, but given the probable rate of amortisation, the contribution of proprietors to the agricultural revolution was relatively modest. Moreover, these investments were undertaken to satisfy the needs and probably the demands of the farmers. Enlarging buildings, for example, offered more shelter to bigger herds of animals or more space to stock grains. Thus, it was the investment of the farmers which contributed the most to the transformation of agriculture.

IV. Farms' animals

At the beginning at least, this investment was also rather modest. According to the *inventaire apres décès* of the richest farmers of the village of Etival-lès-Le Mans – that is, those who left property worth more than 1000 livres/francs – the animal population of these farms was low and, except for pigs, was even declining.

The decline in the number of horses can be explained no doubt by the improvement in tools, as we shall see shortly. The decline in the number of sheep was dramatic. More and more, farmers were abandoning sheep raising. Before the Revolution, half the farmers owned sheep; after 1820, only a quarter of them did. No doubt this was a reflection of the successful competition of the nearby Beauce and of Normandy, both of which were concentrating on sheep farming. But even if the number of farm animals remained stable, their value rose, often dramatically.

Table 8.1 Animal populations per farm in Etival, 1769–1850

Date	Cows	Oxen	Calves	Pigs	Poultry	Horses	Sheep
1769–1788	3.8	5.8	4.3	2.5	14.5	5.7	17.0
1789–1810	3.0	2.6	2.4	1.7	7.0	2.6	6.9
1820–1850	2.3	3.9	2.3	3.9	13.6	2.4	3.5

Sources: AD Sarthe, 4E supp., XVII 36–101, *inventaires après décès.*

Table 8.2 Value of individual farm animals, village of Etival, 1769–1850 (livres)

Date	Cows	Oxen	Calves	Pigs	Poultry	Horses	Sheep
1769–1788	186.6	536.0	113.3	59.2	12.8	245.9	100.9
1789–1810	150.4	423.9	93.6	84.9	14.3	192.1	80.0
1820–1850	255.1	635.5	127.4	119.4	28.9	457.5	93.2

Sources: AD Sarthe, 4E supp., XVII 36–101, *inventaires après décès.*

Unfortunately, there is no direct evidence of why this might be so but there are a number of possibilities: younger and stronger animals; healthier animals; heavier animals because of better nourishment. Whatever the case, more expensive animals required more money to buy replacements and, of course, more profits when it came time to sell them.

There was also a slow improvement in the equipment available to the farmers of Etival. Before 1820, the level of equipment was remarkably low. The price was so low, in fact, that most, if not all tools must have been made of wood. Pioger, our exemplary farmer, had only two ploughs worth only 20 livres. This began to change with the Restoration. For example, René Papin had a harrow with 'iron teeth' in 1821.[7] Mathurin Avice had an iron harrow also; indeed almost all his tools were made of iron.[8] Françoise Dutertre even had an English-made tool, a cart *à la Malborough* which was worth the unprecedented sum of 300 francs.[9]

Where did the money come from that financed these improvements, as modest as they were? Outside family networks, the credit market was almost non-existent. The inventories indicate that debt levels were modest, and, so to speak, 'normal': arrears on taxes and rents; wages owed to farm labourers; and debts owed to merchants and local artisans. Thus the 'agricultural revolution' of the Upper Maine was financed by the profits of the farmers themselves. Since the account books of the farmers have not turned up, the question must remain there.

V. Improvements of the farm after 1850

The inventories become more and more silent on the possessions of the deceased after 1850. But one source does exist that permits us to continue the story. These are the reports of the judges of the local agricultural society which gave prizes to the best farmers.[10] This is a valuable source because it allows an insight into the social and cultural values of the epoch. These reports address themselves of an old debate among French agronomists about what the characteristics were of a good farmer. Certain themes never changed. Thus our judges were equally obsessed with the cleanliness of stables and granges, and by the

[7] *Ibid.*, 4E XVII/99, inventory of 5 June 1821.

[8] *Ibid.*, 4E XVII/100, inventory of 11–12 February 1822.

[9] *Ibid.*, 4E CIV/11, inventory of 2 March 1830.

[10] Bulletin de la Société d'agriculture, sciences et arts de la Sarthe, various dates from 1850 to 1900.

good order of account books. The farmers' wives were always praised for their fine house keeping. By the middle of the nineteenth century, however, several new themes began to appear. The judges awarded prizes for the possession of agricultural machines, for intelligent cattle raising, or for the care in applying fertiliser. They praised innovations like the construction of sluices, construction of cisterns to capture animal urine and rain water, or the crossing of local breeds with English Durhams, or with horses from Normandy. Of course, outstanding farmers like these were exceptions. Relative to the entire department of the Sarthe, they produced three times more cows, horses and pigs than their neighbours.

They also worked the larger properties, where the department as a whole encompassed medium and small properties. But large property was distinguished by more than just size. It devoted more of its resources to cattle raising than small and medium sized properties. They were also relatively more important producers of potatoes and turnips as well as clover, colza and lucern.

This sort of land use explains the relative importance of these farms. It also explains the construction of new buildings on these farms: they required more shelter for larger herds.

We should also note that it was always possible to win a prize without advanced equipment. Of course, a majority of prize-winners had expensive tools like articulated harrows, root cutters and so on. But the number of labourers was much more important. Winning farmers employed many more men and women than their ancestors did. The farm of Bures (62 ha), for example, employed six male and two female farmhands, five or six labourers, and at harvest time, eight more labourers. By contrast, in 1777, the farmer

Table 8.3 Animal populations per farm on 48 prize-winning farms and all farms in the Sarthe, 1862–1877

	Cows	Oxen	Calves	Pigs	Horses	Sheep
Farms	9.3	7.1	9.6	9.8	6.3	18.1
Sarthe	3.2	0.4	1.2	3.8	1.9	2.2

Sources: Line 1: *Bulletin de la Société d'agriculture, sciences et arts de la Sarthe* various dates from 1850 to 1900 13. Line 2: *Enquête agricole*, 1862.

Table 8.4 Land uses of prize-winning farms and all farms in the Sarthe (%), 1862–1877

	Wheat	Barley / Oats	Other Grain	Meadow	Forage	Fodder	Fallow	Other
Farms	16.9	18.4	–	26.9	25.9	7.7	2.3	1.9
Sarthe	13.4	14.2	8.7	23.6	1.0	11.1	19.9	8.1

Sources: Line 1: *Bulletin de la Société d'agriculture, sciences et arts de la Sarthe* various dates from 1850 to 1900 13. Line 2: *Enquête agricole*, 1862.

of La Cantinnière (69 ha) left derisory debts to just one female servant and to two men. There are many examples of this difference.[11]

VI. Conclusion

At this point, the sources become vaguer but it is time to conclude. It is evident that the greatest contribution to the transformation of the countryside around Le Mans came from the tenant farmers. In effect, from the Revolution onwards, productivity ran ahead of rents. No doubt, throughout the period, proprietors had reason to be content, but as time went on, agricultural transformation benefitted those who worked on the soil, the tenant farmers and the hired workers. After so many centuries of struggle and misery, the agricultural revolution began to write an optimistic story.

Bibliography

[Anon.] (1823) *Résumé des comptes moraux et administratifs des hôpitaux et hospices de Paris et des divers établissements de charité et d'administration qui en dépendent pour l'année 1822*, Paris: Imprimerie Madame Huzard.

D'Avenel (1894) *Histoire économique de la propriété, des salaires, des denrées, et de tous les prix en général, depuis l'an 1200 jusqu'en l'an 1800*, vol. 4, Paris: Imprimerie Nationale.

Béaur, G. (2000) *Histoire agraire de la France au XVIIIe siècle: Inerties et changements dans les campagnes françaises entre 1715 et 1815*, vol. 139, Paris: SEDES.

Désert, G. (1975) 'Les Facteurs de l'expansion,' in G. Duby and A. Wallon, (eds), *Histoire de la France rurale*, vol. 3, Paris: Seuil.

Désert, G. (1977) *Une Société rurale au XIXe siècle: les paysans du Calvados, 1815–1895*, New York: Arno Press.

Fosseyeux, M. (1912) *L'Hôtel Dieu de Paris au XVIIe et au XVIIIe siècle*, Paris: Berger-Levrault.

Goy, J. and Le Roy Ladurie, E. (1982) *Tithe and agrarian history from the fourteenth to the nineteenth centuries: an essay in comparative history*, Cambridge (Cambridgeshire), New York-Paris: Cambridge University Press and Editions de la Maison des Sciences de l'Homme.

Grantham, G. (1996) 'The French Agricultural Capital Stock, 1789–1914', *Research in Economic History*, 16, pp. 39–83.

Hauser, H. (1936) *Recherches et documents sur l'histoire des prix en France de 1500 à 1800*, Paris: Presses modernes.

Hoffman, Ph.T. (1996) *Growth in a Traditional Societé: the French Countryside, 1450–1815*, Princeton University Press.

---

[11] AD Sarthe, 4E XVII/ 45, 4, 26 February 1778; *Bulletin de la Société d'agriculture... Sarthe*, xx (1869–70): 219.

Labrousse, E., Romano, R. and Dreyfus, F.-G. (1970) *Le Prix du froment en France au temps de la monnaie stable (1726–1913), réédition de grands tableaux statistiques*, Monnaie, conjoncture 9, Paris: S.E.V.P.E.N.

Le Roy Ladurie, E. (1973) 'Dîmes et produit net agricole (XVe–XVIIIe siècle),' in *Le territoire de l'historien*, Paris: Gallimard.

Morineau, M. (1971) *Les Faux-Semblants d'un démarrage économique, agriculture et démographie en France au XVIIIe siècle, Cahiers Des Annales*, 30, Paris: Armand Colin.

Sauvy, A. (1928) 'Indice annuel des prix de gros en France de 1820 à 1857 et aperçu sur les mouvements des prix depuis 1790', *Bulletin de la Statistique générale de la France*, XVII.

Slicher van Bath, B.H. (1964) *The Agrarian history of Western Europe*, New York: St. Martin's Press.

Sutherland, D.M.G. (2002) 'Peasants, Lords, and Leviathan: Winners and Losers from the Abolition of French Feudalism, 1780–1820', *Journal of Economic History*, LXII, 2, pp. 1–24.

Toutain, J.-C. (1992–93) *La Production agricole de la France de 1810 à 1990: départements et régions: croissance, productivité, structures*, Économies et sociétés 27.

Appendix: Sources and Methods

The calculation of TFP is based on the model in Philip T. Hoffman, 1996. It is possible to derive factor shares, land use, a breakdown of the farm by the fertility of its various types of land, both by arable and by pasture; and the rotations of land for the Le Mans series thanks to on the inventory after death of Martin Pioger, a tenant farmer of the farm of La Grève that was owned by the hospital of Le Mans. He died in 1799.[12] The archives of the hospital itself allow a reconstruction of the rent, but above all the 'expertise communale' of the village of Etival, Pioger's home village[13] chose the farm of La Grève, among others, as a check on its calculations of net revenue for the village as a whole.

Prices

Livestock prices are taken from several dozen inventories after death.[14] For the milk production of an eighteenth-century cow, see AD, Sarthe, HG 637, 'Recette ou profit [...] année commune prise sur 6 ans, 1783–1788,' based on a log kept by Sister B [...] The milk was then converted to butter.

Prices for all grains are local prices from the Le Mans *mercuriale*, for 1783–90, and 1797–1803, as listed in the 'expertise communale' of Etival.[15] Wheat prices falling outside that period have been spliced to the series by using the prices in Labrousse, Romano, and Dreyfus, 1970 for the Sarthe. Butter has been valued at 1.30 francs per kilogram which is the national price in 1776–1800 given by d'Avenel, 1894: 378, 595. For the period following, see the butter prices given in Désert, 1977: 757. Hay, wool, and green beans

[12] AD, Sarthe 4E XVII, 73–4, inventory of 27 prairial An VII.
[13] AD, Sarthe, 3P 1903.
[14] AD, Sarthe, 4E XVII.
[15] AD, Sarthe, 3P 1903.

(the last a proxy for garden production) prices derive from Sauvy, 1928; where it has not been possible to correlate these prices with other known prices, I have substituted the average of the known series for the unknowns. Wood prices: Hauser, 1936: 149–50. Gaps in the series (and there always is a gap between 1793 and 1797), have been filled in by linear interpolation.

Rents

AD, Sarthe, Le Mans , HG 479: Sommier des recettes des rentes et fermes, 1765–An V; HG 606: Rentes et fermes, An V–1810; HG 638: Sommier du revenu des fermes, An XI–1823; plus the dossiers of the individual farms in series HG: 1204–07, 1218, 1224–25, 1231, 1233–34, 1240, 1271–73, 1282–84, 1289, 1295, 1299, 1303, 1321–22, 1332, 1340–41, 1350, 1354, 1357, 1387–88, 1407.

9 The growth of plough team productivity during the nineteenth century in the Île-de-France*

Jean-Michel Chevet, INRA, ADES-UMR 5185, Bordeaux

I. Introduction

The growth of agricultural labour productivity in the eighteenth and nineteenth centuries is at the heart of the debates on growth, whether in France or Great Britain. Each country, in its historiography, holds up the other as a negative example. Increased agricultural labour productivity is often cited as the main reason for the economic growth of England. According to this theory, economies in labour led to the formation of the working class, though this leaves aside the fact that the English population rose from five million to thirty-three million inhabitants in two centuries – a far more effective contribution to the making of that working class. In addition, France was thought to have remained a nation of peasants, in contrast to an industrialised England, because its agriculture and agricultural productivity were less efficient. In this context, agricultural mechanisation is thought to have been one of the most important variables in explaining the improvement of labour productivity in agriculture.

This version of development is built on hypothetical-deductive[1] and ideological premises, and raises more questions than it answers. For example, it has been asserted that the labour employed for a given surface unit shrank greatly in England between 1700 and 1850. However, contemporary evidence does not seem to show this, and the fact that production intensified at this period seems to suggest that the opposite was more likely to be true.[2] Since the answers to these questions are contradictory, it appears more worthwhile to take a new look at the problem, using different sources and approaches. In particular it seems necessary to see how productivity gains were linked to improvements in tillage implements, and to the mechanisation of agriculture, by computing these gains. It is absolutely necessary to use new sources for this purpose, since official agricultural enquiries on the subject of labour, such as that of 1852, were marred by errors because they did not take all the farm tasks into account.

Because of the doubts that arise in studying the history of growth, both of the increase in production and the increase in productivity, it is desirable to use other kinds of information, and discard models hastily built from insufficiently reliable and, above all, too fragmentary data (Allen, 1992). We also have to employ a much finer level of analysis than the overall approaches used hitherto to determine the growth of labour productivity in different countries (Wrigley, 1987). Only when the productivity of labour has been

---

* Translated by Judith Le Goff.

1 The use of this method is not peculiar to economists.

2 For a discussion of all these questions (Allen, 1982; Béaur, 1994; Campbell and Overton, 1991; Chevet, 1994; Grantham, 1991; Hoffman, 1996; Moriceau and Postel-Vinay, 1992).

evaluated and estimated on a new basis, at the local level, will it be possible to put forward some generalisations, far different from those of lazy intellects and vague concepts.[3]

Agricultural accounts, when they are complete and reliable, as in the cereal-growing regions, make it possible to do this,[4] as they include data on labour. Even though this information is almost complete, however, it is still necessary to make some hypotheses when processing the data, and complete them from other sources, such as treatises on agronomy, which became more detailed during the nineteenth century, and the very explicit agricultural theses dating from the turn of the century. It is wrong to think that these documents reflect a different reality from that of the accounts, which – according to some – have their own logic. Those who hold this position forget that the data in these complementary documents are themselves based on accounting records from the farms. Thus any document that casts new light can serve to complete those that are already used. This, I believe, is how agricultural accounts should be used.

However, is it possible to extrapolate from one, or a few, sets of farm accounts to a whole region, which is assumed to be homogenous? What errors are likely to be made in doing this? In short, are the accounts representative or are they only useful for the very small world they describe? It seems to me that the variations from one farm to another, in a given region, are not so great as they are said to be. It should be remembered that the many enquiries made during the eighteenth and nineteenth centuries, which give overall information, usually employed uncritically, were put together from pieces of information which were no more precise, and indeed often less so (because obtained by word of mouth from a few well known farmers), and no more numerous than those we find in farm accounts. Refusing to extrapolate the information from farm accounts to the whole region would, logically, lead to excluding these enquiries themselves. And that, it should be evident, would leave economic history in the silence of the tomb. On the other hand, attempting to construct a model on the base of the accounts, as is done in this paper, will make it possible to confirm or invalidate the data in the enquiries, which is particularly necessary for the study of labour in the nineteenth century. When properly understood, accounts, even those which resemble diaries (*livres de raison*) can make it possible to construct indices, to avoid the pitfalls of surface appearances, to bypass the dead ends of certain methods and thus help renew our present research perspectives.

This article will follow this method, though it does not attempt an overall evaluation of agricultural labour productivity.[5] It will only seek to evaluate the change in the productivity of labour furnished by one of the essential components of farms, the draught team, and only in the French context. To do this, we shall take account of the growth in

---

[3] The use of the terms 'macro' and 'micro', which refer to economics and economic theories, has been avoided deliberately, as has the intermediate zone between the two, which does not exist in economic history.

[4] The rare accounts from tenant farms are, of course, more informative than those from sharecropping regions, which is easy to understand. For this reason, there is more need to turn to other sources when using the latter type of document than the former. This is the price of seeking to understand ancient societies.

[5] For an overall estimate of labour on cereal farms (Chevet, 1994).

area tilled because of the increased cultivation of fallow land. This increase took place at a slow pace during the eighteenth and the first half of the nineteenth centuries, but much more rapidly afterwards.[6]

The improvement in productivity of draught teams in various types of tillage before seeding had three elements: an increase in the pulling power of the team, an improvement in the ploughing implements (reducing friction by using a better line of pull), and the specialisation of tilling implements which, in certain cases, meant that the tasks were performed more quickly. This was the case when grubbers were used instead of ploughs, for example. These improvements, and combinations of them, will be evaluated in the remainder of the paper, using the documents already mentioned.[7]

II. Growth of the surface ploughed by teams in the cereal-growing regions of northeast France[8]

Around 1700 and during most of the eighteenth century, it is relatively simple to determine the extent of ploughed land as well as the total surface area ploughed in a year in the cereal-growing regions. The farms were roughly divided into three sections; the fallow, which was to be sown with wheat, was ploughed three times, sometimes a little more, while the second section, which had previously grown wheat and was to be sown with oats, was ploughed only once. From this it can be estimated that the surface ploughed each year, for a farm of 100 hectares, was 133 hectares, more or less. Progressively, as artificial meadows were slowly introduced during the eighteenth century, the total area of plough land decreased slightly as the artificial meadows remained in place several years, particularly in the case of alfalfa. On the other hand, the amount of ploughing on land under wheat increased slightly. Thus, around 1800, the ploughed area on a farm of 100 hectares can be estimated at 95 ha, and the total surface area ploughed in a year at 155 hectares (see Table 9.1).[9] There appears to have been a slight increase in the work on the land during the course of the century.

Determining the area of ploughing carried out in a year became more difficult during the course of the nineteenth century because of different crop choices made by farmers, some turning to sugar beet production, others to artificial meadows. For this reason, it is necessary to use several examples in order to give an account of the various situations (Heuzé, 1862).

---

[6] On the use of agricultural accounts, Béaur and Chevet (2000).

[7] This work is based on a certain number of sources that will be fully cited later. They consist of agricultural accounts, many articles in the *Journal d'Agriculture Pratique*, the Primes d'Honneur, agriculture theses from the early twentieth century, and agricultural treatises (Chevet, 1994, 1997, 2009).

[8] Only ploughing and equivalent tasks are considered in this study. A forthcoming paper will include harrowing and rolling, which were also carried out more frequently as the century went on.

[9] These calculations were made on the base of a sample of farms in Brie. The proportion of fallow could be even less, as in the Ile-de-France, where it was only about 26%. (Moriceau, 1988, 1994).

Figure 9.1 Cited places in the Île-de-France

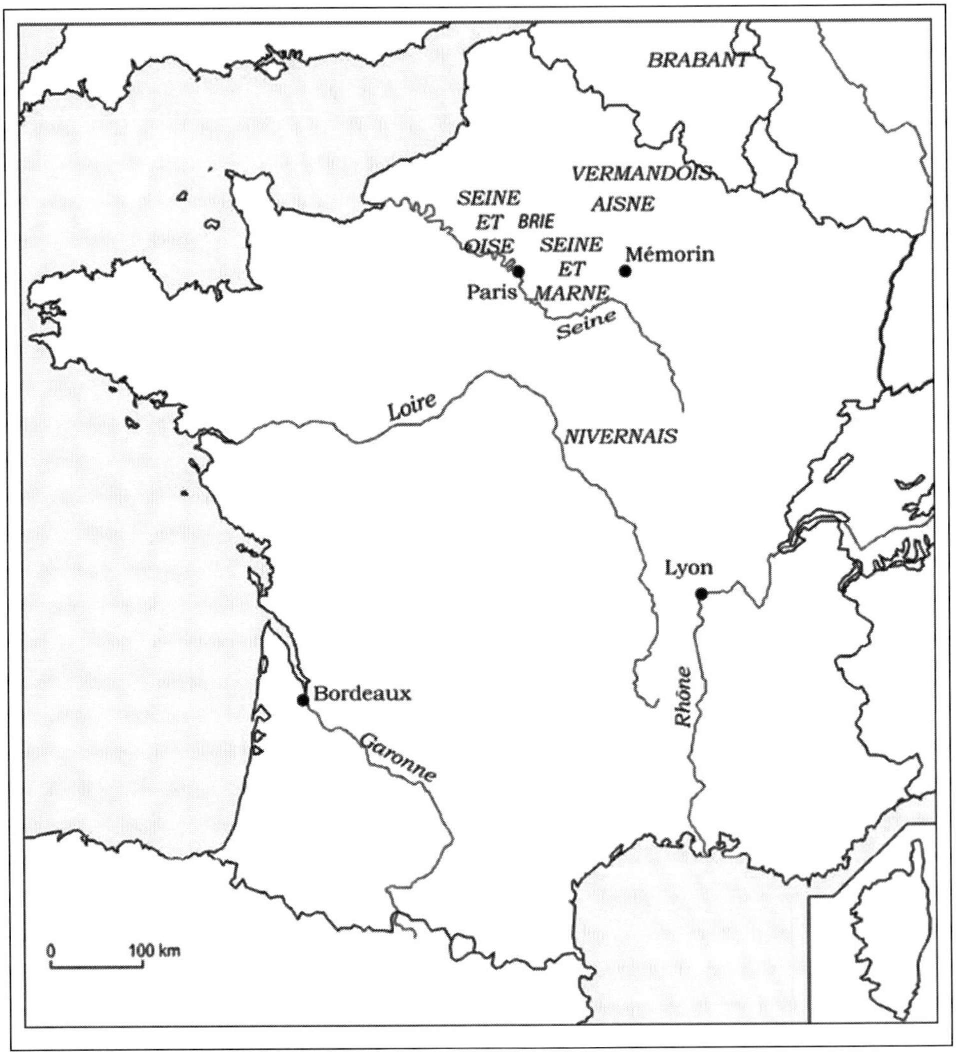

By the end of the nineteenth century, the fallow field had practically disappeared from the farms studied here, as can be seen in the sample (see Tables 9.1 and 9.3 to 9.6) and the crop rotation had been considerably modified. On the farms mainly engaged in sugar production, beets led off the rotation and received the largest number of ploughings. The preparation of the ground for their cultivation began with stubble removal, either with a stubble cultivator or a grubber. This was followed by a deep ploughing, then an ordinary

Table 9.1 Area ploughed on a typical 100 hectares farm in the Paris region at the beginning of the nineteenth century[10]

	Area of farm	Area ploughed	*Area of ploughing carried out*
Wheat	36	36	*126*
Spring sowing	29	29	*29*
Fallow	30	30	*0*
Total of ploughed land	95	95	*155*
Artificial meadows	5	0	*0*
Total	*100*	*95*	*155*

Source: Chevet, 1994; Moriceau, 1994.

ploughing, and then by the use of a scarifier, once or sometimes twice. As the amount of land devoted to beets varied, this meant that all the parcels of land did not follow the same crop rotation. Thus, the area destined for wheat after beets was only given one ploughing and one passage with the scarifier, while for oats sown after wheat the ground was prepared with a stubble cultivator, followed by a plough and a scarifier. On the sugar beet farms the section to be sown with wheat thus received less tillage than that for oats, although the opposite had previously been the case. But when wheat was sown on fallow land, the land received the same tilling as oats. On the other hand, where there was little or no sugar beet, the ground was prepared for wheat with a stubble cultivator, deep plough, ordinary plough and two uses of the scarifier, that is five kinds of tilling instead of three or three and a half during the eighteenth century.[11]

At the beginning of the nineteenth century, as during the eighteenth century, all ploughing was done with an ordinary plough, usually the local type.[12] At the end of the nineteenth century, some of the tasks were done with grubbers or scarifiers, some with stubble cultivators or multi-blade ploughs. These new implements with several blades made it possible to save time. The scarifier was designed to cut the earth at an angle perpendicular to the surface. In order to achieve this, the cutting parts of the teeth were shaped like a coulter. The grubber was used for cutting roots. The working part of it was made up of flat shares with cutting edges. It served to slice off a shallow crust of soil horizontally. In a way, two of the working parts of the plough were made into two separate implements, with many more active parts. The use of these new instruments spread in the first half of the nineteenth century, even at the end of the eighteenth century where the soil was light. Sometimes, on the sugar beet farms, deep ploughing was done with steam engines. However, it seems that, in most cases, teams of oxen were reintroduced for this

[10] That part of the artificial meadow, which, each year, went in and out of the crop rotation must also be taken into account.

[11] On farms where fallow was still practiced, land destined for wheat was ploughed four times.

[12] In some cases a plough without a coulter, or even without a share, would be used.

kind of ploughing. As for the multi-blade ploughs and stubble cultivators, they were not used until the end of the nineteenth century, when some of the problems of draught had been solved (Chevet, 1994: 124–127).[13]

This specialisation meant that the number of tilling implements used on a given surface increased. So, while there was one plough for about 30 hectares in the eighteenth century, at the end of the nineteenth there was one for about 35 ha. When the other tilling implements, grubbers, scarifiers etc., are included this figure falls below the thirty hectares of the eighteenth century. This can be seen in the example of a 140 hectares farm in Brie. It had a stubble cultivator, four Brabant ploughs, three grubbers and a scarifier. This works out as one Brabant plough for 36 hectares, and 16 hectares per tilling implement (Moriceau, 1988).

Tables 9.3 to 9.5 synthesise the preceding information on ploughing. The second column in the tables gives the extent of each crop while the third column gives the surface ploughed for each crop. The fourth column is the total area of ploughing carried out. This figure is obtained by multiplying the area of the crop by the number of ploughings or equivalent operations in the year. The last column converts the work of all the tilling implements to the equivalent in ordinary ploughing. To obtain these figures it is assumed that all preparatory tilling was with an ordinary plough as at the beginning of the nineteenth century, in this case a reversible Brabant plough. Although this calculation is partly theoretical, it makes it possible to measure the effects of implement specialisation.

The surface area worked equivalent to ordinary ploughing has been calculated. To obtain these results it was first necessary to convert each task into the equivalent in ordinary ploughing (see Table 9.2). In the second column of this table is the area worked in a day by each tilling implement. A stubble cultivator, for instance, would work 0.80 ha of ground while an ordinary plough would turn 0.50 to 0.55 ha in a day. It can already be seen that the new implements made it possible to work a greater area in a day because only the area worked in deep ploughing is less. In the third column, the equivalent in ordinary ploughing of each task has been calculated. Thus, to continue with the same example, the stubble cultivation would correspond to 0.66 of ordinary ploughing, meaning that a stubble cultivator would do the 'same work' as a plough in 0.66 of a day, that is, a gain of about a third of a day.

The different equivalents in the third column of Table 9.2 were then used to calculate the area of land prepared for each of the different crops, assuming that the preparation was done with an ordinary plough. Thus, for example, a surface of 10 ha to be sown with wheat, is entered as 20 ha, an ordinary ploughing and a scarifier, in the third column of figures of Tables 9.3 to 9.6, but only for 13.5 in the last column of the same tables, since the work of the scarifier only counts as 0.35 of ordinary ploughing.

Tables 9.3 to 9.5 show that specialisation of tilling implements (grubbers and scarifiers) made it possible to work the land better over a given time. For the farm of Mémorin, the area of land ploughed would have been 64.4 ha thanks to the new

[13] For a discussion of the use of new farm implements see Chevet (1994) and Moriceau (2002).

implements, an increase of 40.5%. Table 9.4 gives an increase of 80% and Table 9.5 one of 34.5% (Chevet, 1994).

Examples of farm crop distributions at the end of the nineteenth century and estimates of areas ploughed for a theoretic area:

Table 9.2 Average day's work, in ha, carried out by different tilling implements at the end of the nineteenth century[14]

	Area worked in one day (in ha)	Area worked converted to equivalent in ordinary ploughing
Stubble cultivator	0.80	0.660
Ordinary plough	0.50 to 0.55	1.000
Deep plough	0.40	1.310
Scarifier	1.50	0.350
Grubber	2.50	0.210
Croskill	3.00	0.175

Source: Heuzé, 1889: 239–240; Lecouteux, 1879: 137–160; Paris, 1978.

Table 9.3 Total area ploughed each year on the farm of Mémorin (Seine-et-Marne)

	Area	Area ploughed	Area of ploughing done	Area of ploughing work in equivalent of ordinary ploughing
Sugar beet	42.8	42.8	128.40	129.47
Wheat	67.1	67.1	172.75	97.35
Oats	60.6	60.6	181.80	110.60
Total of ploughed land	170.5	170.5	482.95	337.41
Artificial meadows	42.4	0.0	0.00	0.00
Total usable agricultural surface	212.9	0.0	0.00	0.00
For 100 ha	100.0	80.1	222.85	158.48

Source: Chevet, 1994.

[14] Preliminary calculations, which need to be refined, show that, for a given area, a team made up 20% of labour on a farm at the beginning of the nineteenth century. A hundred years later, because of mechanisation of other segments of work, which mainly helped to reduce the labour in harvesting and transporting crops, the team made up about 34% of the labour. Over the same period of time, ploughing made up 56% of the work of teams around 1800, but no more than 20% at the end of the nineteenth century.

Table 9.4 Total area ploughed each year on a farm in the Vermandois (Aisne)

	Area	Area ploughed	Area of ploughing done	Area of ploughing work in equivalent of ordinary ploughing
Sugar beet	18	18	54	37.98
Wheat	57	57	216	107.50
Oats	88	88	334	177.00
Flax	8	8	24	15.60
Annual fodder	36	36	75	52.68
Total of ploughed land	207	207	703	390.76
Artificial meadows	43	0	0	0.00
Total usable agricultural surface	250	0	0	0.00
For 100 ha	100	82.8	281.2	156.30

Source: Chevet, 1994.

Table 9.5 Total area ploughed each year on ten farms (agriculture theses)[15]

	Area	Area ploughed	Area of ploughing done	Area of ploughing work in equivalent of ordinary ploughing
Sugar beet	67	67	201	202.67
Wheat	106	106	251	115.58
Oats	64	64	178	113.65
Total of ploughed land	237	237	630	467.90
Artificial meadows	42	0	0	0.00
Total usable agricultural surface	279	0	0	0.00
For 100 ha	100	84.95	225.81	167.71

Source: Chevet, 1994.

It can be seen that this gain was greater on farms where the area of beets cultivated was small. This can partly be explained by the fact that growing beets involved deep ploughing, which was the equivalent of 1.31 ordinary ploughing. Thus the new tilling implements

[15] Sample made up from agriculture theses from the beginning of the twentieth century. They all concerned northeast France.

allowed a significant gain of time. This would have been about 34% from when the ground had been prepared with only an ordinary plough. The gain must then be considered to be real, as the intensification of production necessarily involves extra preparation of the soil.

These gains are not the only ones to be considered, since they only take account of the specialisation of tilling implements and not of the improvements in the so-called ordinary plough over the course of the nineteenth century. The saving of time allowed by the improvement of that plough is the next question to be discussed.

III. The results of improvements to the ordinary plough in terms of productivity gains

Table 9.6 shows the evolution of area ploughed, for 100 hectares, during the nineteenth century. It can be seen from our sample, that the area ploughed in a year decreased by 2.2%. This was due to the increase in artificial meadows, which were not sowed, and consequently not ploughed, each year. The area of ploughings carried out is the sum of all plough-like tilling carried out as has been previously discussed. This increased considerably, going from 155 ha at the beginning of the century to approximately 245 ha around 1900, which was an increase of 58%. In contrast, the area as equivalent of ordinary ploughing only increased 4%, going from 155 ha to about 161 ha. As we have seen, this was because the plough-like tilling with grubbers, scarifiers and stubble cultivators, took up less time, on an equal area, than ordinary ploughing. It was because plough-like tilling was faster that the area ploughed increased. Thus, over the course of a century, because it was given more tilling overall, the land was worked better.

It can also be seen from Table 9.6, that the number of days ploughing, for 100 ha, went from 387 to 307, a decrease of about 20% over a century. This increased productivity of the plough team cannot be attributed to the specialisation of tilling implements, since the area of land ploughed, in equivalent of ordinary ploughing, only increased by 4%. This saving of 80 days in the course of the century allowed teams to be used more in carts, to transport the increased production of grains, straw, hay and new crops. It is necessary to look at areas other than specialisation of tilling implements to explain this saving. This point will be considered in the next section. Two areas need to be explored: team productivity and technical improvements in tilling implements.

Table 9.6 Changes in team productivity in terms of area ploughed in a year during the nineteenth century for an area of 100 ha

	Area ploughed	Area of ploughing done	Area of ploughing work in equivalent of ordinary ploughing	Number of days ploughing
1800	95.0	155.0	155.0	387.0
1900	92.9	244.9	161.3	307.0
Variation	– 2.2 %	+58 %	+4 %	–20.7 %

Source: Calculated from the previous tables

IV. The development of team productivity during the nineteenth century

Before starting to analyse this subject, it is necessary to make a detour by way of the notion of labour with the help of the mathematician Euler. Euler demonstrated, and even set it out in a formula, that the amount of work done by a team was the result of three factors. First the speed, which was intrinsically dependent on the kind of animal used, horses being faster than oxen, but also on the size of the animals, a small horse having, on average, less speed than a larger one. The second factor of team productivity was power. A team of three horses, for example, would be less powerful than one of four horses. The same was true when the weight of the animals varied: the heavier the horse, the greater its power. As these two factors, size and weight, could have helped to change the work of the team, it is necessary to analyse what they really were during the nineteenth century. The third and last element did not concern the team, but the tractive resistance of the tilling instruments: ploughs, harrows, etc. Many factors affected this resistance. The team had to overcome the varying amounts of friction from the implements. Whether the line of pull was well designed or not also contributed to the resistance and the weight of the implement pulled. Tractive resistance also depended on the size of the strip of earth turned: the wider it was, the more labour it took (Gasparin, 1847: 41–50, 67–72; De Gaita, 1857).[16]

When we come to consider the development of the pulling strength and speed of the team there are two different situations. In the cereal-growing regions, the farms stayed loyal to horse teams. In contrast, in the sugar beet regions, from the middle of the nineteenth century on, ox teams, and even mixed teams, began to appear. On these farms, the oxen were bought from regions of plough oxen, such as the Nivernais, as they were used to heavy work.[17] They were then fattened, mostly with beet pulp from the sugar beet factories, and sold in the Paris markets.

It is relatively simple to establish the numbers of horses and oxen, and how they changed over the nineteenth century. This is not the case, however, for the weight of horses at the beginning of the nineteenth century, where the rare information comes from works on agronomy. However, a comparison with changes in the weight of other animals (cows and pigs) confirms what will be said about horses.[18]

V. Changes in the draught force of farms during the nineteenth century

In the cereal-growing plains of northeast France, the horse had long been the plough animal of choice. With the development of sugar beet growing, oxen reappeared as plough and draught animals, particularly for deep ploughing on the land destined for beets, and for pulling the heavy carts in which they were transported. On the other hand, where

[16] Without going into details, the productivity of a team is calculated by multiplying four-ninths of the weight of the team by two-thirds of the speed, the total then being reduced by a fifth.
[17] As the ploughmen refused to drive oxen, it was also necessary to bring ox-drivers from these regions.
[18] Other lines of research, food rations, for example, will be investigated in the future.

Table 9.7 Growth in the pulling power of teams on farms using only horses

	1800	*1900*	*Variation %*
Area worked by team, in ha	40.0	40.00 to 45.00	Max. = 12.5
Number of horses per 100 ha	7.5	9.13	21.5
Number of horses to a team	3.0	3.60 to 4.10	21.5 to 37.0
Weight of a horse in kg	450.0	775.00	72.0
Weight of horses per 100 ha, in kg	3,375.0	7,077.00	109.5
Weight of horses by team, in kg	1,350.0	2,830.00 to 3,185.00	110.0 to 136.0

Source: Calculated from Chevet, 1994; Moriceau, 1994; Ringelman, 1887; Ministère de l'agriculture, 1929.

there were no beets, the horse was still the preferred animal in the plough as well as for wagons and market deliveries. Where oxen were used the two types of draught were complementary to each other. During the period being studied, the draught force of the team underwent great changes, which will now be considered.

The results for the first situation are summarised in Table 9.7. It can be seen that the surface area worked by a team had scarcely varied in a century. In some farms it increased by 5 ha, an increase of 12.5%, in others it remained the same.[19] The number of horses per 100 ha, went from 7.5 to 9.13, an increase of more than 21%. So a team made up of 3 horses around 1800 would have had around 3.6 to 4.1 at the end of the nineteenth century, an increase of 21.5 to 37%. During the same period the weight of horses increased considerably. A horse that would have weighed 450 kg[20] around 1800, sometimes less, weighed 775 kg around 1900, an increase of 72%. Thus the weight of horses per 100 ha doubled in the course of the century, which suggests how great the productivity increase of the team was. However, all the available power of the team was not used simultaneously, some of the horses being substitutes, or working alongside at rolling. Because of this, the real increase in team productivity would have been about 70%, which is still considerable. As well as the increase in weight, there was also an increase in size, as horses were generally taller in the withers, but this is difficult to measure.[21]

On the farms where oxen were reintroduced, the area worked by a team (see Table 9.8), which was 40 ha in 1800, fell to 28 ha in 1900, a decrease of 30%. This decrease is due to the large numbers of oxen, which were slower than horses, but which were needed for the deep ploughing essential in growing sugar beets. This decrease is not entirely realistic,

[19] The sample used in these calculations was taken from Brie, which may explain the differences noted with the sample from the Ile de France, used by J.-M. Moriceau (Moriceau, 1988).
[20] The figure given by A. Tessier for the Beauce has been used, on the grounds that the learned abbé would surely have chosen an average figure. However, other authors give lower weights for the same period. For this reason, the weight in 1800 may have been overestimated (Tessier, 1793).
[21] Although I am convinced this is the case it is not possible at the moment to supply the figures to prove it.

Table 9.8 Changes in pulling power on farms with horses and oxen

	1800	1900	Variation %
Area per team	40.0	28	– 30
Number of horses per 100 ha	7.5	7	– 6.5
Weight of a horse in kg	450.0	705	56.5
Number of oxen per 100 ha	0.0	10	
Weight of an ox in kg	0.0	785	
Number of draught animals	7.5	17	126.5
Weight of horses in kg	3,375.0	4,935	46
Weight of oxen in kg	0.0	7,850	
Total weight of animals in kg	3,375.0	12,785	279
Weight of animals per team in kg	1,350.0	3,580	165

Source: Calculated from Chevet, 1994; Moriceau, 1994; Ringelman, 1887; Ministère de l'agriculture, 1929.

since not all the animals were engaged in ploughing at the same time, and carting was also important on this type of farm. These changes can be evaluated more precisely by taking into account the number of (horse) ploughmen and ox drivers.[22] On these farms, the number of horses decreased by 6.5% but their weight increased from 450 kg to 707 kg, that is, 56.5%, a little less than on the farms that did not grow sugar beet.

The weight of the horses per 100 ha, went from 2,275 kg to 4,935 kg, an increase of 46%. For the same area, around 1900, there were, in addition to the horses, 10 oxen, making a total of 17 draught animals, an increase of 126.5%. In all, there was an increase of 279% in the live weight of draught animals. The increase in the live weight of animals was thus much greater than that on farms not growing sugar beet.

As it was rare for the teams to contain both horses and oxen it is difficult to do the same calculation as above to find out the increase in power of the team. In fact, the area of 28 ha per team is a theoretic figure derived from the average of areas worked by teams of horses and of oxen.[23] However it is worth keeping, as it has the merit of emphasising the average increase of pulling power of 165%, much greater than that on non-sugar beet farms, which, it should be remembered, was 110 to 136%.

An example from Brie will help to demonstrate the development of pulling power on the beet growing farms. In that region, at the beginning of the nineteenth century, a farm of 240 ha had six teams of three to four horses. Around 1900, a similar farm of 224 ha, had two teams of four horses and three teams of three horses, plus three teams of six oxen. In this example, the increase in power of the horse teams, due to their weight and not to

[22] The areas ploughed in Tables 9.7 and 9.8 are somcwhat different from those given in Section I. This is because the figures are averages and the samples were not exactly alike.
[23] This will be discussed in detail at a later date, when the various types of tilling are studied.

their number, was 57% on average. Adding the heavier ox teams more than doubled the weight of animals available for a given surface. Thus a team which in 1800 had a power of 1,350 kg, had 2,115 to 2,820 kg, according to the number of horses, and 4,767 kg when it was pulled by oxen.

It cannot be denied that the draught power of teams in the cereal-growing plains increased considerably during the nineteenth century. Because they overcame the tractive resistance of the plough more easily, the teams did the ploughing more quickly. It is also likely that the stature of these animals increased slightly over the same period, due to better selection, though this has not yet been proven.[24] This gain also contributed to the increase in speed. In an indirect way the increase in pulling power helped to increase the speed of the teams, which explains why the number of ploughing days decreased (Table 9.6) although the work of preparation for sowing increased. In the same way as the increase in the pulling power of the teams, the improvements to the ploughs also meant that the speed of ploughing increased by reducing the tractive resistance. This is the next topic to consider.

VI. Changes in tilling implements resistance to pulling during the nineteenth century

At the end of the eighteenth century, and perhaps even before then, attempts were made to improve to ploughs in order to reduce their resistance to the draught animals. This was particularly true in the French Revolution, a period of great scarcity of horses and manpower (whether this was real or imaginary is not important here). However, it was only during the first half of the nineteenth century that these improvements really took hold, and the new, industrial, ploughs did not appear until after 1850. This was also the period when the use of new tilling implements, the grubbers and scarifiers that have been discussed above, became common. These improvements and changes were made possible by the development of one of the branches of physics, mechanics. The invention of the dynamometer,[25] at around the same time, should also be mentioned as it made it possible to assess the progress achieved by comparing the resistance of different ploughs to traction.

We can get some idea of the progress made in reducing the resistance of ploughs to pulling from agronomy treatises. Better still, since there is information on the traditional Brie plough, it is possible to see what improvements were made to it throughout the nineteenth century. The characteristics of the three types of plough in pulling trials have been compared (Table 9.9); the first type was the old Brie plough which had hardly been modified during the nineteenth century, or even the preceding centuries, the second was an old plough from the region west of Paris as modified by Pluchet, a well-known local farmer, the third, the Leloup was also a modified plough. The dimensions of the strip of earth turned by the three ploughs were not identical, but it is not known if that was owing to the type of plough. For that reason, it has been necessary to calculate the labour

[24] The speed of a horse measuring 1.47 m was 1.23 m/second while that of a horse of 1.62 m was 1.35 m/second.

[25] But were they all properly calibrated?

necessary to move a cubic metre of soil. This trial showed that the Brie plough needed the greatest pulling force. However, the resistance of the Brie plough may have been somewhat exaggerated in order to emphasise the progress made, or there may have been a topographical error. The improvements introduced by Pluchet and Leloup would not explain a reduction of 36% in the resistance to traction, so it may perhaps be better to take 290 kgm as the resistance instead of the 390 given in the literature. For this reason we have used both figures in Table 9.9 and the question remains moot.

Even after making this adjustment, the Brie plough was the most difficult of the three to put in motion. It came far behind the Pluchet, which, however, ploughed more deeply during the trials, 14 cm as opposed to 19 cm, although the width of the strip was identical. Though the Leloup plough took first place for average draught that was because it made the shallowest furrow of the three. When the labour need to turn a cubic metre of earth is counted it can be seen that the Pluchet took least labour: 2.3 to 1.47 times less than the traditional plough and 1.3 times less than the Leloup.

If the accounts of contemporaries are to be believed, this reduction came from improvements to certain parts of the plough. The first was the share, a kind of wedge cutting into the ground; one side was shortened and the other given a more aerodynamic shape. The other essential improvement was to make sure the line of pull was as close as possible to the point of resistance of the plough. Guillaume seems to have introduced this improvement,[26] but he was only applying to ploughs what he had seen done with gun carriages during the Napoleonic wars. The mouldboards were also shaped so as to turn the earth over better and, as time went on, were made out of sheet metal or cast iron, but that did not necessarily mean that friction was reduced. The wheels were also improved which, taken together with the improvements in the actual process of turning the soil, helped to reduce friction, and thus the resistance to traction. Finally, better-constructed ploughs weighed less, which also reduced friction. A better-designed plough was better balanced and easier to control. The ploughman thus had less difficulty in keeping it in the furrow, which also reduced friction.

From the beginning of the nineteenth century on, traditional ploughs were considerably improved by rural artisans, and by farmers spurred on by the spirit of progress. It is

Table 9.9 Draught force necessary to pull various types of old ploughs (in kgm, kilogram-metres – the contemporary unity of measurement)

Type of plough	Width of strip worked	Average draught	Labour to turn 1 m^3 of soil	Weight of plough in kg.
Brie	0.14 * 0.26	390 {290}	12,660 {7,967}	
Leloup	0.12 * 0.28	243	7,235	112
Pluchet	0.19 * 0.26	267	5,415	146

Source: De Guaita, 1857; Laboulaye, 1872; Ringelman, 1887.

[26] He invented the plough which is named after him and one of the first two-blades, which seems to have been used rarely because of its defects.

important to understand that these improvements to the traditional plough owed nothing to industrial production, and were independent of it.

The industrial workshops took up the progress in making new machines in iron and cast iron. The reversible Brabant plough, which used an old idea,[27] became much more common during this period, as did the ploughs adapted to the deep cultivation necessary for beets. However, these ploughs could only be used where the land was drained so that the ploughing could be done on the flat.

Taken as a whole, these improvements made it possible to plough more deeply than in the past (see Tables 9.9 and 9.10). The new ploughs, apart from the Bonnet, designed specifically for deep ploughing, turned the earth to a depth of 16 to 19 cm, more than what than the old Brie plough could do.[28] Only the Pluchet ploughed so deeply. The width of earth turned was, on the other hand, identical; only the Froger ploughed wider. Thus it was not the increased width that explains the increase in the amount of land that the new ploughs could work in a day. The new ploughs tended to be lighter than the older ones, even though they were made entirely of iron and had two plough bodies. This also helped to reduce friction and thus pull resistance.

Still according to the results of the trials, it can be seen that the Pluchet plough, in the first half of the nineteenth century, reduced the pull resistance by about 35%. At the end of the century, the reversible Brabant added to the reduction in draught force. This reduction was 26% for the Ransomes and 80% for the Ball, when compared with the Pluchet.[29] Obviously too much weight must not be placed on these figures, but it seems certain that all kinds of improvements had contributed to reducing considerably the pull resistance of the ploughs. Thus it can be seen that the old ploughs worked slowly and to a

Table 9.10 Draught force necessary to pull different types of new ploughs, in kgm

Type of plough	Width of strip	Average draught	Labour to turn 1 m^3	Weight of plough
Bonnet	0.27 * 0.25	402	5,956	79
Howard	0.17 * 0.23	164	4,194	112
Ransomes	0.18 * 0.23	160	3,865	122
Bella	0.17 * 0.25	135	3,176	
Froger	0.16 * 0.34	173	3,176	130
Ball	0.19 * 0.22	121	2,895	130

Source: Laboulaye, 1879.

27 It seems that this plough may have been used from the 1830s in the Aisne.
28 The ploughing depths given in the trials (see tables) are not what the ploughs were capable of doing. The reversible Brabant was designed for ploughing to a depth of 15 to 20 cm. It is difficult to get an exact idea of the ploughing depth as this varied according to the specific situation.
29 Different results would be obtained using average draught.

Table 9.11 Draught force necessary to pull three types of specialised ploughs, in kgm

Type of plough	Average draught	Work to turn 1 m^3 of soil	Weight of plough in kg
Two blade	253	6,800	
Five-blade scarifier	347 to 505	3,856 to 5,000	299
Seven-blade scarifier	638 to 836	4,352 to 5,300	319

Source: Laboulaye, 1872; Ringelman, 1887.

lesser depth than the new ploughs, particularly as the teams had become more powerful. This explains the reduction in the number of ploughings in Table 9.6.

We have seen that in the nineteenth century much ploughing work was done with grubbers, scarifiers, two-blade and multi-blade ploughs. To take one example, the scarifier only penetrated to a depth of 8–13 cm, but operated over a width of 1.15–1.45 m, a width that increased as time went on. In one operation this implement worked a strip of earth five to six times wider than a plough. Also, it did not take much more draught force because it was pulled by 2 to 4 horses, a number that varied according to the difficulty of the task (4 were needed for old alfalfa for instance).

Even in the least favourable case, the scarifier needed less pull force than that used by the Pluchet, 5,000 to 5,300 against 5,400 kgm, even though it was much heavier than a plough. The old teams could have pulled these machines, and they did so in the light soils north of Paris. But before their use became general in the second half of the nineteenth century they needed to be improved. These new machines were born from the ingenuity of farmers and country artisans, but their use did not become general until the second half of the nineteenth century. Thanks to the specialisation they helped to bring to work in the fields, they made a considerable saving on labour possible.

VII. Conclusion

This study of ploughing work shows that the specialisation of ploughing implements, the increase in the draught force of the team and improvements in pulling of tilling implements, by reducing friction for example, had a big impact on labour productivity, for a growing number of tasks were done in a number of days which decreased significantly during the nineteenth century. In a forthcoming study it will be seen that the other tasks on the farm also underwent a great reduction of labour. This was particularly so for the harvest machines, the reapers, reaper-binders, beet-harvesters and so forth. During the nineteenth century, and particularly during the second half of the century, there were two factors influencing employment in agriculture. On one side, intensification of production increased the need for labour, on the other, mechanisation tended to reduce it. The work of quantifying this double movement will continue after this study of ploughing to cover, even if approximately, the saving in workforce at the level of the farm, a group of farms, and even, by extrapolation, a region. This quantification will make it possible to measure the impact of mechanisation on the rural exodus and industrialisation.

The chronology of the arrival, and more importantly, the generalisation of the new tilling implements on the farms must be identified more precisely. It must also, where possible, be linked to a quantification of farm labour by using agricultural accounts and treatises on agriculture, for if we want to find out about the evolution of agricultural productivity, we have to get beyond vague impressionistic propositions which justify all and any sorts of assertions. In order to achieve this, historians of the countryside in the nineteenth, and also the twentieth, century must stop continually rewriting myths.

We must try to find out exactly what was happening on the farms. All the new implements did not appear at the same time and all of them did not have the same effect on employment. To be sure, an improvement in ploughs can be seen during the first half of the nineteenth century, and it is possible to find some cultivators and grubbers from the middle of the nineteenth century on. However, it seems that at that time the greatest improvements were still to come, in the last quarter of the century for the reapers.

It is reasonable to think that these various improvements lead to a reduction of employment mainly after mid-century, and that it was felt progressively as the improvement of ploughing implements proceeded. For this reason and also because of the progressive cultivation of the fallow and the increase in the volume of production, the amount of employment scarcely decreased during the first half of the century. It must even have increased, as another study has tried to show.

Illustrations

Illustration 9.1. Brie plough, made by M. Leloup

Source: De Guaita, 1857: 450.

Illustration 9.2. M. Pluchet's plough

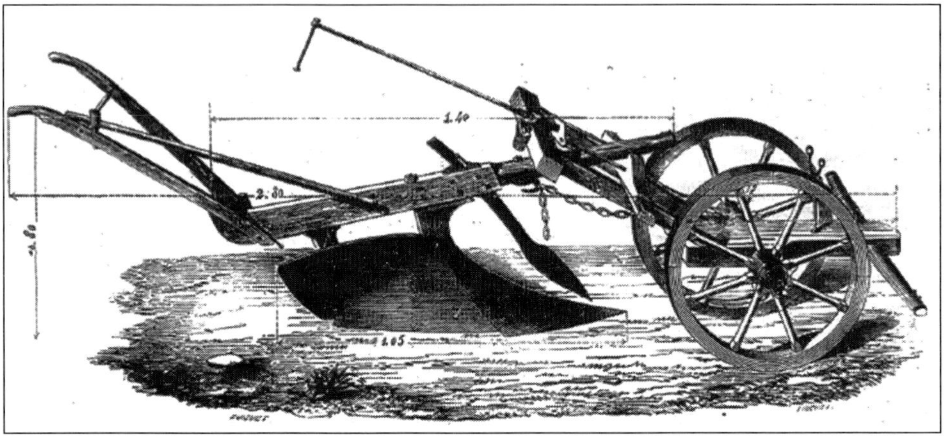

Source: De Guaita, 1857: 455.

Illustration 9.3. Grubber (*extirpateur*)

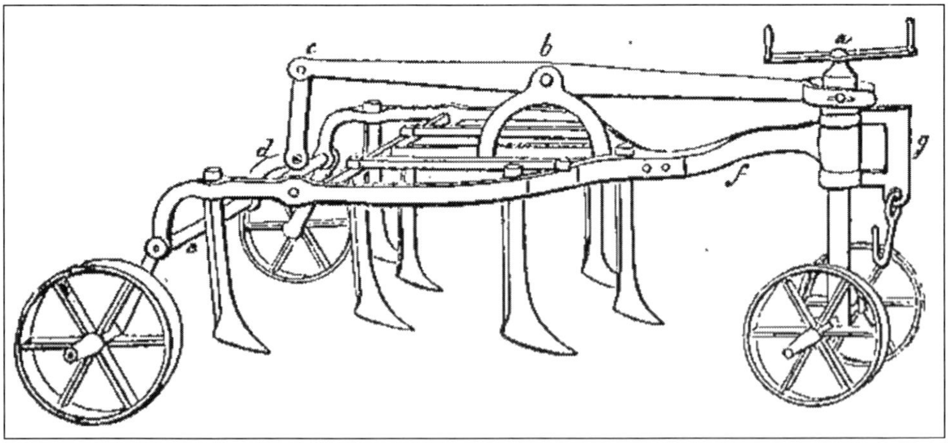

Source: Lefour, 1868: 162.

Illustration 9.4. Scarifier (*scarificateur*)

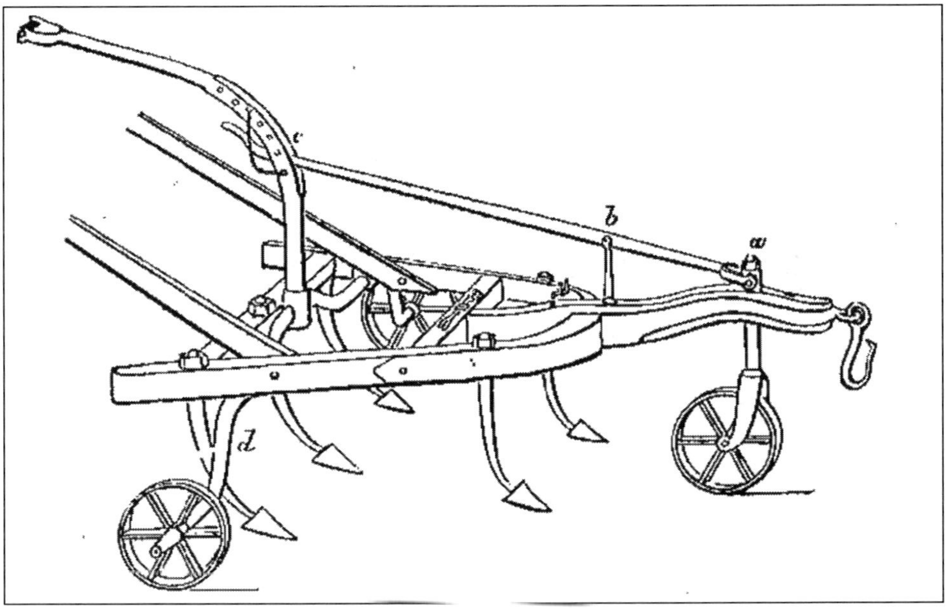

Source: Lefour, 1868: 162.

Illustration 9.5. Double Brabant (reversible) plough

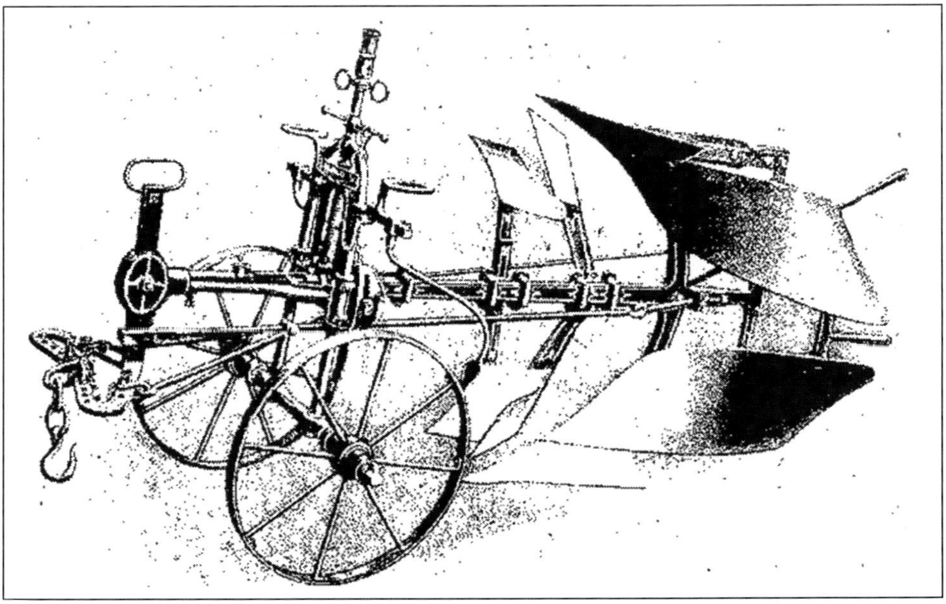

Source: Lequertier, 1921: 32.

The Brie plough, named after the region east of Paris where it was used, always turned the earth over on the same side. For this reason, it was used in 'ridge and furrow' ploughing (*labour en billions*). This was the method of ploughing used on damp and impermeable soil to facilitate the runoff of water in winter. *Billions* were small 'strips' of land, higher in the middle than on their long sides. A furrow was left on each of the long sides for the water to drain. Obviously, these furrows remained unproductive. In damp regions most ploughs were very similar to the Brie plough. The Leloup and Pluchet ploughs (Illustrations 9.1 and 9.2) were improved versions of the Brie plough. These improvements, made in the first half of the nineteenth century, helped to reduce the draught force needed for ploughing.

Lighter and more permeable soils were ploughed in flat 'strips'. There the work was done with a turnwrest (*tourne-oreilles)* plough, the ancestor of the Double Brabant plough (Illustration 9.5), which allowed the earth to be turned to the right or left by moving the mouldboard (*oreille*) at the end of each furrow or by reversing the body of the plough with 1 handle.

As more and better drainage resulted in the levelling of fields in the Brie by the middle of the nineteenth century, cultivation on the flat became possible everywhere, even in naturally damp soils. It was now possible to use improved implements such as Double Brabant ploughs (Illustration 9.5), grubbers (Illustration 9.3) and scarifiers (Illustration 9.4). Thanks to the use of the Double Brabant plough the time lost in turning the plough at the end of the furrow was reduced. There were, however, some difficulties in introducing them into common use. Though the ideas for some of these implements, such as the two-furrow plough and the Double Brabant plough, go back to the end of the eighteenth century, technical problems had to be overcome before their use could become general. It was not until the last third of the nineteenth century, for example, that the use of two-furrow ploughs began to spread.

In general, in all the regions where it was used, ridge and furrow ploughing was an obstacle to the use of improved implements because of the domed shape given to the earth. This type of ploughing made it difficult to use grubbers and scarifiers, but also two-furrow ploughs, scythes for harvesting cereals and all the harvesting implements. Drainage was thus, in most cases, a prerequisite for the use of improved tilling implements, and because of this, for the reduction in agricultural employment.

Bibliography

Allen, R. (1992) *Enclosure and the Yeoman: the Agricultural Development of the South Midlands, 1450–1850*, Oxford: Clarenton Press.

Béaur, G. (1994) 'L'Histoire de l'économie rurale à l'époque moderne ou les désarrois du quantitativisme. Bilan critique', *Histoire & Sociétés Rurales*, 1, pp. 67–97.

Béaur, G. and Chevet, J.-M. (2000) 'Introduction' to the special issue 'Productivité et croissance agricole', *Histoire & Mesure*, Vol. XV, 3/4, pp. 187–201.

Campbell, B.M.S. and Overton, M. (1991) *Land, Labour and Livestock. Historical Studies in European Agricultural Productivity*, Manchester: Manchester University Press.

Chevet, J.-M. (1994) 'Production et productivité: un modèle de développement économique des campagnes de la région parisienne aux XVIIIe et XIXe siècles', *Histoire & Mesure*, IX-1/2, pp. 101–145.

Chevet, J.-M. (1997) 'Quelle "révolution agricole" en Angleterre? A propos de deux livres récents sur l'agriculture anglaise du Moyen Âge au milieu du XIXe siècle', *Histoire & Mesure*, XI-3/4, pp. 389–410.

Chevet, J.-M. (1998 and 1999) *La Terre et les paysans en France et en Grande-Bretagne. Du début du XVIIe siècle à la fin du XVIIIe siècle*. Volume I: *Les hommes et les structures foncières*, Paris: Messene, Volume II: *Les hommes et la production*, Paris, Messene.

Chevet, J.-M. (2009) 'Angleterre capitaliste, France paysanne: la remise en cause du mythe?', in J. Broad, (ed.), *A common agricultural heritage?*, Agricultural History Review, Supplement Series 5, pp. 37–54.

De Guaita, F. (1857) 'Charrues des environs de Paris', *Journal d'agriculture pratique*, tome 1, Paris, pp. 450–454.

Garola, C.V. (1893) *La Pratique des travaux de la ferme*, Paris: J. B. Baillière.

Gasparin, A. de (1843–1851) *Cours d'agriculture*, 5 vols, Paris: La maison rustique.

Grantham, G. (1991) 'The Growth of Labour Productivity of Wheat in the Cinq Grosses Fermes of France, 1750–1929', in B.M.S. Campbell and M. Overton, (eds), *Land, Labour and Livestock. Historical studies in European Agricultural Productivity*, Manchester: Manchester University Press, pp. 348–363.

Heuzé, G. (1889) *La Pratique de l'agriculture*, vol.1, *Les agents de production, les opérations culturales, l'application des engrais, les semailles*, Paris: La maison rustique.

Heuzé, G. (1862) *Les Assolements*, Paris: Hachette.

Hoffman, P. (1996) *Growth in a Traditional Society: the French Countryside, 1450–1789*, Princeton: Princeton University Press.

Laboulaye, C. (1872) 'Instruments d'agriculture', in *Dictionnaire des arts et manufactures, de l'agriculture et des mines*, vol. II, Paris: Librairie du Dictionnaire des Arts et Manufactures.

Lecouteux, E. (1879) *Cours d'économie rurale*, vol. 2, *Constitution des entreprises agricoles*, Paris: La maison rustique.

Lefour, P.A.A. (1868) *Culture générale et instrument aratoires, défrichements, drainage, labours et façons du sol*, Paris: La maison rustique.

Lequertier, R. (1921) *Les Machines agricoles*, Paris: Garnier frères.

Moriceau, J.-M. (1988) 'Un Facteur de progrès agricole au centre du bassin parisien : l'équipement des grandes exploitations de l'Île-de-France du XVIe au début du XIXe siècle d'après les inventaires de fermiers', in M. Baulant et al., (eds), *Inventaires après-décès et ventes de meubles. Apports à une histoire de la vie économique et quotidienne XIVe-XIXe siècle*, Louvain-la-Neuve: Academia, pp. 211–231.

Moriceau, J.-M. (1994) *Les Fermiers de l'Île-de-France, L'ascension d'un patronat agricole (XVe-XVIIIe siècle)*, Paris: Fayard.

Moriceau, J.-M, and Postel-Vinay, G. (1992) *Ferme, Entreprise, Famille. Grande exploitation et changements agricoles: les Chartier (XVIIe-XIXe siècles)*, Paris: éditions de l'EHESS.

Moriceau, J.-M. (2002) *Terres mouvantes : les campagnes françaises du féodalisme à la mondialisation (1150–1850)*, Paris: Fayard.

Paris, A. (1978) 'Charrue et labour à la fin du XVIIIe siècle dans le département de Seine-et-Marne. Une enquête sur l'outillage et les techniques agricoles. Rapport présenté par le citoyen Challan devant la Société d'agriculture de Seine-et-Oise à la séance du 25 ventôse an X', *Ethnologie française*, pp. 48–62.

Ringelmann, M. (1887) *Les Machines agricoles*, Paris: Hachette.

Ministère de l'Agriculture (1936) *Statistique agricole de la France. Résultats généraux de l'enquête de 1929*, Paris: Imprimerie nationale.

Tessier, A.-M. (1793) 'Cheval', in *Encyclopédie méthodique. Agriculture*, Tome III, Paris: Panckoucke, pp. 99–149.

Wrigley, E.A. (1987) 'Urban Growth and Agricultural Change: England and the Continent in the Early Modern Period', in E.A. Wrigley, (ed.), *People, Cities and Wealth. The Transformation of Traditional Society*, Oxford: Blackwell Publishers, pp. 157–193.

10 Agricultural output, costs and incomes in the United Kingdom, 1919–1940

Paul BRASSLEY, University of Exeter

I. Introduction

Advancing age is inevitable, but to discover that one has become an historical source is disconcerting. Yet that is the position in which I found myself when, for the purposes of this paper, I began to think about the conventional image of agriculture in the United Kingdom between the wars. I realised that the image I held in my head probably resulted from conversations I had, when I first began to work on farms in the 1960s, with the farmers who employed me. Several of them had been farming before the war, and the story they told was one of low prices, little government support, low incomes, low outputs, decreasing arable and increasing permanent pasture, and consequently less crop and more animal output. Later, when I began to read the literature, Murray (1955), Whetham (1978), Brown (1987) and Perren (1995) told me much the same story. It seems quite credible, so I don't suppose I would have questioned it if Ted Collins had not given his paper at the 2001 Economic History Society conference in Glasgow, in which he argued, I think, that the interwar depression wasn't real in terms of output and productivity. That started me thinking about how you might measure depression, and I realised that I had already been involved in some work which might shed additional light on the question. So the purpose of this paper is to assess the accuracy of the conventional image, and especially the part of it about incomes.

II. The World Market

Between the wars, the UK was an import economy as far as food and agriculture were concerned. On average, between 1920 and 1939, food, beverages and tobacco formed 45% of UK imports (Liesner, 1989: 46). In 1937–8 imports accounted for 76% of the wheat supply, 60% of the barley supply, 81% of the sugar supply and significant proportions of fruit and vegetable supplies. The pattern was the same in meat and animal products: 50% of beef, 62% of mutton and lamb, 53% of pigmeat, 21% of poultry meat, 91% of butter, 76% of cheese, 39% of eggs and 88% of wool supplies were imported (Britton and Marks, 1989: 166, 181, 192–3, 205, 210, 219, 227, 232–3, 238, 242). Once government support was withdrawn, developments on world markets had a direct effect on the prices received by UK farmers. Interestingly, the more recent examinations of this period (i.e. Martin (2000) and Wilt (2001)) have very little to say about the world market, and Michael Tracy's (1982) work, which gave it the prominence it deserved, seems to have been forgotten recently. There is no space in this paper to tell the whole story, and two illustrations will have to suffice.

The first concerns the wheat trade: world wheat production, inflated by the demand increases of the First World War, was already declining by 1920. Nonetheless, although the net surplus of supplies only amounted to about 7% of production, that was slightly more than the import requirement of the largest importer, the UK (Kains-Jackson, 1919: 217). Here was a sign of structural surplus. The effects of that, and of the impact of more general depression, were seen in the USA ten years later. Maize and wheat prices in 1931 fell to half of their 1929 levels. One quarter of the US population lived on farms, and their incomes fell with these price falls. By 1930 54% of farm families – some 17 million people – earned less than $1000 per annum. The poverty line at that time was set at $2000 per annum. (Reynolds 1995: 28).

Similar problems affected many other countries. Agricultural depression was a world wide phenomenon. In Britain average wheat prices fell from 17s/0d per hundredweight in 1919 to 9s/10d in 1929. Barley prices fell from 21s/2d to 9s/11d per cwt over the same period, and prices of oats similarly decreased. Fat cattle prices nearly halved, as did fat sheep prices, and fat pig prices more than halved between 1920 and 1929 (Stanley, 1929: 219–21). The overall agricultural price index for the UK fell from a peak of 16.33 in 1920 to a minimum of 6.27 in 1933 (1986 = 100). It subsequently rose again, but had only reached 7.38 by 1939. Part of this was the result of inflation and disinflation – the deflated API only fell from 235 to 144 in the same period – but the trend was clear (Brassley, 2000: 83).

Depression, or at least low prices, was by no means unpredicted. As early as 1919 it was clear that government support would at least be controversial, if it continued at all. The Royal Commission appointed to inquire into the economic prospects of the agricultural industry was evenly split, half recommending continued price support and the other half its cessation. The latter group produced, in half a page, a critique of support which predicted future problems with astonishing accuracy:

> It could not, in our opinion, be other than detrimental to the best interests of agriculture were it obliged to conduct its operations on the uncertain basis provided by guaranteed prices. These guarantees can only be given by Act of Parliament, and no Parliament can bind its successors. Political opposition to guaranteed prices is certain. Electoral controversies will rage over the question of the continuance of the policy. A cleavage of interest between town and country is likely. The industry will be distracted by the necessity of interfering in politics. It will be tempted to support its claims by exaggerated estimates of the costs of production – a tendency only too noticeable in much of the evidence submitted to us. It will look to the taxpayer for its profit rather than to the development and improvement of its technique and business methods. In the event of the policy of the guarantees being continued by successive Parliaments, other industries will claim, with as much or as little reason, to be put on the same footing. This in turn will serve to divert the attention of the industry from its own legitimate sphere of action. (R.C. on Agriculture, 1919)

In the event, of course, support was discontinued, and by 1922 Charles Orwin, head of the Agricultural Economics Research Institute at Oxford, was predicting the impact of lower prices:

> [...] There is plenty of room for a further fall in markets before farming of one kind or another ceases to be a remunerative investment, but the country should be

> perfectly clear as to what is involved. The remedy for low prices is the reduction of costs and of output.

The same thing had happened thirty years earlier, he argued. In one of the southern counties, in a hamlet which once sent 44 children to the village school, a farmer, a shepherd and a dog, all living elsewhere, eventually farmed the land by themselves,

> [...] And today there can be seen a deserted village [he provided photographs to prove it] [...] all within seventy miles of London, the centre of a state which imports more food per head of population than any in the civilised world. (Orwin, 1922: 9–10)

II.1. Assessing the impact of low prices

Almost exactly thirty years after Orwin wrote those words, Dr E.M.Ojala published *Agriculture and Economic Progress* (1952). It was derived from his D.Phil thesis, and he struck a nice note of continuity in thanking Orwin for editing the manuscript of the book. It is an interesting and well written work, the substance of which has been almost entirely ignored by historians, who have concentrated on using the data contained in the appendix. This paper continues the tradition. Ojala's appendix does indeed demonstrate that output fell between the wars, that costs fell too, but not by as much, and so farm incomes fell. Ojala's figures are a good basis for discussion – Turner, for example, has argued that a fresh approach to output estimation would not necessarily produce better results (Brassley, 2000: 78) – but they are not without shortcomings:

- they take no account of the independence of Eire in 1922
- they are in current prices, at a time when the value of money was changing
- they omit the war years (although for the purposes of this paper this matters little)
- they leave agricultural incomes aggregated, rather than allocated to land, labour etc
- and so they are not directly comparable with the DNIC (see below).

Much of the remainder of this paper is therefore devoted to adjusting Ojala's data to take account of their shortcomings, and to reviewing the results that emerge.

II.2. Interwar changes in output

The major problem with Ojala's output figures is that they take no notice of the changing value of money and the separation of Eire in 1922. The problem of Irish output is dealt with by Brassley (2000: 79–80), and the resulting corrected figures are listed in table 10.1, which also shows the effect of expressing them in constant (1986) prices and thus in the form of an index. Pre-war figures are included for comparative purposes. Using 1904–10 as the pre-war base period reveals that output reached its interwar minimum in the early 1930s at about 18% below its prewar level.

The 1920–22 current price output peak is revealed to be simply the result of high postwar prices rather than a real output change. Thus prices became important. There were obviously two sources of variation: the general price level, measured by the retail price index (RPI), and the agricultural price level, measured by the agricultural price

Table 10.1 Output of UK agriculture in current and constant prices

	current prices (£million)	RPI (1986 = 100)	constant (1986) prices(£m)	index (1904–10 = 100)
1904–1910	170.55	2.58	6610.5	100.0
1911–1913	188.05	2.68	7016.8	106.1
1920–1922	409.35	6.25	6549.6	99.1
1924–1929	283.67	5.01	5662.1	85.7
1930–1934	245.47	4.49	5467.0	82.7
1935–1939	293.00	4.57	6411.4	97.0

Source: Brassley, 2000: 80–84; constant prices (r) are calculated from current prices (m) using the formula r = m x 100/RPI (Retail Price Index).

index (API). Having been fairly stable in the first decade of the twentieth century, prices began to rise from about 1909, and then doubled in the First World War, reaching a peak in 1920 before decreasing steadily in the 1920s and early 1930s. They bottomed out in 1933/4 but the 1940 price level was still below the 1918 price level. In current price terms the API largely followed this trend, with a marked rise in the immediate prewar years, a peak in 1919–20, a rapid decrease from 1920–22, and a long steady decline to 1933, after which they began to rise again. (Brassley 2000: 80–84). This pattern followed world agricultural price trends (see Tracy, 1982), as would be expected in what was, as we have already seen, an import-dominated agricultural economy.

The decrease in farm prices thus parallelled the overall retail price variations. Farmers sold their output for less, but the purchasing power of each pound was greater. Whereas output in current prices fell by about 60% from its 1920–22 peak to its 1930–34 trough, in constant prices the fall was only about 20%. But because farm prices were falling farmers had to sell more to maintain their receipts. A basket of farm goods that would have brought in £200 (in 1986 prices) in 1920–22 would have realised only £148.5 (also in 1986 prices) in 1930–34. Thus the *volume* of output *rose* between 1920 and 1939 according to these calculations, and even rose a little – 10% or so (from £3,265 million to £3,681 million) – between 1920 and 1934 (Brassley 2000: 84).

While this conclusion may be at variance with the popular conception of the interwar years, it does not seem implausible. Although the total area of agricultural land (i.e. arable plus permanent grass) decreased by about 2.7 million acres, or roughly 10% (Murray, 1955: 22), and the lower priced arable products exhibited decreasing acreages and declining or at best static outputs, production of the higher-priced products increased, as Tables 10.2 and 10.3 demonstrate.

Sugar beet, with the advantage of government support, was the only arable crop to increase significantly, reaching a peak of over 400,000 acres and 4 million tons in 1934, before declining slightly to the levels shown in Table 10.3. Poultry numbers too reached a peak in 1934. Most of the rising milk production went into the liquid trade, leaving the butter and cheese markets to the importers. Farmers were reacting logically, if not

Table 10.2 Contracting or static enterprises, 1920–1939

	Wheat		Barley	
	m. acres	*output (m. tons)*	*m. acres*	*output (m. tons)*
1920–1922	Approx. 2	1.75	Approx. 1.6	1.2
1931	1.25	1.00	–	–
1938–1939	1.70	1.60	1.0	0.9
	Oats		Horses	
	m. acres	*output (m. tons)*	*Numbers ('000)*	
1920–1922	3.20	2.10	950	
1938–1939	2.00	1.70	650	
	Potatoes			
	'000 acres	*output (m. tons)*	*Remark:*	
1920–1922	>700	4–5	Differences due to average yield variations between 5.5 and 7.2 tons / acre	
1931	575	3		
1938–1939	600	4		

Source: MAFF, 1966: 98–129; Britton and Marks, 1989: 218 & 238 (m. = million).

Table 10.3 Expanding enterprises, 1920–1939

	Sugar Beet		Sheep numbers	
	'000 acres	*output (m. tons)*	*(m.)*	
1920–1922	8	0.065	20	
1938–1939	345	3.500	26	
	Catle & calves	Cows & heifers Pigs in milk	Pigmeat production	
	(m.)	*(m.)*	*(m.)*	*'000 tons*
1920–1922	6.7	3.0	2.5	299
1938–1939	8.1	3.6	3.8	423
	Fowls	Egg supplies		
	(m.)	*(m.dozen)*		
1920–1922	29	189		
1938–1939	60	545		

Source: MAFF, 1966: 98–129; Britton and Marks, 1989: 218 & 238 (m. = million).

always rapidly, to market forces, and falling cereal outputs did not imply a decreasing total volume of output. But what mattered to farmers was how much money they made. If costs rose by more than output their incomes would fall, and vice versa, and the next step is therefore to examine cost trends.

III. Cost changes

Ojala defined costs as the value of inputs (feeds, fertilisers, imported animals and seeds, machinery, and miscellaneous expenses) together with land taxes and rates. Agricultural income was therefore output minus these costs. The DNIC – the Departmental Net Income Calculation – is the method currently used for calculating net farm income, and is available as a continuous series from 1970. In 1984 the Ministry of Agriculture, Fisheries and Food published estimates of the DNIC, using the same calculation methods, from 1937/8 to 1974/5 (MAFF, 1984). In other words, it is possible to link Ojala's farm income estimates, which conclude in 1939, with the modern series. It is not the purpose of this paper to do so in detail, but reconciling the two provides a useful check on Ojala's estimates. In addition, the DNIC method disaggregates incomes to a greater extent than Ojala's method, so that it is possible to measure the return to land, labour and capital. What is left, therefore, is the reward to the physical and managerial labour of the nation's farmers, together with the rewards to their own capital invested, and this is termed 'farming net income'. The calculation method is summarised in Table 10.4.

It is also necessary to make two adjustments to Ojala's figures to render them compatible with the DNIC and the output estimates given above. The first involves adding in figures for contract services and farm maintenance (Tasker, 1994: 20) shows how this is done. It appears from Ojala (Ojala, 1952: 214) that these items are included in his miscellaneous expenses, but since MAFF (1984)'s figure for machinery repairs plus fuel and oil is the

Table 10.4 The Departmental Net Income Calculation

	Gross Output (including subsidies)
less	Gross inputs
equals	Gross Product (which is broadly equivalent to Ojala's agricultural income)
less	depreciation
equals	net product
less	labour cost
less	net rent
less	interest
equals	Farming Net Income

Source: Lund and Watson, 1981.

same as Ojala's machinery repairs and fuel, and their miscellaneous expenditure is the same as Ojala's (all for 1937/8 – MAFF – and 1935–9 – Ojala), there is a case for adding in additional contract and farm maintenance costs to the Ojala total to bring it closer to the MAFF total. The effect of this, in various year groups, is to increase total expenses by between about 6% and 9%. The second adjustment requires the elimination of Irish costs before 1922. A similar problem occurs with the output calculation made above, and it was resolved by using Turner's (1996) estimates of Irish output. Unfortunately Turner made no estimates of Irish costs, but it seems reasonable to assume that Irish costs would form roughly the same proportion as Irish output and adjust the pre-1922 figures accordingly. The results of these two adjustments are shown in Table 10.5.

Subtracting these adjusted gross input figures in Table 10.5 from the current price gross output figures in Table 10.1 produces the gross product, which is shown in Table 10.6 in current price terms, and also converted to constant prices and an index.

Table 10.5 Adjusting gross inputs

	Ojala's gross input £m	Ojala adjusted for costs	Irish fraction %	Irish gross £m	Adjusted input £m
1904–1910	70.33	75.95	16.8	12.76	63.19
1911–1913	79.61	86.00	17.1	14.71	71.29
1920–1922	162.58	178.70	17.1	30.56	148.14
1924–1929	126.91	136.66	–	–	136.66
1930–1934	97.44	104.51	–	–	104.51
1935–1939	120.97	129.97	–	–	129.97

Source: see text.

Table 10.6 Gross Product

	Gross Product current £m	RPI	Gross Product constant £m 1986 = 100	Gross Product index 1904–10 = 100
1904–1910	107.36	2.58	4161.24	100.0
1911–1913	116.76	2.68	4356.72	104.7
1920–1922	261.21	6.25	4179.36	100.4
1924–1929	147.01	5.01	2934.33	70.5
1930–1934	140.96	4.49	3139.42	75.4
1935–1939	163.03	4.57	3567.40	85.7

Source: see text.

Comparing Table 10.1 and Table 10.6 reveals that the gross product constant price index (minimum 70.5 in the late 1920s) goes down by more than the gross output constant price index (minimum 82.7 in the early 1930s), which implies that costs were rising more than returns overall. The gross product hits its minimum in the late 1920s because output fell but costs, in real terms, were above the 1904–10 level. Then in the early 1930s, although output fell, costs fell more, so gross product rose, and in the later 1930s output rose significantly, but costs rose somewhat too, so although gross product increased it was still below the 1904–10 base.

This gross product represents the money available to cover depreciation, labour costs, rent and capital costs, with the remainder forming the return to the farmer's manual and managerial efforts and his own capital. Since it is this remainder that will determine how well off the farmer feels, we should now examine variations in depreciation etc to see how it changes this remainder. Tasker (1994: 22 & Appendix I) explains how a depreciation figure can be calculated from the data in Feinstein and Pollard (1988: 277–9), but he does not adjust for Eire. This operation is carried out in Table 10.7, using essentially the same Irish correction factor as used in Table 10.5.

Labour costs and net rent can be calculated from Feinstein (1976), and interest from Tasker (1994), with the standard Irish adjustment. They are shown in Table 10.8.

Table 10.7 Calculating the net product

	Gross Product (£m current prices)	*minus*	Depreciation × 0.83	*equals*	Net Product (£m current prices)
1904–1910	107.36		8.02		99.34
1911–1913	116.76		7.74		109.02
1920–1922	261.21		7.74		253.47
1924–1929	147.01		9.33		137.68
1930–1934	140.96		9.33		131.63
1935–1939	163.03		9.00		154.03

Source: see text.

Table 10.8 Labour, rent and interest, i.e. factor costs

	labour	net rent	interest	total factor costs
1904–1910	46.84	25.47	2.80	75.11
1911–1913	48.97	25.74	3.46	78.17
1920–1922	91.03	21.36	6.67	119.06
1924–1929	72.17	22.36	6.72	101.25
1030–1934	65.80	26.69	5.61	98.10
1935–1939	66.00	23.70	4.40	94.10

Source: see text.

Table 10.9 Calculating net income

	Net product costs	*minus*	total factor costs	*equals*	current prices	Net farm income, in constant prices (1986)	index
1904–1910	99.34		75.11		24.23	939.1	100.0
1911–1913	109.02		78.17		30.85	1,151.1	122.6
1920–1922	253.47		119.06		134.41	2,150.6	229.0
1924–1929	137.68		101.25		36.43	727.1	77.4
1930–1934	131.63		98.10		33.53	746.8	79.5
1935–1939	154.03		94.10		60.00	1,312.9	139.8

Source: Tables 10.7 and 10.8. Current prices are concerted into constant prices using the same RPI conversion factors as those used in table 10.6.

In Table 10.9, these total factor costs are subtracted from the net product to give net income, which is then converted into constant price and index terms.

In Table 10.9 farmers are revealed, probably not surprisingly, as the residual earners. Input costs only vary over about a 20% range in real terms, and factor costs over a 35% range. But net farm income more than doubled after World War I and was then cut by a factor of three for ten years before doubling again. Farmers produced as much as ever or more in volume terms, but the low world prices to which they were exposed reduced their output in real terms by 15–20%. Their input costs rose in the late 1920s before falling in the 1930s, for reasons which are not immediately apparent. Factor incomes fell a little but not much, and the net result was incomes which varied dramatically. But the years of dramatic rise were far outnumbered by those of dramatic fall. This might explain why farmers had bad memories of the interwar years. Those with traditional ideas about mixed farming and employing labour looked back to their grandfathers' stories of the years up to 1870, and remembered, like A.G. Street (1932), the pre-First World war years of their youth when the worst of the depression was past. But nonetheless they responded to market forces and increased livestock output at the expense of arable, while cutting back on labour and economising on building and machinery repairs. As a result, despite the downturn in prices and the fall in incomes, the agricultural industry's use of the nation's land, labour and capital resources was not necessarily wasteful or inefficient. Whether or not it was can only be decided by a Total Factor Productivity (TFP) calculation.

There are various ways of calculating TFP but the one used here – using Crafts' equation (see appendix) – produces results (see Table 10.10) that seem intuitively credible, even if they are not always in complete agreement with other estimates , or indeed entirely devoid of their own problems. And they suggest that TFP rose by about 25% between 1923 and 1939, which may be compared with a negative figure for the Second World war years and a much smaller rise for 1867–1913.

Table 10.10 Total Factor Productivity percentages

1867–1913	4.41
1911–1922	18.57
1923–1939	25.30
1939–1945	–8.89
1946–1965	82.60

Source: Brassley, 2003.

IV. Conclusion

Between 1919 and 1939 UK agriculture maintained and even increased its volume of output while coping with a drastic reduction in capital formation (it was always less than half its First World War level between 1919 and 1935), and a 20% decrease in labour, coupled with a small decrease in the quantity of land used. This resulted in a productivity increase that contrasted markedly with the smaller figure for the 1911–22 period and the negative figure for the Second World War. Several factors probably combined to produce it: changes in the output mix; living off the capital invested in the first world war; mechanisation to some extent; and concentration of effort upon the better land all suggest themselves. But which of these, if any, was the one that really mattered will have to wait for another paper.

Bibliography

Brassley, P. (2000) 'Output and Technical Change in twentieth-century British Agriculture', *Agricultural History Review*, 48 (1), pp. 60–84.

Brassley, P. (2003) *Long run TFP estimates for UK agriculture*, unpublished paper, University of Plymouth.

Britton, D. and Marks, H.F. (1989) *A Hundred Years of British Food and Farming: a statistical Survey*, London: Taylor and Francis.

Brown, J. (1987) *Agriculture in England: a survey of farming 1870–1947*, Manchester: Manchester University Press.

Crafts, N. (1986) *British Economic Growth during the Industrial Revolution*, Oxford: Oxford University Press.

Feinstein, C.H. and Pollard, S. (1988) *Studies in Capital Formation in the UK 1750–1921*, Oxford: Oxford University Press.

Kains-Jackson, C. (1919) 'The Corn Trade in 1919', *Journal of the Royal Agricultural Society of England*, 80, pp. 212–224.

Leisner, T. (1989) *One Hundred Years of Economic Statistics*, London: Economist Publications.

Lund, P.J. and Watson, J.M. (1981) 'Agricultural Incomes: a review of the data and recent trends', *Economic Trends*, pp. 103–122.

MAFF [Ministry of Agriculture, Fisheries and Food] (1966) *A Century of Agricultural Statstics*, London: HMSO.

MAFF [Ministry of Agriculture, Fisheries and Food] (1984) *Departmental Net Income Calculation, Historical Series 1937/8 to 1974/5*, London: MAFF, Statistics Division 1.

Martin, J. (2000) *The Development of Modern Agriculture: British Farming since 1931*, Basingstoke: Macmillan.

Murray, K.A.H., (1955) *Agriculture (History of the Second World War, Civil Series)*, London: HMSO and Longmans, Green & Co.

Ojala, E.M. (1952) *Agriculture and Economic Progress*, Oxford University Press.

Orwin, C.S. (1922) 'Commodity Prices and Farming Policy', *Journal of the Royal Agricultural Society of England*, 83.

Perren, R. (1995) *Agriculture in Depression 1870–1940*, Cambridge University Press.

[R.C. on Agriculture] (1919) The Interim Report of the Royal Commission appointed to Inquire into the Economic Prospects of the Agricultural Industry in Great Britain, Cmd 473, 1919, BPP 1919 VIII.1.

Reynolds, D. (1995) *Rich Relations: the American occupation of Britain, 1942–45*, London: Harper Collins.

Stanley, R.E. (1929) 'Agricultural Statistics, 1929', *Journal of the Royal Agricultural Society of England*, 90, pp. 219–221.

Street, A.G. (1932) *Farmer's Glory*, London: Faber.

Tasker, J.C. (1994) *An Investigation of Farm Income 1867 to 1939*, University of Plymouth, Seale-Hayne Faculty of Agriculture, Food and Land Use, unpublished BSc dissertation.

Thirsk, J. (1997) *Alternative Agriculture*, Oxford University Press.

Turner, M. (1996) *After the Famine: Irish Agriculture 1850–1914*, Cambridge University Press.

Tracy, M. (1982) *Agriculture in Western Europe*, 2nd ed., London: Granada.

Wilt, A.F. (2001) *Food for War: agriculture and rearmament in Britain before the Second World War*, Oxford: Oxford University Press.

Appendix

The TFP methodology used in this paper follows that used by Crafts (1985: 78–9), who uses the expression

$$\frac{\Delta Y}{Y} = \alpha \frac{\Delta K}{K} + \beta \frac{\Delta L}{L} + \gamma \frac{\Delta T}{T} + r^*$$

in which: $\Delta Y/Y$ is the rate of growth of output,

$\Delta K/K$ is the rate of growth of the capital stock,

$\Delta L/L$ is the rate of growth of the labour force,

$\Delta T/T$ is the rate of growth of land,

α, β, and γ are the shares of profits, wages and rents in national income, and r^* is the rate of growth of total factor productivity